The Experience
of Student Teaching

J.M.Clowry

The Experience
of Student Teaching

JOHN W. DEVOR

The American University
Washington, D.C.

THE MACMILLAN COMPANY, *New York*
COLLIER-MACMILLAN LIMITED, *London*

Third Printing, 1965

Library of Congress catalog card number: 63–16366

The Macmillan Company, New York
Collier-Macmillan Canada, Ltd., Toronto, Ontario

Printed in the United States of America

TO

Student teachers
who are anxious to improve themselves
in order to provide better teachers
for the schools of tomorrow

Preface

After working with student teachers for many years, the author has developed this guide to help you prepare for the difficult tasks of your first experience as a regularly employed teacher. While all problem situations cannot be anticipated, the solutions that are included have proved to be valuable and effective. They should suggest the basis, or point of departure, for the resolution of problems in individual circumstances.

The student-teaching experience will be one of the most important factors contributing to your competence and success in coping with daily planning and classroom routine. The immediate applications of the material here presented will be seen, because the author has placed major emphasis on specific examples and suggestions.

A useful portion of the book derives from student-teacher evaluation reports and unsolicited comments by supervising teachers. The anonymity of the individual has been protected by name and place alterations. The author is especially grateful to these persons for their excellent examples and suggestions, and it is hoped that these materials will benefit your future teaching experience.

John W. Devor

Washington, D.C.

Contents

APPENDICES

I. PREPARATION

1. Your Student-Teaching Experience

Since the student-teaching experience usually comes near the end of the undergraduate program for the professional and academic preparation of teachers, it furnishes a very important opportunity for synthesis and application of theoretical learnings that have been provided through other course work. Thus, the concepts, values, and skills which have been learned in a more or less theoretical way through previous course work may be applied and made more valuable to the prospective teacher.

The student-teaching program provides a laboratory for the testing of ideas—a place where the student may encounter real problems, an opportunity for personal growth, and a feeling of reality. All of these factors tend to make the student-teaching experience one of the most interesting and helpful phases of the professional preparation of the prospective teacher.

The process of "learning by doing," which has become axiomatic in educational circles, is basic to the student-teaching experience. In fact, it has been emphasized that "the only way in which one can really learn to teach is by teaching." Of course, it is generally conceded that there are certain understandings regarding human growth and development, methods and materials of instruction, and the American educational system which are necessary for the proper development of skills important to teaching.

Some opportunity should be provided for the prospective student teacher to observe and work with boys and girls in the classroom situation throughout the time of his preservice period of preparation. The number and variety of experiences will be determined by certain factors related to the teacher-education program of the institution involved. Perhaps the most important factor which contributes to the availability of such experiences is the campus laboratory school. It is generally recognized, however, that some opportunity should be provided for every prospective teacher to have some student-teaching experience in an off-campus school, preferably in a public school since this is the type of institution in which he will probably be teaching after graduation. In fact, some firsthand experiences in such schools are valuable prior to the student-teaching period.

DEFINITION OF TERMS

Due to differences in terminology used in connection with teacher education, it is well to define certain terms that are used extensively in this volume. It is understood that several terms may be used interchangeably and that the usage varies with the locality.

The definitions and explanations given below are in accordance with those agreed upon by the Association for Student Teaching and listed in the Thirty-Eighth Yearbook of the Association: [1]

Supervising Teacher: One who teaches children or youth and who also supervises student teaching and/or other professional experiences.
a. Cooperating school supervising teacher: One who performs the responsibilities of a supervising teacher in a cooperating school.
b. Laboratory school supervising teacher: One who performs the responsibilities of a supervising teacher in a laboratory school. One who is a member of a laboratory school staff recognized by the college as qualified to guide a group of pupils and one or more college students, guiding the latter in their understanding and teaching of a given pupil group.

School:
a. Campus or off-campus laboratory school: A school which is controlled and supported (all or in part) by the college and which is

[1] Ernest J. Milner, Editor, "The Supervising Teacher," Thirty-Eighth Yearbook, The Association for Student Teaching: Cedar Falls, Iowa, 1959.

organized as an integral part of the teacher education program to provide significant opportunities to study and relate the various phases of the teacher's activities both in and out of school.

b. Cooperating school: A school which is not controlled or supported by the college but which does provide facilities for professional laboratory experiences in a teacher education program.

c. Off-campus school: (see definition of cooperating school).

Student Teaching: The period of guided teaching during which the student takes increasing responsibility for the work with a given group of learners over a period of consecutive weeks.

Professional Laboratory Experiences: All those contacts with children, youth, and adults in the school and community (through observation, participation, and teaching) which make a direct contribution to an understanding of individuals and their guidance in the teaching-learning process.

Participation: Those experiences of the college student in which he is assisting and working with the regular classroom teacher in teaching activities. This is a part of pre-student teaching and student teaching.

Supervisor:

a. College or university supervisor of student teaching: The college representative who is responsible for supervising a student teacher or a group of student teachers.

b. Off-campus supervisor of student teaching: The college representative who is responsible for supervising student teachers in off-campus student teaching centers.

c. Resident supervisor of student teaching: The college representative, who like the student teachers, is assigned to live in the community in which the student teaching center is located and is responsible to the college for supervising the student teaching experiences in that center.

Directed Observation: All professional observations which have been planned, supervised, and evaluated [referred to as "observation" throughout this volume].

Student Teaching Program: The program of professional laboratory experiences provided in connection with the course which is commonly called "Student Teaching." This program includes all observation, participation and actual teaching involved in such a course. [Author's definition.]

Student Teaching Experiences: All of the professional laboratory experiences provided for the prospective teacher in connection with the student teaching program. [Author's definition.]

Student Teacher: The individual who is assigned to a certain school to carry on the work of student teaching under the direction of a master teacher who is employed by the school system. [Author's definition.]

AIMS OF PROFESSIONAL LABORATORY EXPERIENCES

It is assumed that the student will have had some professional laboratory experiences which may be classified as observation and participation previous to the time when he takes the course designated as "student teaching." The extent and quality of such experiences are determined by the adequacy of preparation provided for the student through the teacher-education institution involved.

The purpose of professional laboratory experiences is, as the name indicates, to provide the prospective teacher with the opportunity of performing as many as possible of the tasks that he will be expected to perform when he starts his first full-time teaching position. In order for the performance of these tasks to be of maximum value to the beginning teacher, they should be performed under the direction and supervision of a master teacher.

The objectives or aims of professional laboratory experiences are essentially the same as the objectives for the entire program of teacher education, since the student-teaching experience usually comes near the close of the preservice preparation of teachers and is a time for summarizing and applying previous learnings. These objectives may well be defined by use of the following two-dimensional chart.

This chart should be interpreted in the following manner. Certain objectives of professional laboratory experiences are to increase the prospective teacher's understanding of basic facts and principles regarding (1) the structure and organization of the

CHART 1

Objectives for a Program of Professional Laboratory Experiences

CONTENT ASPECTS	BEHAVIORAL ASPECTS				
	Understanding of Basic Facts and Principles	Competency in Applying Understanding	Ability to Select, Prepare, Organize, and Use Materials	True Appreciation	Ability to Evaluate
A. The American Educational System					
1. Functions	x			x	x
2. Structure and organization	x			x	x
3. Curricula	x			x	x
4. Relation to other educative agencies	x			x	x
5. Current trends	x			x	x
B. Human Growth and Development					
1. Physical, social, emotional, intellectual, and cultural factors	x	x		x	x
2. Activities of young people	x	x		x	x
3. Motives underlying behavior	x	x		x	x
4. Information about children	x	x		x	x
C. Instructional Methods					
1. Nature of learning	x	x	x	x	x
2. Techniques of instruction	x	x	x	x	x
3. Techniques of evaluation	x	x	x	x	x
4. Techniques of diagnosis	x	x	x	x	x

CHART 1—CONTINUED

Objectives for a Program of Professional Laboratory Experiences

CONTENT ASPECTS	BEHAVIORAL ASPECTS				
	Under-standing of Basic Facts and Principles	Compe-tency in Applying Under-standing	Ability to Select, Prepare, Organize, and Use Materials	True Appreci-ation	Ability to Evaluate
D. Instructional Materials					
1. Patterns of curriculum organization	x	x	x	x	x
2. Learning objectives in teaching fields	x	x	x	x	x
3. Units for instruction	x	x	x	x	x
4. Source materials for instruction	x	x	x	x	x
5. Evaluation instruments	x	x	x	x	x
E. Role of the Teacher in a Democratic Society					
1. Personal, social, intellectual, and moral qualities	x	x	x	x	x
2. Legal requirements	x	x	x	x	x
3. Agencies for employment	x	x	x	x	x
4. Active identification with professional organizations	x	x	x	x	x

American educational system, (2) motives underlying behavior, (3) techniques of instruction, and so forth. Other objectives include ability to select, prepare, organize, and use (1) techniques of instruction, (2) source materials for instruction, and so forth. The program of professional laboratory experiences should also increase the beginning teacher's appreciation of (1) the activities of young people, (2) techniques of evaluation, (3) personal, social, intellectual, and moral qualities of the teacher in a democratic society, and so forth.

If the objectives defined in this chart are kept in mind, the student teacher should receive an adequate and effective series of learning experiences to prepare him for the job of teaching.

The value to be derived from thoughtful application of objectives for a program of professional laboratory experiences is indicated in the following statements by an elementary student teacher:

As I began my twelve weeks of student teaching, I wished to attain certain general aims for myself and for my class. I find that my aims may be classified in a similar manner to those outlined in our student-teaching book. These are:

1. understanding of basic facts and principles (most of which I had learned through course work at the university);
2. competency in applying the understandings;
3. ability to select, prepare, organize, and use instructional materials; and finally,
4. the ability to evaluate objectively and competently.

Whether or not I was able to attain all of these aims can only be judged by someone other than myself. However, with each activity involved in the student-teaching experience, I tried to keep them in mind. I feel certain that consideration of these objectives was an important factor in determining the children's reactions to me. I could never have anticipated such warm acceptance as I received. This friendship was evident during my first week in the school and grew greater throughout the time of my student teaching.

PROFESSIONAL LABORATORY EXPERIENCES: TYPES

Three types of activity should be provided in the program of professional laboratory experiences. These are (1) observation, (2) participation, and (3) actual teaching. The amount of time which should be devoted to each varies with the student teacher and the situation (grade level, type of pupils, situation of the school, etc.). A list of activities which the prospective teacher may accomplish under each of the above headings is given in Appendix A of this volume.

It is difficult to list all of the possible activities which may be classified under the above headings. However, the supervising teacher and student teacher should consider the activities that are provided and list them under the three headings. The rules that may be followed in classifying student-teaching experiences are as follows:

1. Observation includes all activities in which the student teacher is merely an onlooker.
2. Participation is interpreted as any activity in which the student teacher is doing more than merely observing, but in which he is not actually working with students.
3. Actual teaching includes all activities in which the student teacher is actually working with students, either individually or as a group. Playground instruction, field trips, and other similar activities may be considered as actual teaching regardless of their location.

CHARACTERISTICS IMPORTANT TO STUDENT TEACHERS [2]

Many aspects of personality important to student teachers may be mentioned. However, there are six areas of personal characteristics which seem to have great importance in affecting the success or failure of students in student teaching. These may be described as follows:

Interest in Teaching

An individual's interest involves the nature of his purpose in life, the clarity of his plans for the future, his concern for educational problems, the relative emphasis he places upon professional obligations and personal affairs, and the attitude he exhibits toward teaching.

[2] Adapted from unpublished materials produced at Ohio State University.

An individual who is genuinely interested in teaching will possess such personal traits as unselfishness, willingness to assume responsibility, interest in working with youth, and enthusiasm for his profession. He will be characterized by such behaviors as are stated below:

1. He regularly looks for and seizes opportunities to learn about teaching and the varied activities of teachers.
2. He rates personal satisfaction above financial gain.
3. He has a deep-seated altruistic purpose in life.
4. He regards teaching as a professional challenge, not merely as a means to a livelihood.
5. He shows increasing ability to identify and analyze teaching problems.
6. He continually offers to carry higher levels of responsibility.
7. He seeks to broaden the scope of his professional experiences.
8. He is anxious to help with activities outside of the regular school day.
9. He already has clearly defined plans for a career in teaching.

Emotional Balance

The concept of emotional balance involves the mental health and general maturity of the individual. This includes a consideration of the presence or absence of psychoneurotic tendencies, the level of stability, and the way in which new or problematic situations are approached and handled. The presence or absence of such personal traits as poise, dependability, cooperativeness, open-mindedness, self-confidence, loyalty, self-control, stability, and sense of humor are involved. The following examples of behavior indicate positive evidence of emotional balance:

1. He adjusts well to new or unusual situations.
2. He meets obligations promptly and efficiently.
3. He exhibits maturity of thought and action.
4. He exhibits no psychoneurotic tendencies or mannerisms.
5. He meets problematic situations with independently planned courses of action.
6. He acts with judgment appropriate to his level of maturity.

7. He accepts criticisms without resentment, is willing to learn.
8. He is able to work well with a group.
9. He is able to see humor in situations involving himself as well as others.
10. He assumes responsibility for the results of his own actions.

Ability to Attract, Interest, and Get Along with Others

An individual's ability to work effectively with youth depends upon his genuine interest in them and his understanding of adolescents and their problems. He must be able to speak their language. Some skill in working with groups is important. Getting along with young people will be facilitated if the individual has such traits as personal magnetism, animation, resourcefulness, patience, fairness or impartiality, cheerfulness, and kindliness.

One's skill in getting along with others will be evidenced by such behavior as:

1. Conversing freely with students; promoting a friendly atmosphere.
2. Securing the confidence, respect, and cooperation of the group.
3. Adjusting readily to the age, grade, and ability level of the students.
4. Being resourceful in helping a group or individuals plan and carry out regular work and creative activities.
5. Having a generally neat and attractive appearance.
6. Exhibiting no objectionable voice, speech, sight, or hearing deficiencies.
7. Demonstrating acceptable patterns of speech and action.
8. Showing leadership by contagious enthusiasm for the task at hand.
9. Being consistent in dealing with problems of management and discipline, generally refraining from snap judgments, particularly in situations of emotional stress.

Skill in Human Relations with Peers and Adults

An individual's skill in getting along with peers and adults involves his ability to meet people graciously and enter easily into conversation with them, a genuine interest in other people, respect for their opinions, willingness to compromise differences, and faith in the sincerity of one's fellow men. Significant personal traits are friendliness, politeness, courtesy, geniality, tact, sincerity, appreciativeness, and optimism.

Some suggested evidences of skill in relations with peers and adults are the following behaviors:

1. He looks for and expects to find good in other people.
2. He tries to cooperate even under difficult circumstances.
3. He appreciates assistance and suggestions from others.
4. He demonstrates ability to follow directions.
5. He receives satisfaction from playing any role well, even though secondary in nature.
6. He meets everyone easily and graciously.
7. He respects opinions differing from his own and makes a genuine effort to compromise whenever possible, without violating major convictions or beliefs.
8. He gives credit to others when credit is due.
9. He generally refrains from harsh or undue criticism of others.

Intellectual and Professional Energy

This concept involves the individual's essential vigor, the creativity of his imagination, his performance under pressure, his general level of accomplishment, and his ambition. Such personal traits as initiative, forcefulness, originality, perseverance, purposefulness, and zealousness are involved here.

Some behavior evidences of this concept are suggested below:

1. He is able to stand up well under pressure.
2. He is ambitious without being personally aggressive.
3. He is challenged to extra effort by problems which are difficult or seem impossible of solution.
4. He exhibits facility in proposing ideas and solutions.
5. He shows ability to initiate and carry out proposed courses of action to solve problems.
6. He is stimulated by everyday experiences and environment to independent investigation, study, and skill development.

7. He sustains consistent effort to reach long-range objectives.
8. He practices good health habits, is mentally and physically vigorous.

Breadth of Interests

An evaluation of an individual's breadth of interests involves a consideration of the scope of his school activities, community activities, work experiences, and leisure-time pursuits. The extent of the individual's participation, the level of leadership responsibility successfully undertaken, and the quality of discernment and judgment developed are emphasized. The individual with great breadth of interests will generally become more tolerant, observant, and sociable, and more understanding, resourceful, and sensitive to the needs and problems of individuals and society.

The following examples of behavior indicate positive evidence of breadth of interests:

1. He has occupied positions of leadership in several different groups or organizations.
2. He receives genuine satisfaction from working with people.
3. He shows interest in many different community activities and projects for social betterment.
4. He seeks experiences in all phases of the school and with a wide range of types of students.
5. He is willing to try new activities and to accept challenging responsibilities.
6. He enjoys the role of both participant and spectator in a wide variety of indoor and outdoor activities.
7. He exhibits a wholesome curiosity in the familiar, the strange, the bizarre, the unusual.
8. He tends to reflect on the deeper significance and meaning of various experiences.
9. He respects and attempts to understand people of other races, creeds, and colors.

Personal Appearance

Perhaps the best rule for student teachers to remember, with reference to personal appearance, is that they should consider themselves in the same light as if they were regular teachers in the school. Thus, they will wish to dress in a manner similar to the regular teachers.

The following examples of behavior indicate positive evidence of proper understanding of personal appearance:

1. The young lady uses good judgment in the use of cosmetics.
2. The student teacher does not try to look too collegiate. (A suit coat is usually more appropriate than a college sweater.)
3. The student teacher keeps his clothes spotless and well pressed.
4. The student teacher should keep his shoes well polished.
5. The young man should be smoothly shaved and have his hair well trimmed.
6. It is well for the young man to wear a dress shirt and an appropriate tie.

The student teacher should remember that the privilege of participating in the student-teaching program is made possible by the courtesy and cooperation of many school officials and teachers in the public schools. It is arranged for those students who have demonstrated their eligibility according to the requirements of their particular curriculum. In return for this opportunity, the college and the public schools expect him to put forth his best efforts to the end that the students with whom he works may have the best possible learning experiences. It is only as the student teacher realizes his responsibility to the public school and the importance of his being a favorable representative of the college that he can receive the greatest benefit from his student-teaching experience.

RELATIONS OF THE STUDENT TEACHER WITH THE SUPERVISING TEACHER

The student teacher's relations with, and attitude toward, his supervising or cooperating teacher affect greatly the value he receives from the student-teaching experience. It is not expected that he will agree with everything the supervising teacher does. However, supervising teachers are chosen for this work because of their preparation for the job of teaching and because they have demonstrated both their ability to deal with young people and their interest in teaching as a profession. Therefore, it is expected that the student teacher will cooperate with his supervising teacher to the fullest possible extent and will reserve judgment regarding his actions until ample opportunity has been provided for him to carry on the same activities.

The following quotations indicate wholesome relations between student teachers and their supervising teachers. The first two statements were made by elementary student teachers and the last three by students at the secondary level:

Miss Blank, I feel, was a very good supervising teacher. Her kindness and patience made me feel at ease from the very beginning. She did much toward making my experience an enjoyable one.

✿   ✿   ✿

Mrs. Smith is an older teacher with a wealth of experience. She is a "comfortable" type of person, and you feel at home with her immediately. She has traveled quite extensively, and I enjoyed hearing about her travels. This fact also enriches the studies for the children as she relates her experiences in various countries . . . through the use of slides.

✿   ✿   ✿

I have taught under the supervision of Mrs. A. C. Jones, a very talented and hard-working teacher. It would be a difficult task to find someone who could adequately fill her position. Even though she has many duties and responsibilities, Mrs. Jones is consistently faithful in discharging all of them. . . . Another sterling quality of my supervising teacher is her gracious manner of giving public recognition to her student teacher. Many times during the past weeks, Mrs. Jones has expressed to the students her appreciation for something which I had done. . . . Mrs. Jones has been helpful in every way, offering worthwhile suggestions and giving sound advice where they were needed. I feel that success of my student teaching is directly related to her thoughtfulness and capable guidance.

✿   ✿   ✿

Mr. Person, my supervising teacher, put me at ease at once. I was glad that he had prepared the class for my coming. I appreciated the opportunity to see methods in action by observing his teaching and that of others at Southern.

❄   ❄   ❄

As a supervising teacher, Mrs. Person was tops. Without her help, my teaching efforts would have been of little value. In conferences, or just in lunchroom chats, she conveyed to me her positive outlook on teaching.

Reporting to the Supervising Teacher

If you have not previously met your supervising teacher, you should first report to the office of the principal of the school to which you have been assigned. Wait for the principal (or someone designated by him) to introduce you to your supervising teacher.

Be considerate of your supervising teacher. He will gladly give of his time to help you become oriented to the new surroundings, but you should not expect him to pay special attention to you when he has thirty or forty students for whose education he is responsible at this particular time. As soon as an opportunity presents itself, have an informal conference with him. During this conference, or at least, at an early one, you should secure the following:

1. A complete schedule of the teacher's curricular and extra-curricular activities.
2. A schedule of all classes in the school.
3. A list of all materials, such as textbooks, reference books, maps, charts, apparatus, etc., used by the students in classes taught by your supervisor.
4. Class rolls for all classes taught by your supervising teacher and, if available, seating charts of all classes.
5. Any special suggestions concerning future observations.
6. Sources of information (such as cumulative records) that will help you get acquainted with the pupils.[3]
7. A knowledge of school regulations.
8. The time when staff members are expected to begin and close the school day.

Observing Proper Relations with the Supervising Teacher

The following behaviors will help in your interpersonal relations:

1. Respect the opinions of the supervising teacher.
2. Adhere to a neutral policy in school relationships.
3. a. Divulge no information not intended to leave the classroom.
   b. Take no part in criticism of one staff member by another.
4. Respect teaching procedures of your supervising teacher.
5. Consult your supervising teacher on all matters of policy regarding
   a. classroom management
   b. discipline
   c. other factors
6. Be regular and prompt in attendance.
7. Assist the supervising teacher in every possible way.
8. Plan with your supervising teacher the initial activities in which you may be engaged.

[3] Remember that these are confidential data and must be treated as such at all times.

RELATIONS OF THE STUDENT TEACHER
WITH HIS STUDENTS

The best rule for the student teacher to follow in his relations with students is to hold the same relationship with students that the supervising teacher maintains. This means that he should be a friend and helper, but that he should be careful about becoming too familiar with his students. Since the student teacher is usually quite young—in fact, often very little older than the youth with whom he works—it is particularly easy for him to become too familiar with them and thus decrease the probability of his having a successful student-teaching experience. Young people prefer their teachers to act as adults. They desire and appreciate better the friendship and assistance of someone whom they respect and admire.

The following statements of student teachers describe their relationships at the beginning of their student-teaching experience:

Miss Smith and each boy and girl helped to make me feel as though I had been with them all year.

o   o   o

I must admit that when I arrived at Blank Junior High, I was a bit nervous. . . . My reservations were soon pacified by Miss Jones, my supervising teacher. She said I would sit in front of the class and act as a "second teacher"; that way, she said, the class would feel more at ease when I took over, and I wouldn't be a complete stranger to them.

Sometimes, even the surprise of being placed in a different situation from the one expected may work for the good of all concerned, as described by a student teacher in the following words:

When I was assigned to the John Olds Elementary School, I was supposed to work under another teacher, who became ill. I had visited this other teacher and found her to be such an excellent teacher and the pupils so bright that I immediately became attached to them. When I went to the school on Monday, February 9, 1959, and the principal, Mrs. Schools, explained to me that I must be assigned to a new teacher, I felt a pang of disappointment. The pupils in the new class were considerably slower, and I felt I couldn't learn as much by working with a slow group as with a bright one. However, after having met Mrs. Blank and the new class, I became as attached to them as to the other group, and even more so, as time went on.

One junior-high-school student teacher makes the following observations regarding the beginning of his student-teaching experience:

I was a bit tense about student teaching when I thought of an experienced supervising teacher breathing down my neck at all times. Mr. Jones, however, proved to be different from my connotation of a supervising teacher. His naturalness and poise, easy-going manner and helpfulness set my insecure feelings to flight. I really enjoyed working with him.

Observing Wholesome Relations with Students

The following rules will help you maintain proper relations with your students:

1. Be impartial at all times.
2. Refrain from being the third party in an argument between students.
3. Avoid intimate social relationships.

4. Do not be a perfectionist—develop sympathy, tolerance, patience, and understanding in working with others.
5. Set a good example in word and deed.
6. Plan your work in such a way that your students will have confidence in your ability and knowledge.
7. Do not try to look too collegiate; a college sweater is not usually appropriate to wear in the classroom.

One student teacher expresses her observations regarding relations between first-grade pupils and herself in the following way:

I consider the most important lesson I learned was that of being firm but friendly and showing the children that you mean what you say. I found that first-graders can usually see the reason for classroom and playground rules. Sometimes they seem hurt after being corrected, but they understand fairness. I also noted that often they can quote the rule, but that practicing it is another thing!

A junior-high-school student teacher makes the following statement regarding her mistake with regard to her relations with students at the beginning of the student-teaching period:

As is the case with most beginning teachers, I became so friendly with the students that I was not tough enough with them. I realize that in order to have a really well-disciplined classroom, I will have to start out more sternly than I would like to do, and later I can ease up a little. It is essential to begin right.

Two senior-high-school student teachers make similar observations:

It was an education in itself to observe how the adolescent mind works. The students were friendly and easy to get acquainted with. One of my biggest obstacles to overcome will be that of being too easy on the students. As Miss Blank [supervising teacher] has said, "Be polite, but very firm from the first. Keep them busy and let them know you mean business. This will help you to command their respect." Mr. Smith's [supervisor] comments on this subject, too, have eased my thinking concerning the inevitable discipline problems most young teachers face.

✿   ✿   ✿

One of the first lessons brought home to me was that getting along with fellow students is completely different from getting along with students over whom you have authority. They can be your friends but not your "buddies." I learned by experience that which I had read in books—that all students must be shown interest, understanding, and love.

RELATIONS OF THE STUDENT TEACHER
WITH THE COLLEGE SUPERVISOR
OR DIRECTOR

The college supervisor or director of student teaching is the one person to whom both the student teacher and the supervising teacher should feel responsible. If any serious difficulty develops between a student teacher and his supervising teacher, his pupils, or their parents, it is the college supervisor who is usually called upon to assist in rectifying the misunderstanding and smoothing the way for the student teacher to continue his work.

The student teacher should consider the college supervisor to be his helper in any difficult situation. When the college supervisor visits your classroom, it is only for the purpose of determining how he may better help you to get the best possible experience during the time of your student teaching. His conferences with you and with your supervising teacher are conducted for the same purpose. The seminar which the college supervisor holds with all student teachers at regular intervals is intended to be a session in which you ask questions and discuss problems that have arisen during your student-teaching experience.

The reaction of one elementary student teacher toward her university supervisor is indicated in the following quotation:

I would like to thank you for all of the guidance you've given me in my student teaching. I always looked forward to your coming to visit. You have a wonderful way of putting student teachers at ease.

RELATIONSHIP OF THE STUDENT-TEACHING PROGRAM TO THE ONGOING ACTIVITIES OF THE COOPERATING SCHOOL

Since the best student-teaching experience is the one which is the most comprehensive, it is important that the student teacher have opportunities to participate in all of the ongoing activities of the cooperating school. If for any reason this is impossible, the goal should be "as wide a participation as possible."

It is often true that the student teacher, as well as the regularly employed teacher, gets to know his pupils better and that his rapport with everyone connected with the school is improved more through informal contacts that are made through extra-class activities than those made through regularly scheduled class work. For this reason the student teacher should participate in all of the activities of the school which time permits.

The importance of such breadth of experience is indicated in the following statement by a supervising teacher:

The student teacher planned and taught an excellent project entitled "Living in Our World." He checked on progress, he evaluated, he considered individual differences, he graded the students, and he determined how he could teach more effectively.

In observing and participating in the Dramatic Club, he gained experience he felt would be useful in his teaching.

Reactions of student teachers toward variety of experience are indicated in the following statements:

. . . I thoroughly enjoyed all of our seventh-grade teacher meetings. While there, I found out what some of the other duties of a teacher are besides just classroom work. I began to realize how teachers must always try to learn more about the subjects which they teach and new ways to present old material. The conferences which I had with Miss Blank [the supervising teacher] were very beneficial to me. She was never too busy to take time to talk to me. She was always willing to answer my questions and help me in any way she could. . . . I believe that the time I spent in preparing lessons, making out tests, grading papers, etc., will prove invaluable to me when I begin teaching on my own.

❋   ❋   ❋

I have had experience in making monthly school reports and in keeping daily attendance records. I have administered and graded the California Mental Maturity Test. I have had the responsibility of grading daily classroom work.

I have observed the activities that have been going on in all of the other classrooms of the school. I taught the classes one full day by myself when Mrs. Jones [the supervising teacher] was ill. . . .

I believe that during my twelve weeks of student teaching, Mrs. Jones has given me every experience that I shall meet in my own classroom. She has given me experience in using all available audio-visual equipment.

Having had experience in teaching, and knowing what I wanted to gain from teaching, Mrs. Jones has succeeded in giving me the desired experiences. I was ready to make my desires known when, early in the program, Mrs. Jones asked me to write a paper on the experiences in which I wished to take part.

Another student teacher expresses some of the values of having varied experiences as follows:

Mrs. Smith has charge of many extracurricular activities. Thus I found myself cutting and sewing bandages for the Student Council.

Also, the annual senior class-night program was under our supervision. This gave me an opportunity to plan and to work on a project which was not directly related to my field. I gained valuable experi-

ence in learning how to handle a large group of students as well as learning how to direct a group of high-school students at work on a class project. . . . From this experience I certainly gained a greater appreciation of teenagers.

One rather timid student teacher says:

Small tasks such as turning on the lights, erasing the board, closing and opening windows, checking room temperature, etc., helped me to gain poise and confidence in the classroom.

One young man makes the following comments:

A major factor which contributed a great deal to my friendship with the students was my taking a sincere interest in their sports. I attended all of their home basketball games. I also traveled with the players, cheerleaders, and other students on several of their trips to other schools. It was great fun, and I enjoyed it thoroughly.

Your success as a student teacher and as a beginning teacher will be determined largely by your knowledge of subject matter and your ability to work effectively with coworkers and students. Consideration for the opinions of others and genuine interest in their activities are essential to wholesome interpersonal relations.

Respect and concern for the individual and with his needs and problems is a prerequisite to good teaching.

SUGGESTED READINGS

At the end of each chapter of this book you will find a list of reading materials which may be helpful to you in solving problems and gaining the maximum from your student-teaching experience.

SELECTED REFERENCES

Brembeck, Cole S., *The Discovery of Teaching.* Englewood Cliffs, New Jersey: Prentice-Hall, Inc., 1962. Chapter 1 gives a description of beginning teachers' impressions of the teaching experience.

Burton, William H., *The Guidance of Learning Activities.* New York: Appleton-Century-Crofts, Inc., 1952. In Chapters 1, 2, and 3 a specific learning situation is presented quickly and as a whole, with special reference to certain details which have meaning when seen in relation to the total situation.

Byers, Loretta, and Elizabeth Irish, *Success in Student Teaching.* Boston: D. C. Heath and Company, 1961. Chapter 1 is a discussion of the factors involved in making a good start in student teaching.

Chandler, J. B., *Education and the Teacher.* New York: Dodd, Mead and Company, 1961. Chapter 16 is an excellent statement of professional and personal satisfactions in teaching.

Grambs, Jean D., William J. Iverson, and Frank K. Patterson, *Modern Methods in Secondary Education.* New York: The Dryden Press, 1958. In the revised edition, Chapters 1 and 2 discuss the adjustment of the prospective teacher to the high-school situation and to the student-teaching experience.

Gruhn, William T., and Harl R. Douglass, *The Modern Junior High School.* New York: The Ronald Press Company, 1956. Part I provides a background in the distinctive contribution of the junior high school.

Kettlekamp, Gilbert C., *Teaching Adolescents.* Boston: D. C. Heath and Company, 1954. Chapter 3 is an excellent discussion of the student-teaching experience.

Kyte, George C., *The Elementary School Teacher at Work*. New York: The Dryden Press, Inc., 1957. Chapter 1 deals with the purposes of an elementary-school program and ways in which these purposes may be implemented.

Mehl, Marie A., Hubert H. Mills, and Harl R. Douglass, *Teaching in the Elementary School*. New York: The Ronald Press Company, 1950. Chapter 24 describes the teacher as a person.

Risk, Thomas M., *Principles and Practices of Teaching in Secondary Schools*. New York: American Book Company, 1958, second edition. Unit I is a discussion of foundations of successful teaching in secondary schools.

Sharp, D. Louise, ed., *Why Teach?* New York: Henry Holt and Company, 1957. An excellent collection of essays about teachers and teaching.

2. Getting a Successful Start

In order for you to accomplish the maximum in your student-teaching experience, it is necessary that your first few days in the cooperating school be enjoyable as well as challenging. Most students have a feeling of insecurity and uncertainty when they begin their student teaching, even though they have had previous experiences in working with young people. This is a natural reaction whenever a person is starting a new job or changing to a new location. However, it is probably more noticeable with beginning teachers than with individuals who are starting in many other types of work because of the fact that they will be in charge of a relatively large group of youth. This feeling of insecurity has been stated by certain student teachers as follows:

My student-teaching experiences were undertaken with fear and trembling. Little did I know, when I came to Blank Junior High School for the first time, what was in store for me. I had no idea that I would have an interest in so many things before the quarter was over. Had I known that I would be helping with a variety of events, I would probably have thrown up my hands in despair. I did not know, however, and since I moved into the situation gradually, it was not nearly so frightening as I had expected.

   ✿ ✿ ✿

When the words "student teaching" were mentioned at the beginning of this quarter, I immediately felt a shiver go up and down my spine. This student teaching was a completely new and different kind of experience from any course I had previously had in college.

   ✿ ✿ ✿

I entered our sixth-grade room here at Western that first Monday with much fear and trembling. However, Mr. Blank made me feel very much a part of the Western family the moment I stepped through the doorway into the room. I greatly appreciated the way in which he gave me a guided tour through the building, introducing me to many of the staff members along the way. Any new situation is rather frightening, but Mr. Blank helped to lessen my feeling of being new and made me feel more at ease by "showing me the ropes."

In spite of all that can be done previous to the time of student teaching, some prospective teachers do not have the correct impression of what is meant by this experience. This is illustrated by the following statement:

By some misconceived idea, I had established the thought in my mind that student teaching would be "glorified fun," a time when studying would cease. However, after my first few days of observation, *I discovered that student teaching was the time when studying really began.*

GRADUAL INDUCTION

One of the best ways for the student teacher to become more secure in presenting learning experiences and dealing with an entire class is through gradual induction. This is true in any line of work, but it is especially important for you as a beginning student teacher, since you must usually build self-confidence in standing before so large a group. In order to do the best possible job, you must feel as much at ease as possible when dealing with such a "large group."

The following quotations indicate the feeling of the student teacher in this regard:

My period of observation was my time for "easing into the saddle" of teaching. I learned the children's first names the first day I was in the classroom, and I soon began to associate likes and dislikes, interests, needs, and personality characteristics with these names.

*　　*　　*

When I entered my student teaching, most of the experiences were new to me. I found it difficult, at first, to adjust myself to being before the class. I feel that my adjustment was made easier because I was permitted to gradually work into the group and to develop confidence in my work as I proceeded.

I appreciated the fact that Mr. Smith [supervising teacher] didn't push me into something until I felt I was ready. . . . Gradually, I increased my load by taking one reading group at a time for a week. . . . Finally, it grew to the point where I had full responsibility of the room. This was really a wonderful experience for me.

Student teaching should not begin with a "sink or swim" technique. However, sometimes circumstances arise which give the student teacher the feeling that he is being put on the spot in starting his actual teaching, as the following statement indicates:

Actual teaching came early in my experience. My supervising teacher was called home about the third day I was there. I found myself in a situation that was rather uncomfortable—at least until the substitute arrived. Not having prepared the lesson, I had to make decisions in a hurry. However, I found that it was not as difficult as I had anticipated.

The rate at which the student teacher can successfully be inducted into the more difficult student-teaching experiences depends on a number of factors. Perhaps the most important of these is the student teacher himself. Some students are ready to enter into actual teaching soon after they start their student-teaching experience. On the other hand, it sometimes happens that they are not actually ready to take over the entire class, even after several weeks of observation and participation.

Another factor which determines the best rate of induction is the age and grade level of the students involved. At the elementary level the student teacher may start almost at the very beginning of his student-teaching experience to do some actual teaching, at least with individual pupils or small groups. On the other hand, in the senior high school it is usually best for the student teacher to have a relatively long period of orientation before undertaking the more difficult responsibilities.

A third factor relating to induction to student-teaching activities is the type of students in the class. The economic and social standing of the students and their intellectual ability determine the time which should be provided for the student teacher to observe and participate in the less difficult activities before attempting the more difficult tasks.

The persons who can best determine the time when the student teacher should enter into more difficult experiences are the supervising teacher and the student teacher. However, it has been found that some supervising teachers have a tendency to rush the student teacher into actual teaching before he is ready, while others are afraid to turn the teaching work over to the student teacher and thus do not give him the experience that he should receive. Both of these situations present a problem to the student teacher. The first is likely to cause him to be frightened and unable to do his best job. In the second type of situation the student teacher will probably become bored and dissatisfied, and feel that he is not getting the experience that he needs. It is natural for the regular teacher to feel his responsibility for the best possible instruction of the students in his class, and rightly so. However, the student teacher must be given some opportunity to "try his wings." Otherwise, he will enter his first classroom as a regular teacher without having the best possible preparation.

One senior-high-school student teacher expresses in the following words her satisfaction with the gradual induction process that was used by her supervising teacher:

The first real problem I had to face in learning to be a teacher was considerable self-consciousness about facing a group of bright youngsters only a few years younger than myself. I had dreaded my first actual teaching ever since I had enrolled in the "Introduction to Education" course nearly two years earlier. But, very fortunately, my supervising teacher had more confidence in me than I had in myself and, somehow, I found that I could get up before the class and talk and write on the blackboard and even walk around the room naturally as "a real teacher."

YOU AND THE SCHOOL PROGRAM

As a student teacher, you should remember that your presence in the classroom may make it necessary for the supervising teacher to adjust his program. Each student teacher is an individual, with certain abilities and certain shortcomings. The modern teacher is aware of the necessity of individualizing instruction for his pupils. Similarly, it is necessary for the supervising teacher to determine, through conferences and other observational techniques, the type of person with whom he is working.

It may be necessary for the supervising teacher to change some of his routines in order to provide essential experiences for the student teacher. As a matter of fact, this may be a good thing for the experienced teacher to do. However, it is usually a difficult situation, since the experienced teacher tends to "get in a rut" and feel that his way of doing things is best. Supervising teachers often report that the student teacher has "put them on their toes," and they feel that it has been valuable for them to have worked with a student teacher.

It is easy for the student teacher to lose sight of the inconvenience which his admission to the cooperating school may entail and to think only of his own problems and plans. Remember that student teaching is a cooperative process, and it must be so considered at all times.

KEEPING A DAILY LOG

One practice which will help you to gain the most possible benefit from your student-teaching experience is the keeping of a comprehensive daily log of activities, problems, answers, and suggestions which are encountered during the entire time of your student teaching. Time spent in such activity is always worthwhile, since such a log will be valuable not only while you are taking student teaching but during your first year in a regular teaching position (see Appendix B for a specimen).

Included in such a log should be the following:

1. Methods, devices, and procedures used by your supervising teacher in improving the teaching-learning situation.
2. Ways in which problems are solved by your supervising teacher and other individuals involved in the teaching-learning situation.
3. Specimens of all plans that you develop (see Appendix C).
4. Comments regarding the usefulness of such plans, and suggestions for their improvement.
5. Sociometric and/or case studies (see Appendices D and E).
6. Student-teaching and conference reports.
7. Criticisms and suggestions made by your supervising teacher and your college or university supervisor.
8. A *daily* record of time spent in observation, participation, and actual teaching.
9. Any other material that may be beneficial to you at a later time.

An elementary-school student teacher expresses her attitude regarding the keeping of a log in the following manner:

The observation of my teacher, Miss Black, helped me feel more prepared when it came to teaching. Taking notes on each child during this period helped me to get to know the names of the children and what each child was like. Keeping a log gave me many ideas to use in my actual teaching experience.

SELECTED REFERENCES

Brembeck, Cole S., *The Discovery of Teaching.* Englewood Cliffs, New Jersey: Prentice-Hall, Inc., 1962. Chapter 2 is a discussion of the problems that the student teacher faces in beginning his work.

Grambs, Jean D., William J. Iverson, and Franklin K. Patterson, *Modern Methods in Secondary Education.* New York: The Dryden Press, 1958 (Revised Edition). Chapter 12 deals with classroom management and the place of the teacher in this process.

Klausmeier, Herbert J., and Katharine Dresden, *Teaching in the Elementary School,* Second Edition. New York: Harper and Brothers, 1962. Chapter 1 provides information and illustrations which should help the beginning elementary student teacher to understand the philosophy and procedures which are important in the modern elementary school.

Kyte, George C., *The Elementary School Teacher at Work.* New York: The Dryden Press, Inc., 1957. In Chapter 1 the philosophy of the American elementary school is discussed with practical applications.

Mills, Hubert H., and Harl R. Douglass, *Teaching in High School.* New York: The Ronald Press Company, 1957. Chapters 1, 2, and 3 include the modern concept of teaching, the role and objectives of the teacher, and the characteristics of the effective teacher.

Ohlsen, Merle M., *Modern Methods in Elementary Education.* New York: Henry Holt and Company, Inc., 1959. Chapter 2 refers to problems involved in the learner-centered classroom.

Risk, Thomas M., *Principles and Practices of Teaching in Secondary Schools.* New York: American Book Company, 1958 (Second Edition). Chapter 7 gives some general principles related to learning activities in school.

Schorling, Raleigh, and Howard T. Batchelder, *Student Teaching in Secondary Schools.* New York: McGraw-Hill Book Company, Inc., 1956. Chapter 2 presents the orientation of the secondary student teacher.

Wingo, G. Max, and Raleigh Schorling, *Elementary School Student Teaching.* New York: McGraw-Hill Book Company, Inc., 1955. Suggestions are made in Chapter 1 for getting started in student teaching.

II. OBSERVATION

3. Observation: Physical, Personnel, Instructional, and Management Characteristics

Your success as a student teacher will be determined largely by your observation of teaching-learning situations in which the superior teacher is involved. Opportunities for observation should have been provided previous to the time of student teaching in connection with other professional courses. The more contact the prospective student teacher can have with youth of the age he is planning to teach, previous to actual student teaching, the better prepared he should be for such work. If the teacher-education institution has a laboratory school, this is the most convenient place for pre-student-teaching observation and participation. However, it is necessary to have some opportunity for such experiences in connection with the student-teaching experience.

It is helpful to the prospective teacher if some observational activities can be continued throughout the period of student teaching, since the participation and teaching experiences provide more sound bases for observing the methods and procedures followed by other teachers. The value of observation in the education of teachers is indicated by the fact that many school systems provide a visiting day for every beginning teacher, during which he may go to other schools in the local system or in nearby cities for the purpose of gaining new ideas regarding methods, devices, and procedures that he may use in improving his own teaching. Some school systems make provision for one or more visiting days for each teacher each year, regardless of the number of years of teaching experience that the individual has had. Since every successful teacher must be on the lookout for new ideas and techniques for use in his own teaching, the value of such a practice is apparent.

Preparation for observation, and guidance throughout the observation period, are especially important for the individual who has not had previous teaching experience. This preparation should be provided largely by the teacher-education institution through pre-student-teaching course work and through a good student-teaching guide. However, the supervising teacher can do much to facilitate the observation process through conferences with the prospective student teacher and by preparing the way for the student teacher.

WHAT OTHER STUDENT TEACHERS SAY

The following statements of student teachers regarding observation give some idea of the benefits which you may obtain through such activities:

Before actually taking over the class, I spent approximately forty hours observing the students and the teacher's methods. This period of observation enabled me to approach my actual teaching with some knowledge of the students' individual aptitudes and the methods employed by the teacher.

            ✿   ✿   ✿

Observing a number of days helped me to overcome the feeling of insecurity and fear I felt toward student teaching at the beginning of the quarter. It helped me to become familiar with the methods of Mrs. Blank's [supervising teacher] teaching of various subjects as well as to become acquainted with the pupils—their names, attitudes, and personalities. I was able to familiarize myself with the routine of the daily schedule and better understand the teaching procedures before I began actual teaching.

            ✿   ✿   ✿

My period of observation was very helpful. From it I learned to know the students and some of their characteristics. It also helped me to know the very bright students and those who were not so bright. By observing my supervising teacher, I was able to learn some of the techniques which she used in teaching, thus helping me much in preparing to teach.

❀   ❀   ❀

I learned to observe children to see why they act and do things as they do. In this way, I could teach more effectively and be more understanding toward them. I also became acquainted with many techniques and approaches to help in teaching.

❀   ❀   ❀

In my observation of the children, I saw thirty-seven different personalities, some who easily adjusted to school and others who rebelled when they could not have their own way. I longed to study each one extensively and help them individually, but the time would not permit. I saw improvement in both behavior and work during my short time with them.

❀   ❀   ❀

I was especially grateful for the first two weeks which I spent in observation. During this time I was able to learn all of the pupils' names, and I endeavored to find out their individual likes, dislikes, hobbies, and abilities. When this was accomplished, I found that it was easier for me to establish good rapport. I also found out later, when I started teaching, that it was much easier for me to teach because of this knowledge.

❋   ❋   ❋

By observing the first two weeks, I obtained helpful information about methods and basic ideas which served as a background for teaching my units. I had a chance to preview texts and materials for use in the course. During this period, I had time to acquaint myself with this age level of pupils and to learn their behavior patterns and interests.

GETTING THE MOST FROM OBSERVATION

In order for an individual to receive the maximum of benefit from observation, he must know what to observe, how (and how not) to conduct himself during the time of observation, and how to make the best possible use of the ideas obtained. Throughout this chapter and Chapter 4 you will find suggestions which, if followed, will aid you in observation. At the end of each of these chapters are questions and problems which should also make your observation more meaningful.

It is recommended that you use the notebook in which you are keeping your log of student-teaching experiences to record your observations of physical, personnel, and instructional characteristics as well as factors relating to classroom management and extraclass and professional activities that are evident in the school in which you are observing. It is also recommended that you answer the questions at the end of each chapter as you proceed with your student teaching. Many of these questions may be answered while you are observing the teaching-learning situations. Others should be considered in conference with your supervising teacher and other persons who are connected with the student-teaching program. Still others may be used when you are planning your work or evaluating your student-teaching experiences.

The more time and effort you spend in answering the questions that are provided throughout this book, the more benefit you will receive from your student-teaching experience. Your student-teaching log will prove to be valuable when you begin your first regular teaching position as well as during your student-teaching experience.

PRELIMINARY OBSERVATION

It is well for you to visit the classroom in which you are to observe before the class assembles. This should be done previous to the time when you begin your student-teaching experience. If you have not been introduced to your supervising teacher, you should present your credentials and, if convenient, spend a few minutes in informal conversation. If time permits, your supervising teacher will probably show you around the room and, possibly, introduce you to other teachers and give you a guided tour of the building. The principal or another person who is in charge of all student teachers in the building may provide a period of orientation before you actually begin your student-teaching experience.

OBSERVING PHYSICAL CHARACTERISTICS
OF THE CLASSROOM

Since the teacher has control, to a large extent, of physical factors in the classroom, it is important for the student teacher to gain knowledge regarding such matters. The effects of ventilation, heating, and lighting on students and teacher should be noted. In fact, you will have much more time to consider such factors while you are observing than after you get into the more difficult phases of teaching.

It is a commonly recognized fact that the teacher may become so involved in his teaching that he forgets about some of the routine duties that are important to the teacher and students. You should notice evidences of lack of attention to physical characteristics of the classroom so that you will be less likely to disregard the needs of yourself and your students when you begin teaching. It may be that your supervising teacher follows the practice of having certain students who are responsible for some of these routine tasks. If so, you should notice how well they assume these responsibilities and consider ways that you might improve the situation.

There are times when everyone involved in teaching and learning become oblivious to physical surroundings. In fact, this usually is the time when the best teaching is being accomplished. At such times it is quite possible that the student teacher may notice the need for certain adjustments that will contribute to the development of a better classroom atmosphere.

Ventilation

One of the physical characteristics of the classroom which greatly influences the quantity and quality of work that can be accomplished is the ventilation, or lack of it. While you are observing, you have an excellent opportunity to study the effects of proper and improper ventilation on the students and the teacher.

Notice the ventilation system that is in use. If it is a forced-air system, study the entire plan which has been provided and determine its strong points and weaknesses. It may be possible to talk with the engineer who is in charge of the heating and ventilation system. He can probably provide information regarding defects which might not be noticeable to a casual observer. If windows are used for ventilation, notice the arrangement of such openings. The circulation of air is usually improved by opening windows at both top and bottom.

In schools with a forced-air system of ventilation, there is likely to be a set of regulations to be followed by all persons in the building. If this is true, you should ask for a copy of the regulations and study them to determine ways in which the operation of the ventilating system might be improved.

Heating

One physical characteristic which is actually a phase of ventilation is the heating of the classroom. The best temperature for optimum working conditions where little exercise is involved is from 68° to 72°. You have undoubtedly noticed that when the temperature in your study room gets higher than 72°, you begin to feel drowsy and you are unable to do your best work. Notice the effects of changing temperature on the students and teacher. Determine whether there is anything you can do to correct any deficiencies.

Lighting

Notice the arrangement for natural lighting in the classroom. Does the seating arrangement make the best possible use of the available natural light without causing glare on chalkboards and desks? Artificial lighting should be adequate for cloudy days without undue glare. The eyes of students and teachers alike are among their most prized possessions and need to be carefully guarded.

You may be able to make some suggestions for the arrangement of seats, desks, etc., for more satisfactory illumination. The student teacher has time to make a thorough study of the lighting arrangements and may be able to give suggestions to the supervising teacher regarding changes that may be made. Adjustment of window shades may be a part of the student teacher's work during his time of observation.

Bulletin Boards and Other Decorations

What has been done, and what more can be done, to promote learning by increasing the attractiveness of the classroom? Among the first duties which you may assume will be the assistance of your supervising teacher in preparing bulletin-board displays and arranging flowers, aquariums, and other decorative and useful materials for the improvement of learning. Your supervising teacher may suggest that you take over the job of arranging bulletin-board displays under his general supervision. It is often true that the student teacher has greater artistic ability than his supervising teacher, and any good supervising teacher is happy to have the assistance of his student teacher in such matters.

One student teacher describes his activities regarding physical characteristics of the classroom in the following way:

This course has made it possbile for me to see and understand the physical characteristics of both the classroom and the school. It has made me realize that the teacher has a big responsibility in the regulation of the physical factors in the classroom. He has the responsibility of controlling the sunlight by raising or lowering the shades, of controlling the air by raising or lowering the windows, and of seeing that maps, books, charts, pictures, and bulletin boards are adequately placed and contribute to the attractiveness of the room. By observing and working with these physical factors during student teaching, I now know that I will have to consider these important things as a part of my job when I enter the teaching profession. I will know what physical characteristics to look for when I enter a school building or a classroom.

GETTING ACQUAINTED

In order for the teacher to perform effectively the complicated job of teaching, he must become well acquainted with his students—know their individual likes and dislikes, aptitudes and interests, as well as their intellectual abilities. Your previous training in theory courses in education should provide an excellent background for your study of individual students and the class as a whole. The more firsthand work you have had with young people, the better prepared you will be to begin your work as a student teacher. However, regardless of the amount of contact you have previously had, your first job in student teaching is to get acquainted with the persons with whom you will be working.

During your time of observation, you will have an excellent opportunity to learn much about your students. Your supervising teacher will help you by providing you with a seating chart so that you can relate names with students and, while class discussion is being conducted, discover some of the characteristics of individual students.

What to Look For

One indication of the types of students in a class, as well as the quality of teaching, is the attitude of the students. If some of them appear to be listless and inattentive, you should try to determine the reasons for it. You may wish to take notes for use in discussion with your supervising teacher at the close of the class period or during your conference period.

Special aptitudes and interests will also be apparent. You

should take note of these characteristics so that you can make use of them when the time comes for you to actually work with the students. The more you learn about your students while you are observing, the better prepared you will be for the work of actual teaching.

One student teacher in an elementary classroom gives the following report of her observational experiences:

My period of observation was very helpful in orienting me to the class. Observing enabled me to learn the names of the students, the routines of the classroom, and the general behavior of the class. I became aware of individual personalities and the class "personality." Mrs. Blank was especially helpful in drawing my attention to specific behaviors and giving me a background of most of the children in the class. One of the most valuable aspects of observation was being able to watch Mrs. Blank as she worked in the classroom.

The Profile Chart

One very interesting and helpful device for use in studying individual students is the profile chart. In preparing such a chart, it is well to choose two students who appear to be quite different in certain important characteristics and observe each over a period of fifteen or twenty minutes. By noticing the attitudes and activities of each student for certain intervals, the percentage of application may be calculated.

Specimen studies involving the profile chart are given in Chart 2. Additional profile charts are given in Specimen Case Study II, Appendix E.

OBSERVING METHODS, DEVICES, AND PROCEDURES OF INSTRUCTION

Observation of the way in which the supervising teacher goes about the job of teaching is one of the most important phases of the student-teaching experience. In the first place, this helps you to become acquainted with pupils and teacher. Second, such activity gives you the opportunity to increase your understanding of basic facts and principles regarding instruction through observation of the use of such facts and principles in an actual classroom situation.

You are being introduced to a real teaching-learning situation with real pupils, and you should take advantage of the opportunity to profit by observation of the personnel involved. Your previous training in theory courses is to be supplemented by concrete experiences and thus made more meaningful. The time of observation, if properly used, should contribute much toward your understanding of the students and the procedures so that you will be better prepared for the time when you will have responsibility for carrying on the work.

Since the success of the teacher in motivating pupils to maximum performance depends largely upon methods, devices, and procedures used in the teaching-learning situation, the importance of observing a superior teacher and noting his activities is obvious. Of course, the only way in which the prospective teacher can determine the methods best suited to his own personality is through actual teaching experience. However, by observing good teaching-learning situations and noting the methods, devices, and procedures used by the superior teacher, you will be better prepared for the task of teaching than you would otherwise be.

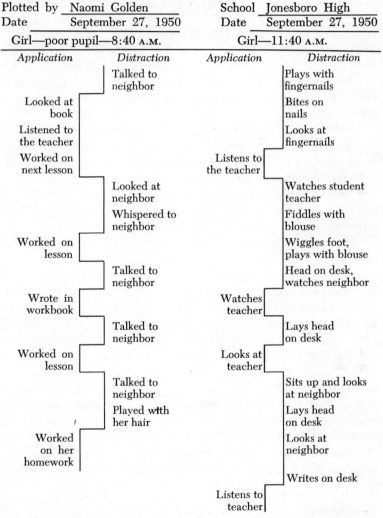

What to Look For

One phase of the teaching-learning situation which you should be able to determine by observation has to do with objectives or goals. Two sets of goals may be in evidence. They are (1) the objectives which the teacher had in mind when planning the work and (2) the obvious goals of the students. Of course, under optimum circumstances these goals should be similar, if not identical. However, this is seldom the case even in an excellent teaching-learning situation.

Three types of goals or objectives should be in evidence: understandings, skills, and attitudes. By observing the interpersonal relations and the activities that are evident, you should be able to determine at least part of the objectives of both teacher and students. Consideration of the needs of students and the methods, devices, and procedures that are used should give you a fairly accurate picture of the teaching-learning situation.

Many methods, devices, and procedures may be used by the supervising teacher in guiding his students toward the objectives or goals which he feels are desirable. Identify the means which are being used by the supervising teacher, and determine the ends toward which the students are being guided. Notice evident changes in behavior of students. If you are permitted to observe a group of students over a sufficiently long period of time under the direction of a superior teacher, you should be able to observe definite changes in mental, emotional, and social characteristics of the learners. More objective evidence of such changes may be provided by evaluation procedures. Note the specific procedures which the supervising teacher uses in evaluating changes which are taking place. Confer with your supervising teacher about such methods, and determine whether the conclusions you drew from observation are in harmony with the supervising teacher's evaluation.

Questioning

One of the most important and effective methods at the disposal of the teacher is questioning. It is adaptable to all types of subject matter and to informal as well as formal teaching situations. The fact that it is the oldest method of teaching is no indication that it is out of date. The types of questions used and the way in which questions are stated determine to a great extent the quality of learning. Student teachers and beginning teachers often encounter difficulties in the phrasing and use of questions. Their questions may be ambiguous or over the heads of their students. Much can be learned regarding the art of questioning by observing a superior teacher.

Desirable behaviors which may be developed in students through proper types of questioning include (1) reflective thought, (2) understanding of facts and principles, (3) application of information, (4) appreciations and attitudes, (5) critical thinking, and (6) cause-and-effect relationships. Questions may be used to create interest, arouse purposes, develop mind-set, or to test designated achievements. Notice the types of questions that are used by your supervising teacher, and determine the purposes which may be accomplished by (1) factual questions, (2) questions requiring yes-or-no answers, (3) leading questions, and (4) thought questions. Confer with your supervising teacher about his reasons for using various types of questions, and determine whether they correspond to your observed reactions.

One student teacher in an elementary school produced the following list of questions to develop understandings regarding the geographic features of the Netherlands and their effects on its population:

1. Locate the Netherlands on the globe.
   a. What special geographic problems face the people in the Netherlands?
   b. How do these problems affect the people?
   c. How do the Dutch people live (1) in cities, (2) in villages, (3) on farms?
   d. Mention some characteristics of the Dutch people.
2. Describe the climate of the Netherlands. How does this climate affect the people?
3. How do the people in the Netherlands—their land and mode of

living—compare with people in other countries that we have studied?

4. What activities and research can we perform to learn more about the Netherlands?

The following questions were developed by a junior-high-school student teacher to help his students understand the influence of territorial expansion on the development of our way of life:

1. Why didn't the term "the West" always apply to the same region?
2. What three types of men played an important part in settling the West?
3. What were the first settlements in the Old Southwest? Why were they settled, and by whom?
4. Under what government did we have the writing of the Ordinance of 1785 and the Northwest Ordinance?
5. Name the states that were located in the Old Northwest.
6. Give the points in the Ordinance of 1785. How did the law regulating the sale of land affect the settlers? Why were land companies organized?
7. Give the provisions of the Northwest Ordinance. Why was this ordinance important?
8. How did conditions in the West promote a more democratic way of life?
9. Give some characteristics of the typical Westerner.
10. How was the Indian problem settled in the Northwest? Name the states that were formed from the Old Southwest. From the Old Northwest.
11. What two requests did the Western Congressmen make? How was the sale of land in the West changed after 1820?

The above lists of questions should help to lead the learners to an understanding of basic facts and principles regarding geography and history, as well as develop appreciation and critical thinking. Cause-and-effect relationships are also emphasized.

A senior-high-school student teacher developed the following questions to bring out the moods that are expressed in writing:

Pippa Passes

The year's at the spring
And the day's at the morn:
Morning's at seven;
The hillside's dew-pearled;
The lark's on the wing;
The snail's on the thorn;
God's in his heaven—
All's right with the world!
—BROWNING

With Rue My Heart Is Laden

With rue my heart is laden
For golden friends I had,
For many a rose-lip maiden
And many a lightfoot lad.

By brooks too broad for
leaping
The lightfoot lads are laid;
The rose-lipped girls are
sleeping
In fields where roses fade.
—HOUSEMAN

1. How may these two poems signify joy and sadness? How did the poets probably feel when writing these lyrics?
2. How do these poems make you feel when you read them? Do they appeal to your emotions?
3. Discuss possible meanings of the poems. Do the last two lines of Browning's poem suggest faith, perhaps faith in the essential goodness of life?
4. Why is Houseman sad? Does he mean that all of his friends have left him to go to sleep somewhere, or does he suggest that, as certain as night follows day, all loveliness passes away?
5. How does the use of such adjectives as "golden," "rose-lipped," and "lightfoot" help us to understand certain qualities of his friends?
6. Write one or two sentences which encompass the thoughts expressed by the two poems. Do these sentences sound as beautiful as the lyrics themselves?
7. On the basis of this discussion, may we say that the poets have interpreted our experiences or that they have said things that we understand? Have they interpreted our thoughts in a new light?

The use of questions to stimulate fruitful discussion is illustrated by the following:

TEACHER—"Are unions good or bad for the individual?"
JOHN   —"I think they are good. My dad is a painter, and he says he is earning twice as much money since he joined the union."
FRANK   —"I think they are bad. My father owns a painting business. He says that if he did not have to pay his painters so much,

MARY   he could charge less, get more contracts, and make more profit."

MARY   —"It looks to me as if John's father has benefited but Frank's father has not."

PETE   —"I think unions are bad because they make everything manufactured by union companies so much more expensive."

JOAN   —"That is true, but if the goods were not more expensive, that would mean that all the workers would be making less money and have less to spend."

TEACHER—"It appears, then, that unions have elements of both good and bad. We have discovered an important principle—that there are very few things that are all good or all bad, and that being able to think in terms of *degree* of good and bad is the mark of an intelligent person."

Since the type of question that is used determines to a great degree the objectives or goals that are reached through the teaching-learning process, it is well to compare these two phases of the situation which you are observing and relate methods to goals.

In any well-adjusted and well-motivated class, questioning should be in three directions: teacher to student, student to teacher, and student to student. In fact, one of the best indications of interest is the number and quality of questions directed by students to the teacher or to other students. The superior teacher will usually turn such questions back to members of the class if they are directed to him. Note examples of this type of learning that are evident in the class which you are observing. Also, note differences in the quality of such participation in various classes. The degree of homogeneous grouping that is found will determine to a great extent the quality of questioning by the students.

OBSERVING CLASSROOM MANAGEMENT

Classroom management is closely related to methods, devices, and procedures of instruction. In fact, it is true that the use of instructional methods and materials which are conducive to a

wholesome teaching-learning situation is the most important factor in classroom management. The observation of ways in which
the superior teacher handles situations which might otherwise
develop into unsatisfactory teaching-learning relations is of inestimable benefit to the student teacher.

You should not mimic the idiosyncrasies of your supervising
teacher, but by observing a teacher's actions, you should get some
ideas regarding possible ways in which certain situations may be
handled. It is generally conceded that beginning teachers have
more difficulty with classroom management than with any other
phase of teaching. Even adequate knowledge of subject matter
and teaching methods does not guarantee that the teacher will
be successful in setting up a wholesome teaching-learning situation. However, observation of a teacher who is demonstrating
good techniques of classroom management should help the student teacher in this regard when he begins his actual teaching.
The statements of a number of student teachers are of interest
here:

One of the first things I noticed was the good classroom atmosphere.
I think it is one of the best I have ever seen and one in which students
can work effectively. The students feel equal and work well together.
It is a democracy where students feel free to express their ideas, because they know their teacher will respect them even though he may
not agree with them. The students love their teacher.

I noticed how the students were treated as adults. If students are
treated as adults, they will feel a responsibility to act more like adults.

                         *   *   *

I observed the democratic classroom in action, and I liked what I saw.
I liked to see the students doing the major part of the work and making
decisions, because I knew they were learning responsibility. They learn,
too, that if they abuse their privileges, they will be taken away from
them. This is not only a law of democracy, but it is a law of life.

These and similar statements by student teachers indicate
something of the importance of observation as a means of providing understanding regarding proper and improper types of
classroom management.

What to Look For

What methods, devices, or procedures does your supervising teacher use to facilitate the beginning of classwork? One of the most important phases of classroom management is concerned with helping students to get settled down at the beginning of the school day or class period and following an active play period. The overexuberance of youth and the opportunities for freedom that are provided by the intermission between classes, the play period, or the lunch period often get the students so keyed up that they have difficulty in getting started on the learning experiences that should be characteristic of the well-organized classroom. The wise teacher will develop certain devices and procedures which will facilitate this process. At the elementary level this may mean having the students rest with their heads on their desks for a few minutes while soft music is being played. The secondary-school teacher will have different methods of helping his students to get started on the work at hand. Since, during your period of observation, you will have the opportunity (which you will not have when you are in an actual teaching situation) of sitting back and observing the procedures followed in beginning a class session, you should gain much which will be of value to you when you take over the direction of a group of students yourself.

Notice any evidence of the inability of certain members of the class to get settled down. Is it apparent that the same individuals have this difficulty most often? Notice what your supervising teacher does to assist these students in cooperating so that the entire class will not be retarded. Note the success or lack of success of such procedures. Does the teacher always use the same tactics in such situations? It is quite probable that the teacher may need to resort to a number of different procedures in order to facilitate the beginning of class or group work.

It is often true that certain classes will have much more difficulty in getting started on the work at hand than will others. This may be due to a number of causes:

1. It is true that no two classes are alike. In schools where an attempt is made at some form of homogeneous grouping, there will probably be a greater difference between classes than will be found when a more heterogeneous group plan is employed. However, regardless of the type of grouping employed, it is always true that some classes have more difficulty in getting started on profitable learning activities than do others. This fact emphasizes the need for varying procedures on the part of the teacher with different groups. In your observation, try to determine the ways in which your supervising teacher handles such situations.
2. The type of situation from which the students have come may have a great deal to do with their actions. For example, if there has been a pep assembly or similar type of activity immediately preceding the class period, the students will naturally be in such a state of mind that it will be difficult for them to change to more subdued classroom activities. The experienced teacher should be aware of such conditions and should vary the procedures to fit the situation.
3. The type of teacher who has been in charge of the class during the preceding period has an effect on the students. Excellent teachers will vary in their approach to problems involved in classroom management. Some teachers lean more to the authoritarian or traditional philosophy, while others emphasize the democratic approach. When a group of students comes

into an altogether different atmosphere from a classroom where they have experienced one of these types of classroom management, it is often difficult for them to adjust to the change. This is not necessarily a reflection on either of the teachers involved. However, it may increase the difficulties encountered in getting the class started on desired and desirable learning experiences.

You may observe other factors which affect the teaching-learning situation. Make a note of such factors and the ways in which your supervising teacher meets them.

The following statements illustrate the attitude of student teachers with regard to their observational experiences:

If I achieved any success at all in my teaching, I would attribute it to the many things I observed from my supervising teacher, . . . her methods of teaching, her handling of teacher-pupil and pupil-pupil relationships, and her wonderful attitude toward the teaching profession itself.

✿   ✿   ✿

I didn't have much chance to observe the children. Since there are so many things to do in the second grade, I [soon] started helping and teaching the pupils. But the time when I did have the opportunity to observe was very helpful. I wasn't sure what to expect from seven- and eight-year-olds, but from watching them I have learned much that will be of value in my teaching.

✿   ✿   ✿

After observing my supervising teacher at length, I observed other third-grade teachers. Being well acquainted with Miss Smith's methods, I was able to reject or expand upon certain aspects of her program after seeing other teachers present the same material in a different way.

One secondary student teacher expresses his feelings in the following manner:

In the teaching profession good classroom management is an important device in successful teaching. The course in student teaching has helped me to understand, observe, and put into practice the factors involved in good classroom management. The conditions or situa-

tions that make it difficult for a class to get settled down at the start of a class period were made evident to me. I had the opportunity to observe the methods and devices used by my supervising teacher to get the class quieted down and started. . . . Other pointers which I learned about classroom management were how to check the roll, distribute materials, and carry on routine duties with a minimum of confusion. . . . These pointers should be of great benefit to me in the future in carrying out classroom management.

The first few minutes of a given class period are extremely important in setting the stage for the entire period. However, for the best possible teaching-learning situation there must be well-planned activities in progress throughout the period. The type of activity and the length of time which should be devoted to each activity will, of course, be determined by the age and grade level of the students concerned and the type of subject matter.

Within a given class there will probably be individual students who will need some special attention during the class period. Notice specific instances of this kind and the methods used by your supervising teacher in each situation. Since even a superior teacher may sometimes fail to do or say the best thing in a difficult situation, you may notice certain instances which you feel might have been handled more diplomatically. However, you should keep these ideas to yourself until you are in a similar situation. You may find that the supervising teacher's procedure was not so far off as you had thought. It is sometimes well to discuss such procedures with your supervising teacher during the conference period, but you should be very careful not to give the impression that the actions or words are being adversely criticized. Remember that your supervising teacher has had much more experience than you have in dealing with classroom difficulties, and even if he does make a mistake now and then, he is probably doing a good job in the long run. You are not his supervisor, but you are observing his procedures for the purpose of gaining as much help as possible for use when you are in a similar situation.

The following statement of a student teacher illustrates the attitude which is usually best in such a situation:

A student teacher may give his opinion, but he must also realize that the supervising teacher has had many years of experience and should know what he is doing. . . . The supervising teacher should have the last word at all times. The student teacher can make mental notes of such experiences and profit by them in his teaching.

Closing the work period is another important phase of the teacher's work. It is sometimes true that the teacher will become so absorbed in the work at hand that he will not notice the time. On the other hand, he may start the necessary activities involved in proper closing of the period at a time which will cause too much wasting of learning time. Notice the methods, devices, and procedures which are used by your supervising teacher in facilitating the closing of the work period without wasting the last five minutes. The collection of books, papers, and/or other materials, together with necessary housekeeping chores, may become a definite waste of time if not conducted in a proper manner.

If the students have had proper guidance in the closing activities of a work period, there will be evidence of cooperative effort on their part. However, even under the best conditions there may be individuals who will precipitate difficult situations, and the wise teacher will deal with such offenders in a way that will prevent their making a habit of such actions.

The way in which students leave the room is another indication of previous guidance on the part of the teacher (or the lack of such guidance). However, you should not be too quick to blame the teacher for improper actions on the part of students. The time of day, the day of the week, the weather, certain school events, and many other factors will affect the behavior of students.

QUESTIONS AND PROBLEMS

1. What are the advantages and disadvantages of the heating and/or ventilating system in use in the school where you are observing?
2. What rules should be followed regarding the admitting of natural light into a classroom? Are these rules satisfied in the room in which you are observing? If not, what changes would you suggest?
3. Are the artificial lights adequate in the room in which you are observing? If not, what suggestions would you make regarding rearrangement or other improvements?
4. What has been done to promote learning by increasing the attractiveness of the room in which you are observing? What suggestions would you make for improving the situation?
5. Select two students who are quite different in certain characteristics and study them over a period of time, noting their participation in classwork and evident interest, ability to stick to a job until it is completed, and other evidences of good or poor work habits.
6. What are the objectives or goals of the teacher and class you are observing, as evidenced by emphasis on certain methods and by teacher-student interrelationships?
7. Give examples of questions which may be used to accomplish the various types of behavior that are desirable in students.
8. Analyze questions that are raised by teacher and students

while you are observing a class. Are they clear and definite? What is the evident purpose of the questioner? Are there evidences of understanding of principles, of interests, and of changes in attitudes?

9. State several principles relating to usefulness of various types of questions.

10. Which types of questions used in the class which you are observing appear to be most effective?

11. Develop a set of questions over a unit or block of subject matter which you may be teaching, using questions which will help to accomplish desired objectives. State the objective or objectives which each question should help to accomplish.

12. Make a list of procedures which may be followed to facilitate the beginning of classwork during a given period.

13. State five rules or principles that the teacher should observe in order to accomplish the maximum during a class period.

14. What methods, devices, or procedures may be used in facilitating the closing of a class period without wasting too much time?

SELECTED REFERENCES

Baruch, Dorothy, *New Ways in Discipline*. New York: McGraw-Hill Book Company, Inc., 1949. The nondirective approach to classroom management is developed in detail.

Burton, William H., *The Guidance of Learning Activities*. New York: Appleton-Century-Crofts, Inc., 1952. Chapters 7 and 8 include a discussion of characteristics of the learner and his relationships with other members of the group, which may be used as a guide to the student teacher in observing classroom personnel.

Grambs, Jean D., William J. Iverson, and Franklin K. Patterson, *Modern Methods in Secondary Education*. New York: The Dryden Press, 1958. Chapters 15 and 16 concern problems connected with adjustment to school life and examples of right and wrong ways of handling such problems.

Jenkins, Gladys Gardner, Helen Shacter, and William W. Bauer, *These Are Your Children*. Chicago: Scott, Foresman and Company, 1953. An excellent discussion of characteristics of preschool and elementary-school children.

Klausmeier, Herbert J., and Katharine Dresden, *Teaching in the Elementary School*, Second Edition. New York: Harper and Brothers, 1962. Chapter 16 is an excellent discussion of mental health and discipline in the elementary school.

McGuire, Vincent, Robert B. Myers, and Charles L. Durrance, *Your Student Teaching in the Secondary School*. Boston: Allyn and Bacon, Inc., 1959. Chapter 2 gives excellent suggestions for the beginning student teacher.

Ohlsen, Merle M., *Modern Methods in Elementary Education*. New York: Henry Holt and Company, Inc., 1959. Chapter 2 is a discussion of discipline in the learner-centered classroom.

Olson, Willard C., *Child Development*. Boston: D. C. Heath and Company, 1949. Chapters 1 and 2 give an overview of child development and the relation of education to such development.

Schorling, Raleigh, and Howard T. Batchelder, *Student Teaching in Secondary Schools*. New York: McGraw-Hill Book Company, Inc., 1956. The adolescent and problems involved in teaching are discussed in Chapters 2, 6, and 7.

4. Observation: Extraclass, Community, and Professional Characteristics

The greater the variety of observational experiences that you can have during your entire period of student teaching, the better prepared you will be to carry on the many and varied activities expected of you in an actual teaching situation. All phases of the teacher's activity in connection with the school, both curricular and extracurricular, should be included in the experiences of the student teacher. Since you may not be privileged to participate in all such activities, it is especially important that you at least have the opportunity to observe your supervising teacher and others when they are carrying on these activities. Of course, the more actual experience you can have with all activities of the teacher, the better will be your preparation for teaching. However, observation is a very important phase of such experience, even after an individual has had extensive practice in participatory and actual teaching activities.

OBSERVING EXTRACLASS ACTIVITIES

It is generally expected that the teacher will accept responsibility for supervising certain activities of students outside of the classroom. The teacher who insists that his job is confined to the four walls of his classroom is almost certainly doomed to defeat. On the other hand, the person who accepts opportunities to mingle and work with pupils outside of the classroom often makes contacts that are extremely valuable in the conduction of classroom activities.

Since it is the purpose of the student-teaching program to

provide the prospective teacher with experiences similar to those he will encounter in an actual teaching situation, you should avail yourself of the opportunity to observe as many types of extraclass activities as feasible in a given situation. There are many such activities in which you will be able to participate, but there are more which you can only observe. The more opportunities you have to observe club activities, assembly programs, athletic contests, pep rallies, and other extraclass activities, the better prepared will you be to participate in such activities when you are placed in an actual teaching position. Of course, you should be provided with opportunities to observe all types of classroom and extraclass activities before you are called upon to participate in such activities. This will give you more confidence and increase the probability of your success when you actually undertake such activities.

Hall Duty

One responsibility which most teachers have is some form of hall duty. This often involves standing outside the classroom door while students are passing through the halls. You may be asked to help with this duty quite early in your student-teaching experience. Regardless of the amount of responsibility that you have in hall duty, it gives you an excellent opportunity to observe students when they are in an informal activity. As you become better acquainted with your students, you will notice more and more characteristic actions while they are passing from room to room between classes.

If there are certain students, such as proctors, who are stationed at various places in the halls to assist with the passage of their fellow students, you may learn much by observing their work. In a well-organized student body, such individuals receive valuable experience in dealing with others through this activity.

Another similar activity which you may encounter early in your student-teaching experience is the fire drill. The teacher is expected to see that his students get out of the building in good order. There is a possibility that there may be an actual fire in the building in which you are doing your student teaching. For this reason, the importance of cooperation during fire drills is especially great. You may be able to help your supervising teacher in this regard.

On the School Grounds

In most secondary schools the average teacher has very little responsibility for playground duties excepting before school begins in the mornings. In some schools, particularly junior high schools, the teachers take turns with playground and bus duties. When your supervising teacher has any duties of this kind, it is well for you to be on hand to learn as much as possible and to help with such supervision.

Elementary-school teachers are usually expected to be on the playground whenever their pupils are having their play period. This is one place in which you, as an elementary student teacher, can be of great service to your supervising teacher almost from the beginning of your student-teaching experience. You will also get better acquainted with your pupils and be able to do better work in the classroom if you assist with playground activities.

In the Lunchroom

Many secondary schools provide a separate lunchroom for faculty members. However, certain teachers are usually delegated to eat in the students' lunchroom and serve as proctors. It is common practice to have two or three teachers at a time serving as lunchroom proctors for a week or more. Thus, each teacher will have one or more weeks of such duty during the school year. The student teacher has an excellent opportunity to assist his supervising teacher with this task. In fact, it might be well for you to volunteer for such duty even when your supervising teacher is not expected to serve. It will provide an excellent opportunity to observe your students in an informal situation, and it will help you to become better acquainted with them. Of course, the supervising teacher should be consulted before undertaking any activity in the school.

Clubs

Club sponsorship is one of the most common types of extra-class activity for which the secondary-school teacher is responsible. It is well for the student teacher to visit all clubs in which he may be interested, if this can be arranged. This gives you an opportunity to observe the students in a more informal situation than the regular classes. You may be permitted to assist with one or more clubs at a future time, thus gaining much valuable experience in working with students.

The following statements by student teachers indicate the value which they receive from extraclass activities:

I was introduced to a wide variety of experiences other than actual teaching. I learned the routine of the home room and the attendance register, assisted with the Science Fair, participated in a parent-teacher conference, learned to set up and operate audio-visual equipment, assisted in administering and grading standardized tests, attended teachers' meetings and student assemblies, performed demonstrations, prepared laboratory materials, took inventory of stockroom—in short, became aware that a high-school teacher's work involves much more than classroom instruction.

                              *   *   *

In addition to my in-class activities, I sat with student-council meetings, current-affairs club meetings, etc. By my attendance, I helped in showing faculty support of athletic events and a dramatic production. I sat with a seminar on international relations in which representatives of six embassies spoke to the students and answered their questions, a major three-day activity into which the students had put much preparation.

Some of the activities mentioned above may be termed participatory activities, but most of them would be classed as observation. Of course, observational and participatory activities should be provided throughout the time of student teaching, and both types of activity may be provided at any point in the student-teaching experience, along with actual teaching. However, it is usually true that observation will be more characteristic of earlier than of later activities.

One student teacher at the junior-high-school level gives the following description of his distributed observational activities:

Observation existed as a separate activity for only two days. Even on the second day of student teaching, I began participating in administrative duties. I eventually completed twenty-five clock hours of observation, but not within the first two weeks, as I had expected. Mrs. Blank felt that I didn't need much observation and spurred me into clerical activities immediately. Observation, therefore, had to be picked up from time to time as the opportunity was provided. It often became a vital tool for studying difficult problems during times of disciplinary crisis.

The above description illustrates excellent adaptation of the student-teaching experiences according to the individual needs and characteristics of the student teacher. The grade level and type of class would also have some bearing upon the length of time which should be spent in observation at the beginning of the student-teaching period and the amount of observational experience throughout the time of student teaching.

Assembly Programs

As a student teacher, you will probably have little to do with assembly programs other than observing them. Your supervising teacher may ask you to help supervise the group for which he is responsible during an assembly program, but under ordinary circumstances this will mean merely enjoying the program. Your main duty in connection with such programs will probably be to take note of the plan used. In many junior and senior high schools, the students have an important place in the planning and execution of assembly programs. However, there are always certain faculty members who are quite active behind the scenes. Your supervising teacher will be able to give you much of the background regarding the organization of faculty and student body for all extraclass activities. If your supervising teacher is not directly concerned with the planning and execution of assembly programs, he can refer you to the faculty members who are involved in this work, and you can get valuable information by talking with them and, perhaps, observing rehearsals and planning sessions in preparation for the presentation of such programs.

Athletic Contests and Pep Rallies

As was mentioned by one of the student teachers previously quoted, attendance at athletic events is one of the principal ways of becoming better acquainted with students and improving rapport between the student teacher and those with whom he is working. The student teacher, being especially interested in such contests in his own college or university, may also be more interested in events that are taking place in the school in which he is taking student teaching than are some of the experienced teachers. However, the length of time that a person has been teaching is not necessarily an indication of his interest in athletic activities. The teacher who is most interested in working with young people is likely to be interested in their athletic activities, even though he may have reached the age at which he can no longer participate actively in such events.

Pep rallies are to be expected preceding any important athletic event. These can be conducted in such a way that they are enjoyable for all concerned. On the other hand, they may develop into the wrong type of activity if they are not properly supervised. Faculty members should always be on hand for such events, and they may provide active leadership in connection with the preparation and execution of rallies. You will undoubtedly have opportunities to assist your supervising teacher and/or other faculty members with this responsibility.

School Publications

In any secondary school, certain faculty members have responsibilities connected with school publications. The amount of responsibility and the work involved are determined by the type and size of the school. It is well for the student teacher to have opportunities to observe activities relating to school publications even though his supervising teacher may not be directly involved in this work. If you will talk with your supervising teacher about this matter, he can probably arrange for you to at least observe school publication activities.

School Traffic Patrol

This activity, also, depends upon a number of factors, including size and location of school and the grade level of the students involved. Most junior high schools and elementary schools located in metropolitan areas have some sort of safety-patrol organization among their students. If the school in which you are working has such a plan, it is well for you to learn as much as possible about it. Your supervising teacher will be glad to make necessary arrangements.

School Savings

Many schools have some form of school bank which is responsible for the handling of the sale of savings bonds or other types of investment. This gives students an excellent opportunity for valuable experience, and it also gives the student teacher opportunities to assist with the work or, at least, to observe the organizational structure involved and the place of faculty members in this program.

In the Library

The student teacher should have opportunities to talk with the librarian of the school to which he is assigned and to observe the workings of the school library organization. You may have opportunities during your actual teaching to take groups of students to the library for work periods. It is therefore important for you to observe in the library and confer with the librarian soon after you begin your student-teaching experience.

One student teacher expresses her idea of the importance of varied observation in the following words:

For the first few weeks, I observed. This gave me a chance to study the pupils, learn their names, and build up self-confidence before actually teaching. At this time I learned various things about the school and its organization. I have observed a science program, a slide program, films, a PTA meeting, a faculty meeting, a spelling contest, an operetta, class elections, the beginning of a unit, and study hall.

Another student teacher writes about certain participatory as well as observational activities which proved to be helpful experiences:

During my student teaching, I observed in other classes also to compare methods and add new ones. Mrs. Smith also took me to teachers' meetings. During my ten weeks I chaperoned a dance and several field trips, and worked with the French Club and the National French Honor Society. These, though extracurricular activities, all added up to the responsibilities of a teacher and made me feel more a part of the entire organization.

OBSERVING COMMUNITY ACTIVITIES

The teacher is evaluated on his activities and relationships in the community in which he is teaching as well as on his success in the classroom. Many times, interest and service in the community determine to a great extent the difference between his success and failure as a teacher. It is apparent, then, that the beginning teacher should consider his strengths and weaknesses with reference to community activities and avail himself of opportunities to be of service to the community outside of the school.

You, as a student teacher, should consider a list of community activities in which you may participate or at least observe. Your supervising teacher will help you compile a list of such activities and arrange times for you to observe as many types of activity as possible. It may be that your supervising teacher will have a special interest in a number of community activities. If so, you may have an excellent opportunity to accompany him.

Since you cannot hope to participate in many community activities, it is best that you observe as many as possible and then determine one or more in which you are particularly interested. If you have specific skills (artistic, musical, etc.) you may find one (or more) type of community work in which you will naturally fit. It may be in line with your work in the school. Types of community work which are more general in nature include the Y.M.C.A., Y.W.C.A., and churches. It may be that you have had previous experience with one or more of these organizations. If so, you will probably wish to continue with the same type of work.

Certain activities in the school, such as Hi-Y and Y-Teen groups, are directly connected with community organizations. Thus, you may become involved with such work both in the school and in the community.

As a rule, the more closely the school activities are connected with community activities and organizations outside of the school, the better will be the teaching-learning situation. For this reason, the student teacher's observation of, and participation in, community activities is important.

OBSERVING PARENT-TEACHER CONFERENCES

You may have opportunities to observe some conferences between your supervising teacher and the parents of some of the boys and girls in your classes. If so, you should gain much in your ability to understand parents and to maintain proper rapport with them.

Opportunities for such conferences are usually more frequent at the elementary-school level, but they are by no means limited to this level, as the following quotation from a senior-high-school student teacher indicates:

I had the privilege of sitting in on a parent-teacher guidance conference during my stay at Brookville. Bill, one of our students in Spanish, was doing very poor work and had received a progress report stating that he was in danger of failing Spanish for that quarter. The parents called the school and requested a conference. I attended this conference, held between the parents, the guidance officer, and my supervising teacher. I helped my supervising teacher gather and compile all data necessary for this conference and to ascertain as nearly as possible just what we believed Bill's problems were. The conference itself was very educational as far as showing me what to expect as a teacher [was concerned]. Bill never completely overcame a low-ability level, but after the conference we observed increased effort on his part and improved study habits.

OBSERVING PROFESSIONAL RELATIONS

The teaching profession is beginning to realize the importance of collective effort for the furtherance of the best interests of its members and of the pupils who are taught. The teacher who is loyal to his profession and who conscientiously adheres to a code of ethics based upon the best experiences of the members of his profession is likely to be the type of teacher who will lead his pupils to accept and practice proper ethical relationships.

Many student teachers will have had experiences with the Student N.E.A. previous to the time of student teaching. They may also have been members of F.T.A. clubs in high school. In this way they have probably acquired some understanding of the importance of professional organizations and proper professional relations in teaching.

One very important opportunity which you have as a student teacher is to observe professional relations among members of the faculty of the school in which you are taking your work. Since you are not an actual faculty member, you are in a position to make more objective observations than might be possible if you were an employed teacher. If you notice any situations in which proper professional relations are not exhibited, it may be well to discuss them with your supervising teacher or with other student teachers. However, it must be remembered that you are actually a visitor in the school, and therefore you must be careful not to give the impression that you are destructively critical of any regular faculty members or other employees in the school system. It may even be best for you to keep such observations to yourself and to refer to them when you are in a similar situation in a regular teaching position.

It may be helpful for you to read a number of codes of ethics which have been produced by professional organizations and apply these rules in connection with your observations. Make your own code of ethics by combining ideas that are found in codes that you have read and any ideas that may present themselves to you as a result of your student-teaching experience.

One excellent guide to professional relations, which was developed by a committee of professional educators and has been revised a number of times, is The Code of Ethics of the National Education Association of the United States. Thoughtful consideration of this code should be helpful to the prospective teacher and to the experienced teacher. The latest revision of the code was issued in 1963 and is reproduced here by permission of the National Education Association.

THE CODE OF ETHICS FOR THE EDUCATION PROFESSION [1]

PREAMBLE

We, professional educators of the United States of America, affirm our belief in the worth and dignity of man. We recognize the supreme

[1] National Education Association, Committee on Professional Ethics, *The Code of Ethics for the Education Profession* (tentative), Washington, D. C., 1963. This code is subject to final approval by the 1963 NEA Representative Assembly. If adopted as the code governing the NEA, it will be referred to all professional teaching organizations for their consideration and possible adoption.

importance of the pursuit of truth, the encouragement of scholarship, and the promotion of democratic citizenship. We regard as essential to these goals the protection of freedom to learn and to teach and the guarantee of equal educational opportunity for all. We affirm and accept our responsibility to practice our profession according to the highest ethical standards.

We acknowledge the magnitude of the profession we have chosen, and engage ourselves, individually and collectively, to judge our colleagues and to be judged by them in accordance with the applicable provisions of this code.

Principle I. Commitment to the Student

We measure success by the progress of each student toward achievement of his maximum potential. We therefore work to stimulate the spirit of inquiry, the acquisition of knowledge and understanding, and the thoughtful formulation of worthy goals. We recognize the importance of cooperative relationships with other community institutions, especially the home.

In fulfilling our obligations to the student, we—

1. Deal justly and considerately with each student.
2. Encourage the student to study varying points of view and respect his right to form his own judgment.
3. Withhold confidential information about a student or his home unless we deem that its release serves professional purposes, benefits the student, or is required by law.
4. Make discreet use of available information about the student.
5. Conduct conferences with or concerning students in an appropriate place and manner.
6. Refrain from commenting unprofessionally about a student or his home.
7. Avoid exploiting our professional relationship with any student.
8. Tutor only in accordance with officially approved policies.
9. Inform appropriate individuals and agencies of the student's educational needs and assist in providing an understanding of his educational experiences.
10. Seek constantly to improve learning facilities and opportunities.

Principle II. Commitment to the Community

We believe that patriotism in its highest form requires dedication to the principles of our democratic heritage. We share with all other citizens the responsibility for the development of sound public policy. As educators, we are particularly accountable for participating in the development of educational programs and policies and for interpreting them to the public.

In fulfilling our obligations to the community, we—

1. Share the responsibility for improving the educational opportunities for all.
2. Recognize that each educational institution may have a person authorized to interpret its official policies.
3. Acknowledge the right and responsibility of the public to participate in the formulation of educational policy.
4. Evaluate through appropriate professional procedures conditions within a district or institution of learning, make known serious deficiencies, and take any action deemed necessary and proper.
5. Use educational facilities for intended purposes consistent with applicable policy, law, and regulation.
6. Assume full political and citizenship responsibilities, but refrain from exploiting the institutional privileges of our professional positions to promote political candidates or partisan activities.
7. Protect the educational program against undesirable infringement.

Principle III. Commitment to the Profession

We believe that the quality of the services of the education profession directly influences the future of the nation and its citizens. We therefore exert every effort to raise educational standards, to improve our service, to promote a climate in which the exercise of professional judgment is encouraged, and to achieve conditions which attract persons worthy of the trust to careers in education. Aware of the value of united effort, we contribute actively to the support, planning, and programs of our professional organizations.

In fulfilling our obligations to the profession, we—

1. Recognize that a profession must accept responsibility for the conduct of its members and understand that our own conduct may be regarded as representative.

2. Participate and conduct ourselves in a responsible manner in the development and implementation of policies affecting education.

3. Cooperate in the selective recruitment of prospective teachers and in the orientation of student teachers, interns, and those colleagues new to their positions.

4. Accord just and equitable treatment to all members of the profession in the exercise of their professional rights and responsibilities, and support them when unjustly accused or mistreated.

5. Refrain from assigning professional duties to non-professional personnel when such assignment is not in the best interest of the student.

6. Provide, upon request, a statement of specific reason for administrative recommendations that lead to the denial of increments, significant changes in employment, or termination of employment.

7. Refrain from exerting undue influence based on the authority of our positions in the determination of professional decisions by colleagues.

8. Keep the trust under which confidential information is exchanged.

9. Make appropriate use of time granted for professional purposes.

10. Interpret and use the writings of others and the findings of educational research with intellectual honesty.

11. Maintain our integrity when dissenting by basing our public criticism of education on valid assumptions as established by careful evaluation of facts or hypotheses.

12. Represent honestly our professional qualifications and identify ourselves only with reputable educational institutions.

13. Respond accurately to requests for evaluations of colleagues seeking professional positions.

14. Provide applicants seeking information about a position with an honest description of the assignment, the conditions of work, and related matters.

Principle IV. Commitment to Professional Employment Practices

We regard the employment agreement as a solemn pledge to be executed both in spirit and in fact in a manner consistent with the highest ideals of professional service. Sound professional personnel relationships with governing boards are built upon personal integrity, dignity, and mutual respect.

In fulfilling our obligations to professional employment practices, we—

1. Apply for or offer a position on the basis of professional and legal qualifications.
2. Apply for a specific position only when it is known to be vacant and refrain from such practices as underbidding or commenting adversely about other candidates.
3. Fill no vacancy except where the terms, conditions, policies, and practices permit the exercise of our professional judgment and skill, and where a climate conducive to professional service exists.
4. Adhere to the conditions of a contract or to the terms of an appointment until either has been terminated legally or by mutual consent.
5. Give prompt notice of any change in availability of service, in status of applications, or in change in position.
6. Conduct professional business through the recognized educational and professional channels.
7. Accept no gratuities or gifts of significance that might influence our judgment in the exercise of our professional duties.
8. Engage in no outside employment that will impair the effectiveness of our professional service and permit no commercial exploitation of our professional position.

Attendance at professional meetings is usually expected of all regular teachers and should, therefore, be a part of the work of the student teacher. Often the supervising teacher will invite his student teacher to attend faculty meetings with him. At the first such meeting, the student teacher may be introduced to the faculty as a whole and be made to feel that he may consider himself a part of the faculty even though he does not legally hold such a relationship.

Of course, attendance at professional meetings should be entirely voluntary on the part of the student teacher, and the supervising teacher, who knows the local situation, should always be permitted to exercise his own discretion as to which meetings the student teacher should attend. Most principals and other members of a faculty are, as a rule, happy to have student teachers visit their faculty meetings. In fact, if this is not the case, there are probably some improper relationships existing in the faculty itself. However, since you are a visitor in the school, you should remember that the principal, your supervising teacher, and the other faculty members have a right to determine whether and when you will be welcome to visit their meetings.

The student teacher is almost always welcome at meetings of regional, state, county, and other educational associations, and he should avail himself of the opportunity to attend such meetings. It is often true that the supervising teacher will invite his student teacher to be his guest at such meetings and will do everything in his power to help him get acquainted with teachers from other schools and school systems.

Parent-teacher meetings are also important in the life of the student teacher. If the school in which you are placed has an active Parent-Teacher Association, you will have an opportunity to get acquainted with the parents of the students in your classes and, perhaps, help to overcome part of the misunderstandings which parents sometimes have regarding student teachers and the student-teaching program. It is natural for parents to desire the best possible teaching for their boys and girls, and it may be that, because of some unhappy experience, they have the idea that they "do not want to have their boys and girls practiced upon." In other words, the parent-teacher meeting can be a means of "selling" the student-teaching program to the patrons of the school in which you are working.

The following reactions of student teachers indicate the value they derived from professional meetings and observation of professional actions:

Faculty meetings at Northwest High School proved to be occasions to be anticipated. I had no idea that these routine meetings could be interesting as well as educational. I had never attended meetings of that nature, and I found them very enjoyable. The refreshments were welcome after a hard day in the classroom, and the educational portions of the programs were just as welcome, for to be "the taught" instead of "the teacher" for an hour was a refreshing experience. The same democratic spirit which was evident in the classroom was present in the faculty meetings. I especially liked the meeting at which we discussed and evaluated the method of evaluation which was then in use. It meant much to me to be accepted as a teacher by the other teachers and to be offered their friendship. Mr. Smith's [the principal] kindness and consideration have made a lasting impression upon me, and it was a joy to be able to help him by substituting for other teachers during difficult times.

* * *

Through association with teachers in casual contacts and teachers' meetings, I developed better professional attitudes.

* * *

I got a better view into the working of the school programs by attending a Parent-Teacher Association meeting and a couple of faculty meetings.

The value which the student teacher can receive from all types of extraclass activities is well illustrated in the following student teacher's statement:

Another important factor that I learned in student teaching was the many responsibilities of the teacher other than those in the classroom. I found that the teacher has to help maintain proper conduct in the halls, in the lunchroom, in assembly programs, in the library, and at athletic contests and pep rallies. The teacher is expected to help keep order on the school grounds and take his turn at bus duty. He is responsible for helping with clubs and assisting with the conduct of money-raising campaigns. He has to make reports to parents and to school officials. The good teacher has many community activities in which to participate. He has many professional meetings to attend, and he has a code of ethics to live by.

Another student teacher describes the values of varied types of observational activities in the following words:

For the first week of my training I observed a class of thirty-seven sixth-graders . . . my first step toward being a teacher. I felt it my duty to know each child before I tried to teach him. During that week I made a seating chart, memorized names, associated behavior patterns with faces, and graded papers. . . . I learned techniques of question-and-answer discussions, what patterns to follow when giving directions, and, most valuable, how to control the class. This, I feel, is the hardest part of teaching for the new teacher. However, by employing my supervising teacher's methods and my own, I did have discipline.

Another very important experience which I had during this first week was that of attending a parent-teachers' meeting. Although I had known the children for only a short time, it wasn't hard to know which were their parents. I gained very valuable knowledge about the children through talking with their parents.

One student teacher was able to become better acquainted with the home life of some of her pupils, as indicated in the following quotation:

In connection with observation, I was also able to visit the homes of the boy and girl about whom I made my case studies. I think, to really understand children and to be able to help them as much as possible, a visit to the homes is necessary.

Of course, visiting a student's home would necessarily have to be cleared with your supervising teacher and possibly with your principal. In some situations it would not be considered proper for a student teacher to visit the homes of his pupils. The student teacher quoted was doing her work in a relatively small town, and her supervising teacher was favorable toward home visitation since she knew all of the circumstances.

Observation is valuable for the experienced teacher as well as for one who has never held a regular teaching position, as indicated by the following statements of an elementary student teacher:

The observation period was very helpful. Although I had never taken student teaching before, I had taught for a year in a private school and I always felt that I had missed a great deal by not having watched a good teacher at work in her classroom. Mrs. Brooks is a very good teacher. It is a real joy to watch her work with her students. . . . By observing her teaching methods, I found much that helped me later on, when I began actual teaching.

The importance of worthwhile observation in the development of the student teacher cannot be overemphasized. Even the observation of events and situations which are not up to standard may be valuable to the prospective teacher by helping him to avoid similar situations when he is placed in an actual teaching position. We should learn through the mistakes of others as well as through our own experiences. Therefore, the prospective teacher should have as many opportunities as possible to observe other teachers and leaders.

QUESTIONS AND PROBLEMS

1. List ten specific extraclass activities with which a teacher may be expected to help.
2. What should be the duties of the sponsor of a club in a junior or senior high school?
3. List ten possible community activities in which the teacher may be expected to participate. Mention special qualifications which the teacher should have in order to be successful in directing these activities.
4. Formulate a code of ethics for your own use, incorporating factors which you have observed in other codes and which you feel are most important for the successful teacher.
5. List evidences of good and poor professional relations which you have observed in the teachers with whom you have been working. Consider your own strengths and weaknesses with reference to professional relations, and propose ways in which you might improve in this regard.
6. Write a brief summary of the events which take place in a professional meeting which you attend. Note indications of good and poor professional relations.

SELECTED REFERENCES

Brembeck, Cole S., *The Discovery of Teaching*. Englewood Cliffs, New Jersey: Prentice-Hall, Inc., 1962. Chapters 13 and 14 give an interesting discussion of the relationships of the teacher with the community in which he is teaching and the parents of the pupils in his classes.

Hymes, James L., Jr., *Effective Home-School Relations*. Englewood Cliffs, New Jersey: Prentice-Hall, Inc., 1953. This book describes ways of bridging the gap between the home and the school.

Jones, James J., and Irving W. Stout, *School Public Relations: Issues and Cases.* New York: G. P. Putnam's Sons, 1960. Common issues in American public education, which affect school public relations, are identified and illustrated by carefully chosen cases.

Kyte, George C., *The Elementary School Teacher at Work.* New York: The Dryden Press, Inc., 1957. Chapter 15 refers to democratic control and discipline in the elementary school, including the place of student government and teacher-parent cooperation in achieving such control.

Logan, Lillian M., and Virgil G. Logan, *Teaching the Elementary School Child.* Boston: Houghton Mifflin Company, 1961. Chapter 15 gives excellent help for teacher-parent relationships.

Mehl, Marie A., Hubert H. Mills, and Harl R. Douglass, *Teaching in the Elementary School.* New York: The Ronald Press Company, 1950. Chapter 21 includes special educational problems, extra-class activities, the teacher, and the community.

Ohlsen, Merle M., *Modern Methods in Elementary Education.* New York: Henry Holt and Company, Inc., 1959. In Chapter 20 the importance of wholesome parent-teacher relationships is discussed.

III. PARTICIPATION

5. Participation in Routine and Extraclass Activities

Participation provides the prospective teacher with opportunities to perform some of the more simple tasks connected with teaching-learning situations. You are still an observer, but you are more than an observer. In addition to the more-or-less passive experiences involved in observing, the student teacher is given opportunities to assist his supervising teacher with routine activities and other relatively simple duties and, thus, is gradually introduced to the more difficult work of the teacher.

Certain activities that are regularly encountered by the teacher in the course of his classroom duties may require an excessive amount of time unless they are properly organized and executed. Since it is important for you, as a student teacher, to have opportunities to perform as many as possible of the duties which you will be called upon to perform in an actual teaching position, you should gain experience in all of the routine activities involved in such a situation.

Among these activities are: checking attendance of students; checking causes for absence or tardiness; collecting and giving receipts for fees; distributing, collecting, and arranging instructional materials; assisting with reports; and adjusting window shades and windows. Doubtless, many other activities which are necessary in the teaching-learning situation will be evident to you or to your supervising teacher. Many of these routine activities may be performed by the student teacher early in his experience, while others should not be attempted until you have become acquainted with the students and feel at home in the classroom.

Participatory activities are often distributed throughout the period of student teaching, and this is as it should be, since some of these activities are more difficult than observation. The mixing of student-teaching activities is well illustrated by the following statement by a student teacher in secondary-school art:

Observation, participation, and teaching are all mixed into one in an art class. During the first few classes I came to know the students and their work and they came to know me. I walked around the class talking with them and making comments on their work. The students seemed to want to see how much I really knew about my subject. Once they discovered, to their satisfaction, that I was qualified, they took criticism from me very well.

RECORDS: ATTENDANCE AND SCHOLASTIC

Among the records which must be kept and with which the student teacher may help early in his student-teaching experience are attendance records, records of school marks, and records of fees paid by students. If the students are seated in a definite arrangement, you should make a seating chart showing the location of each student in the classroom. By studying this chart while you are observing the class, you can learn the names of the students and certain distinguishing characteristics of each. This will greatly facilitate your work when the time comes for you to take over the more difficult phases of your student-teaching experience. After studying this seating chart for a few days, you may use it in checking the attendance and thus become better acquainted with the students. If regular seats are not assigned, you may call the roll or use whatever method your supervising teacher uses. If this arrangement is followed, you may ask the students to raise their hands as you call their names, in order that you may become better acquainted with them. It will greatly facilitate your job of getting acquainted if the students have regularly assigned seats. However, you must go along with your supervising teacher's plan in this regard and make the best possible progress in learning about the students with whom you will be working.

One very important way in which you may help your supervising teacher is in checking excuses for absence and tardiness, if such excuses are used in the school in which you are working. Much of this work will probably be done in the school office. However, there will be some duties related to excuses that will have to be accomplished in the classroom. You will need to consult with your supervising teacher to learn about the system in use in your school. It may be that your supervising teacher will insist on carrying out this duty himself, in order to check on the possibility of students using invalid excuses. If so, you may learn much by being near your supervising teacher during this time.

The marking of students is another type of activity with which the student teacher should have some experience. Of course, this must be done in consultation with your supervising teacher, especially near the beginning of your work with students. Your supervising teacher may insist on having the privilege of making the final evaluation of the students' work. However, you should have some opportunity to participate in this activity, even though your evaluation may not be final. When you begin actual teaching, when you are in complete charge of a class for a few days, you should have much more to do with the evaluation of your students' work than you will have when your supervising teacher is doing the teaching.

Regardless of the amount of experience in evaluating student progress that you may be privileged to have during your student teaching, it is extremely important for you to learn as much as possible about the system of marking that is used in your school and the method of recording marks, averaging grades, and all other factors related to this very difficult phase of the teacher's work. It will be interesting for you to note the amount of emphasis that is given to school marks. Confer with your supervising teacher about this matter, and, if possible, talk with the principal and/or others connected with the school to determine their philosophy regarding evaluation and marking of students.

The recording of marks in the teacher's register is another activity which the student teacher can perform early in his experience. This will be helpful to you in learning about your students and will also assist your supervising teacher.

Another type of record-keeping which is often required of the teacher involves the collection of school fees. You may be a valuable assistant to your supervising teacher in such activities, and at the same time you may learn important procedures for later use.

The number and type of fees will be determined, to a certain extent, by the type of subject matter and other factors. However, especially at the senior-high-school level, there are always opportunities to assist in selling and/or collecting tickets for school games, programs, and other activities. In art, science, industrial arts, and other classes there may be fees or rentals that must be collected by the teacher. Certain of these administrative duties may be accomplished by other school officials or by the student council or individual students. However, the teacher often has much responsibility for seeing that they are accomplished. You may provide assistance in carrying out such duties.

Participation in the routine activities of the classroom and the benefits derived therefrom are illustrated by the following quotations:

I became conscious of the working machinery of the class when I began to assist the teacher with classroom activities. I marked papers, kept roll, kept study periods, entered grades on the permanent roll sheet, and assisted pupils in class during work periods.

❁　　❁　　❁

Participation began early and has continued throughout the quarter. First of all there was clerical work, from correcting papers to filling out the monthly statistical report on attendance. This gave me a good picture of the many duties outside of actual teaching which a teacher must perform. Along with this, I was in charge of study hours and home-room periods.

❁　　❁　　❁

Doing the paper work and participating in activities and conferences showed me the problems and the routine facing the teacher. Keeping the roll and making out the monthly attendance, for example, gave me training which I will value when I begin teaching. Mr. Schools pointed out what a neglected but important phase this is. A big thrill was helping to make out the report cards. This experience taught me to be critical, yet objective, about looking at the total student.

INSTRUCTIONAL MATERIALS

In every class, regardless of the type of subject matter involved, there is need for distributing and collecting instructional materials and arranging and caring for such materials after they have been used by the students. You may be very helpful to your supervising teacher in filing clippings, pictures, and other instructional materials so that they will be available for future use. Such materials are often contributed by students, and, after being used in present classes, they should be filed in such a way that they can be easily located for future use.

Reference books and supplies are used in all types of class work. These materials must be checked out to students and collected after being used. The student teacher can be of great assistance in such routine duties even early in his student-teaching experience.

The checking of written work, drawings, and other products of students' activities may often be done by the student teacher with the approval of the supervising teacher. It is understood that your supervising teacher should have the opportunity to make final decisions regarding the marking of students' work. However, you may gain insight by working with your supervising teacher in evaluating the products of students' endeavors, and it may be that, before you finish your student-teaching experience, you will have opportunities to make final evaluations of such work.

The number and kind of routine activities with which you may be involved must be determined by your supervising teacher in line with the policies of the local school administration. However, the rule regarding such participation is the same as has been mentioned previously—that the number and variety of such experiences be as great as possible in a given situation.

The following statements by student teachers indicate some of the routine activities which they felt were valuable experiences for the prospective teacher:

Along with the gradual leading into the work of teaching the entire class, I graded papers, learned to operate the projector and ditto

machine, and became better acquainted with individuals by talking
with them or by playing games with them during the noon hour.

❖   ❖   ❖

A neat classroom has become one of my goals for my own room. The
example of my supervising teacher has been excellent. . . . Our ideas
were shared; then we wove them together. Each one tried to give
the other equal opportunity to express ideas and opinions. We've had
to compromise, too. In grading the students' notebooks, each of us
read each one of them, put down our own grades and remarks, and
then shared our findings together.

❖   ❖   ❖

My participation was very helpful in that it helped to acquaint me
with the different responsibilities that a teacher has. Grading papers
also helped me to become better acquainted with the pupils and
learn their capabilities.

❖   ❖   ❖

There are many things besides actual classwork that go into teaching,
such as ditto work, record-keeping, etc. I was glad for the opportunity
to learn these things, too.

❖   ❖   ❖

There are many things to be learned about a school system which
greatly assist the teacher in understanding her work and in doing it
more efficiently and effectively. Some of these in which I have had the
privilege of special coaching are the testing program, the system of
textbook supply, the use of film and filmstrip projectors, the making
of reports, and teacher-parent counseling. These were much more
meaningful to me since I was in the actual school situation in which
they were employed and was permitted to participate whenever possible.

REPORTS: IN SCHOOL AND OUT

Another type of routine duty with which the student teacher
should have some experience is the making of reports. It is true
that the supervising teacher, who is legally responsible for all
activities in connection with the school program, including reporting, will wish to have the final decision concerning the issuing

of reports to parents and school officials. However, the student teacher should at least have opportunities to work with the supervising teacher in the making of reports.

It may be that your supervising teacher will permit you to prepare report cards, with the understanding that he will check them before they are released. If not, you should be permitted to discuss the reports with your supervising teacher. The final decision regarding grades and comments to be given on report cards should, of course, be the responsibility of the supervising teacher.

Reports to school officials are often rather complicated. The slightest error in such a report may cause a great deal of difficulty and loss of time for the person whose job it is to compile the composite report for the school. However, since this is one place where the beginning teacher is likely to have trouble, you should have some opportunity to work with reports to school authorities, even though your supervising teacher will probably need to check your work carefully before submitting it to the person who does the clerical work for the school.

Reports to students may be in the form of individual conferences, as well as report cards. In fact, such conferences are often scheduled at the time when report cards are issued, and may include parents as well as students and teacher. It is well for the student teacher to be an observer, at least, in such conferences. The amount of participation which may be permitted will depend upon the age and grade level of the students and other factors. The supervising teacher must determine the extent to which the student teacher can participate without causing any difficulty.

EXTRACLASS ACTIVITIES IN SCHOOL

As a student teacher, you can be very helpful to your supervising teacher and learn much by assisting with extraclass activities. In many schools it is customary for the teachers to stand outside their rooms when students pass between classes. This is especially true in junior high schools. By assisting with this work, you may relieve the supervising teacher for other duties within the classroom or elsewhere and at the same time become better acquainted with the students in an informal situation.

Supervision of the lunchroom is another activity which may be shared with the student teacher. This duty is usually assigned to teachers on a rotating basis so that no one will feel that he is being given an excessive amount of such work. You may even volunteer to help teachers other than your own supervisor, if there is need for such assistance. As a general rule, the more contacts the student teacher can have with all faculty members in the school in which he is working, the better his experience will be and the more favorable will be his impression on everyone in the school and in the school system as a whole.

Club activities also provide excellent opportunities for the student teacher to have experience in working with students in informal situations. It is possible that there will be one or more clubs which will interest you especially and with which you have worked as a high-school or college student. Such activities will provide valuable experience to you and also give you opportunities to be of service to the faculty and students with whom you are working.

The student teacher can also be used as a talent source for assembly programs. It is quite possible that you have had similar experiences in connection with your high-school and college work. Participation in assembly programs in the school in which you are working will give you excellent opportunities to demonstrate your talents before the student body and faculty, thus increasing your self-confidence and, at the same time, improving your status with students and faculty members. You may also help a student or a group of students in preparing a play, a musical number, or some other contribution for an assembly program.

You may be helpful to your supervising teacher by sitting with the group of students with whom you are working during assembly programs. In many schools the teachers are expected to supervise their own groups, and any help that you can provide will be greatly appreciated.

It is possible that your supervising teacher may be responsible for planning and presenting one or more assembly programs during your student-teaching experience. If so, you may assist with such work, either directly or indirectly.

Athletic contests and pep rallies provide excellent opportunities for the student teacher to gain valuable experiences and at the same time provide valuable assistance to faculty members. The fact that you are probably more interested in such activities than are many experienced teachers gives you an advantage and can greatly improve your relationships with the students. Activities in which you may participate include assistance with ticket sales and ticket collection for athletic contests and other public programs, the training of cheerleaders, and the supervision of pep rallies.

The student teacher in English, or even in other subject-matter fields, may have opportunities to work with students on school publications. It may be that your supervising teacher will have some responsibility for such work. If so, you will have a special advantage. Otherwise, your supervising teacher may be able to arrange with those who do have this responsibility to permit you to assist them. If you have had previous experience with the publication of school newspapers or yearbooks, you will have a decided advantage in your student teaching.

The school librarian will probably welcome any assistance that you may provide. The supervision of students, when they are doing research work in the school library, can be especially helpful to the librarian and to your supervising teacher, and at the same time provide you with valuable experiences in preparation for your future work.

The benefit and enjoyment derived by student teachers from their work with students in extracurricular activities are indicated by the following quotations:

Working with the dramatic club was interesting. Although my part in helping with it was small, it was still valuable. It was worthwhile to see how the two directors of the club worked with the students.

❀   ❀   ❀

I enjoyed the various activities of the school. When I started teaching, there was a musical play called *Little Women* in rehearsal. I worked on stage and helped a few with their parts. The students seemed to have a very good attitude while working on the play.

At noon I have played volleyball on a number of occasions. This I enjoyed. Then I went to Mammoth Cave with the juniors and seniors. I received some experience toward improving my ability to work with young people while on this trip.

❀   ❀   ❀

I was very fortunate to have the opportunity to be a supervisor of some junior-high-school students at lunch. This was one of the most delightful . . . experiences I had during my student teaching. It was at their table that I learned the interests of the students and could talk freely with them. The students at this time seemed to relax, and in many instances they forgot that I was their teacher and acted as if I were just "one of the kids." I learned what junior-high-school students like and dislike and what, at that age, they value most. This is one of the first steps that must be taken before a student teacher can get through to the students both in and out of the classroom. It was here that I also learned what most of the students did when they were through with their school day. Most of the information that I gained could never have been learned in the classroom or even [by] just talking with the students before or after a class.

The student teacher in an elementary school may not have as many opportunities to assist with extraclass activities as will the secondary-school student teacher, but there are some such opportunities, as indicated by the following quotations.

One fifth-grade student teacher makes the following statement:

I feel that my student-teaching experience was very well rounded, as I had opportunities to supervise the children not only in the classroom but also in the halls, on the playground, in the lunchroom, and at the different programs.

Other elementary student teachers made the following observations:

Playing with the children was fun. One can never begin to imagine the amount of energy children have. Leading the children in games helped me learn how to give directions and to think of little things to make the games more enjoyable.

❊   ❊   ❊

In helping supervise the pupils in cleaning the playground, I became aware of how children can delight in working to make their environment look better and how good citizenship can start in the lower grades. I also came to know some of the boys and girls better as individuals, and it gave me a chance to be with . . . [them] outside of the classroom, thus helping me to see them in a different phase of life and therefore getting to know them better as a group.

COMMUNITY ACTIVITIES

Many types of community activities are open to the interested student teacher. Some of these activities, such as scouting, may be located in the school building. However, most of them will be in churches, Y.M.C.A. or Y.W.C.A. buildings, or other community centers. There is a possibility that your supervising teacher will have some responsibilities in connection with such activities. If so, you may be given valuable experience by helping him with this work. Church and civic organizations are always glad to have assistance with youth groups, and you may gain much valuable experience through such work.

One student teacher at the senior-high-school level makes the following statement about the value of experience with extraclass activities:

I was fortunate in that I was able to participate in a wide variety of activities in addition to the regular classroom experiences. . . . Each of these activities served as a valuable learning experience to me. . . . The responsibility of the teacher in each of those situations took on a new light. I was able to see the interrelationship of many of the activities in which the teacher participates and how they are related to the needs of the students. Many of the principles of education thus came to have more meaning for me.

QUESTIONS AND PROBLEMS

1. Make a seating chart, showing the location of each student in the classroom (if regular seats are assigned). Check the roll at the beginning of each class period.
2. What system of marking is used in the school in which you are doing your student teaching? What are the advantages and disadvantages of this system? Discuss this matter with your supervising teacher.
3. What evidences are there of excessive or insufficient emphasis on school marks? What factors determine, to a certain extent, the emphasis that is placed upon school marks in a given school?
4. What fees or rentals are required of students in the school in which you are located? What system is used in keeping records of fees that are paid by students? Is this system satisfactory? If not, what suggestions would you make for its improvement?

5. What reference books and supplies are available for use by students in your school? What system is followed for the distribution, collection, and records of curriculum materials? Is this system satisfactory? If not, what suggestions would you make for its improvement?

6. Discuss the method of reporting to parents and school officials which is used in the school in which you are working. What are the advantages and disadvantages involved? What suggestions would you make for improving this system?

7. What plans are followed to keep students informed regarding their progress in school work?

8. Discuss the question of hall duty with your supervising teacher and with the principal or vice-principal of your school.

9. What responsibilities do teachers have for bus duty and lunchroom supervision in the school in which you are doing your student teaching? Are the arrangements satisfactory? If not, what changes would you recommend?

10. What are the responsibilities of teachers in your school regarding assembly programs, athletic contests, pep rallies and other all-school affairs? In what ways can you help with these responsibilities?

11. What publications are produced in the school in which you are working? What can you do to assist with the production of these publications?

12. In what ways can you assist the school librarian?

13. Discuss with your supervising teacher the types of community activities in which he participates. What can you do to assist with these or other activities in the community where you are working?

14. Is there an adult program sponsored by the school in which you are working? If so, arrange to visit these classes and determine ways in which they differ from those in the regular school.

SELECTED REFERENCES

Burton, William H., *The Guidance of Learning Activities*. New York: Appleton-Century-Crofts, Inc., 1952. Chapter 6 includes a comprehensive study of the learner and the learning process.

Clark, Leonard H., and Irving S. Starr, *Secondary School Teaching Methods*. New York: The Macmillan Company, 1959. Extraclass responsibilities of the teacher are discussed in Chapter 15.

Harrison, Raymond H., and Lawrence E. Gowin, *The Elementary Teacher in Action*. San Francisco: Wadsworth Publishing Company, Inc., 1958. Chapter 15 gives suggestions for the teacher in conducting extraclass responsibilities.

McGuire, Vincent, Robert B. Myers, and Charles L. Durrance, *Your Student Teaching in the Secondary School*. Boston: Allyn and Bacon, Inc., 1959. The teacher's relations with the community are considered in Chapter 5.

Stratemeyer, Florence B., Hamden L. Forkner, and Margaret G. McKim, *Developing a Curriculum for Modern Living*, Second Edition. New York: Bureau of Publications, Teachers College, Columbia University, 1947. An interesting report on a group of fifth-grade learners is given in Chapter 8.

6. *Planning Your Work*

Planning is an essential phase of successful teaching. Even the experienced teacher must prepare definite plans covering the learning experiences involved. This preparation should consist first of thorough study and mastery of the subject matter to be taught, and second, of planning the way in which it should be taught. The importance of thorough preparation in both subject matter and method cannot be overemphasized. It is the teacher's best assurance that the students will profit from his teaching.

Since planning is such an important phase of successful teaching, it is essential that you have sufficient practice in this activity under the direction of your supervising teacher. You have doubtless had some practice in constructing teaching plans and resource unit plans previous to the time of student teaching. However, since you are now in a situation where you will be using your plans in teaching, they are likely to be more complete and useful than those you have previously constructed.

Planning cannot be considered except in connection with actual teaching. Regardless of the amount of preparation you have done previous to the time of teaching a given unit or block of work—and such preparation is an absolute necessity for optimum success in teaching—daily planning must constantly accompany the teaching process. This is true regardless of the amount of experience that the teacher has had, but it is especially true with the student teacher and the beginning teacher.

Planning is, of course, a cooperative activity involving your supervising teacher and your students as well as you. Your supervising teacher is responsible for the intellectual development of the students in the classes that you will be teaching. He is, therefore, anxious for you to do the best possible job when he permits you to undertake actual teaching. For this reason he will wish to assist you with your planning, both previous to your time of teaching and while you are teaching a unit or block of work. His suggestions and criticisms will be of inestimable value to you in planning your activities.

Teacher-student planning is also essential to the best possible teaching-learning situation. The amount of such planning that is necessary is determined by the type of subject matter being taught and the type of students with whom you are working; however, a certain amount of planning must be carried on continuously with your students in order for maximum learning to be accomplished. Any plan must be sufficiently flexible to permit changes during the class period as the situation requires.

The following statements of elementary student teachers are indicative of their attitudes regarding the importance of proper planning.

I have also found it helpful to always come to school well prepared, with a definite plan of what I am going to do during the day. It is important, however, to let the children help you plan and to read the written plans from the board every morning.

                              *   *   *

It was not until I tried to teach my unit on "sound" that I realized how much preparation is needed as to background knowledge, method of presentation, and the gathering of materials. After spending much time gathering pictures pertaining to sound . . . and trying in vain to borrow some science equipment from my high school, I thought that it would be a marvelous idea to have well-equipped libraries, solely for teachers, where pamphlets, films, pictures, etc., could be borrowed on any subject taught in the elementary school.

Secondary-school student teachers make the following statements regarding the importance of planning their work:

I learned the importance of having an aim—of stating just what I planned to teach and why. I learned the significance of having a long-range planned program, of knowing exactly the work to be covered from day to day, and of holding to schedule (not inflexibly); for while subject matter is important, it may, at times, be subordinated to pupil personality needs.

* * *

When I began planning for my own teaching experience, I began realizing another aspect of teaching: the amount of time and knowledge that goes into a single unit of material—first, organizing and including all of the material that the students should know about this single subject; second, planning and collecting all visual aids that will help put the material across; and third, planning actual experiences where the students can put the material learned, skills and ideas, into practice. These experiences must give the student enough freedom to use his own imagination and creativity in putting these techniques into practice. A fourth consideration is planning evaluations that will give the individual student knowledge of his progress, especially in areas where he needs to continue to work. In the over-all plan, in weekly and day-to-day plans, a great deal of time, effort, and thought is required by the teacher. This is the aspect of teaching that most laymen, myself included, do not usually consider when thinking of the teaching profession. Nor do they appreciate the skill that is needed to plan for each learning experience of the student.

* * *

The degree to which I had made my preparations for the day often determined its success and my general attitude.

PREPARATION FOR THE CONSTRUCTION
OF TEACHING PLANS

The plan which you will construct and use for your student teaching will be determined largely by the plan used by your supervising teacher. However, you should have opportunities to use your own ideas and construct your own plans rather than use your supervising teacher's plans without adaptation. The amount of original work which you may do depends upon the subject matter and the supervising teacher. If there are certain ideas which you have for the improvement of the class work but which are not in agreement with your supervising teacher, it is usually best to make a note of them and use them when you are in your own classroom situation, rather than to antagonize your supervising teacher by insisting on using materials of which he does not approve.

THE UNIT PLAN

The type of plan which will be best for use in your student teaching will, of course, be determined by the type of subject matter involved and the situation in which you are placed. However, it is well to have some sort of relatively long-range plan to use as a guide in preparing your daily and weekly plans. This may be some form of a unit or block plan, covering the work of two or more weeks.

Regardless of the type of subject matter involved, the first step in developing any plan is *to determine the objectives or aims* which should be achieved, or at least approached, through a study of the work to be provided. Two types of aims may be included: first, the teacher's aims, and second, the students'. The second type is the more important. Regardless of the quality of the aims that the teacher has for the students in his class, little will be accomplished unless he stimulates the students to develop aims of their own which are in line with the objectives which he hopes to have them achieve. For this reason, in developing a set of objectives for a unit of work, it is best for the teacher to put himself in the place of his students (or at least

try to do so) and state the objectives from their viewpoint. Of
course, it is hoped that the achievement of the students' objectives will coincide fairly closely with the teacher's aims.

The second step which should be considered in developing a
unit plan is *consideration of the content or subject matter* involved. What learning experiences can be provided which will
assist the students in attaining (or working toward) the objectives which are set for the unit of work? Unless there is a definite
relationship between the learning experiences to be provided
and the objectives to be reached, there is little or no value in the
learning experiences. As you prepare your resource and teaching plans, you should continually try to relate the proposed learning experiences to one or more of the objectives that have been
previously set.

One phase of planning which has a definite relationship to the
consideration of content or subject matter is the *choice of resource materials.* The type and number of resource materials
available will be determined by the subject matter involved, the
location of the school (urban or rural), the amount of money
which has been spent or is available, and many other factors.
However, the resourceful teacher is continually finding new materials which are valuable in teaching, and students are continually adding to the teacher's supply of resource materials, if the
proper attitude is maintained. In fact, one problem which the
teacher often faces is the selection and retention of valuable resource materials contributed by students, and the discarding of
not-so-useful materials without offending the students or causing
them to lose interest in their work. As a student teacher, you will
probably have to rely principally on the resource materials which
have previously been collected or made available. However, it
is often true that resource materials are added to your supervising
teacher's collection as a result of your work in the school. This is,
of course, always welcomed by the supervising teacher. You may
be able to start your own collection of resource materials while
you are doing your student teaching. This will be valuable to you
when you get into your first regular teaching position.

The third step in planning is to determine the *teacher activities* which will contribute most to effective teaching and learning. This, also, will be determined by the type of subject matter involved and the location, as well as other factors. Teacher activities may include preliminary and preparatory activities which will arouse interest and pave the way for the best possible use of the learning experiences to be provided for the students. An experiment, a clipping, a motion picture, or other audio-visual activity may be quite effective in preparing the students for the work of a unit. There will, of course, be certain teacher activities throughout the progress of the unit, many of which you may not foresee when you are making your preliminary plans. However, the more complete your planning, the greater will be the probability of your success in teaching the unit.

The fourth step, and one of the most important, to be accomplished in planning work for a class is *the choice of learning experiences* for the students. One question which the teacher must always bear in mind is "What learning experiences may be provided which will enable the students to get as much as possible out of the unit or block of work that is being planned?" Since the principle of "learning by doing" is so important, it is necessary for the teacher to plan ahead to provide activities which will give his students guidance in learning the greatest possible amounts in the time available. It will undoubtedly be true that many activities will develop throughout the progress of a given unit of work which were not anticipated when you made the preliminary plans. However, the more complete your plans, the more likelihood there will be that your students will learn what they should as a result of their study activities.

The fifth step which should be considered in planning a unit of work is the process of *summarizing the work* and relating the various phases in such a way that the students can get an over-all picture of the entire unit and relate it to others which have preceded or will follow. This is necessary for proper understanding and use of the material involved. You may not be able to effectively plan this phase of the unit until the time comes for carrying out this step, but it will be well for you to do as much as possible in this regard.

The final step in planning is *consideration of evaluation procedures and materials.* Of course, evaluation should be a continuous process running throughout a unit or block of school work, and some attention should be given to continuous evaluation when you are making your preliminary plans. Nevertheless, the probable procedures to be followed and instruments to be used in the final evaluation of the work of the unit should be planned before teaching. Evaluation should always be directly related to the objectives or aims that were set at the beginning of the unit plan. In other words, you should ask yourself such questions as the following: What are the objectives or aims which I hope my students will have achieved upon completion of this unit or block of work? In what way(s) can I best determine their progress toward these objectives? Evaluation will be used in determining marks or grades which will be awarded to the students upon completion of the work involved. However, the emphasis in all evaluation should be placed on the achievement of objectives.

THE DAILY LESSON PLAN

If the unit or large block plan has been properly constructed, it is a relatively simple matter to plan each day's work so that it will fit into the total picture and contribute a maximum to desired learnings. The type of lesson plan to be used will depend upon the type of subject matter and the requirements and expectations of the supervising teacher and school authorities of your cooperating school. Many schools have a more-or-less definite system for the development of daily plans. Your supervising teacher will help you in determining desired procedures.

The steps to be followed in developing daily lesson plans are essentially the same as those involved in the unit type of plan. However, one important phase of the daily plan which may not be obvious in the unit plan is *the assignment.* This should be given a prominent place in the day's activities, not left to the last minute of the period and therefore probably misunderstood by a majority of the students. Your supervising teacher will be able to give you some good pointers for the making of assignments.

Specimen Plans

Your supervising teacher will probably have some plans which he has been using for a number of years and revising periodically. It may be that he has had such extensive experience that he does not often need to refer to his plans in teaching. However, he should have some definite plans on which he bases his instruction. It will be to your advantage to analyze these plans thoroughly as well as to study plans that are provided in professional literature. Plans which you have constructed in connection with previous course work should be helpful to you. However, you will doubtless need to revise such plans and adapt them to the situation in which you are teaching. As a rule, the more specimen plans you can examine, the more ideas you will be able to formulate for use in developing your own plans.

The importance of planning in preparation for teaching is indicated in the following quotation from the report of a student teacher:

I felt that my greatest need was in unit and lesson planning and in organizing and following through in activities. In this I got as much practice as possible by assisting my supervising teacher in every way possible.

This is the statement of an experienced teacher who was taking student teaching to satisfy a requirement for certification.

Another student teacher makes the following statement about planning:

In lesson preparation I have discovered that the teacher cannot prepare lessons haphazardly and expect good response on the part of the students. It is difficult for the teacher to present something which he himself does not know, and it is more difficult for the students who have to listen. It seems to me that . . . the discipline problem is very much taken care of when lessons are well planned and presented in an interesting manner.

Another student teacher makes this observation:

I found that preparation was the hardest part of teaching, but all of the hard work was rewarded when I graded the first test I had given.

I found that as a whole the class showed that they understood the lessons we had studied together. Somehow I feel that I did more learning than teaching during the time of my student teaching.

Specimen plans are given for your guidance in Appendix C of this volume. A few representative plans have been chosen in various subject-matter fields and at various grade levels to provide assistance for the student teacher, regardless of the area in which he is doing his work.

QUESTIONS AND PROBLEMS

1. Analyze plans provided by your supervising teacher or given in professional literature to determine the following: (a) objectives or aims, (b) content, (c) resource materials, (d) teacher activities, (e) learning experiences, (f) approach to the unit, (g) summary, and (h) evaluation devices and procedures.
2. What are the objectives of the unit(s) or block(s) of work which you will be teaching?
3. Make a list of available resource materials which may be used with the unit(s) or block(s) of work which you will be teaching.
4. State specific procedures which you plan to use in arousing student interest and otherwise preparing the class for the unit(s) or block(s) of work which you will be teaching.
5. What method(s) do you plan to use in your teaching? Why do you consider such a method(s) to be appropriate?
6. Develop various types of evaluation instruments (tests or other types) for use with the work that you will be teaching.
7. Develop one week's lesson plans for a unit or block of work which you will be teaching.

SELECTED REFERENCES

Association for Supervision and Curriculum Development, *Creating a Good Environment for Learning*, 1954 Yearbook. Chapters 4 and 5 give illustrations of teacher-student planning.

Burton, William H., *The Guidance of Learning Activities*. New York: Appleton-Century-Crofts, Inc., 1952. Chapters 12, 13, and 14 describe the method of planning and developing units with an analysis of an illustrative unit at the fifth-grade level.

Faunce, Roland C., and Nelson L. Bossing, *Developing the Core Curriculum*. New York: Prentice-Hall, Inc., 1958. Chapter 10 describes the process of planning instruction for core classes.

Grambs, Jean D., William J. Iverson, and Franklin K. Patterson, *Modern Methods in Secondary Education*. New York: The Dryden Press, 1958 (Revised Edition). A guide for planning and providing materials for teaching and learning is found in Chapters 6, 7, and 8.

Gruhn, William T., and Harl R. Douglass, *The Modern Junior High School*. New York: The Ronald Press Company, 1956. Part II illustrates planning instruction in many fields.

Klausmeier, Herbert J., and Katharine Dresden, *Teaching in the Elementary School*, Second Edition. New York: Harper and Brothers, 1962. Chapter 5 provides excellent suggestions and illustrations for the development of unit and lesson plans.

Kyte, George C., *The Elementary School Teacher at Work*. New York: The Dryden Press, Inc., 1957. The unit of work is explained in Chapter 6, with a concrete example of the process of cooperative planning in the development of such a unit.

Leonard, J. Paul, *Developing the Secondary School Curriculum*. New York: Rinehart and Company, Inc., 1953. Chapters 15, 16, and 17 provide many excellent examples of units of work.

Logan, Lillian M., and Virgil G. Logan, *Teaching the Elementary School Child*. Boston: Houghton Mifflin Company, 1961. The integrating of learning experiences for elemetary-school pupils is discussed in Chapter 6.

7. *Interpersonal Relations*

The teaching-learning process is dependent for its success on the interpersonal relations that obtain. Your relations with your supervising teacher will, from the beginning, influence your success as a student teacher, as will also your relations with your students. Interpersonal relations among students are influenced by your relations with your supervising teacher and with your students. Thus, all such relations that take place in the classroom and in extraclass activities have an important bearing on your success as a student teacher and as a regular teacher.

The observations of one elementary student teacher in this regard are appropriate to this discussion:

I shall summarize first the impact of the classroom on my interpersonal relationships with the teacher and children.
1. There is never enough time to give each child the individual attention he could use.
2. Two adults in a classroom tend to keep children more dependent on adult help. It makes more difficult the task of creating an atmosphere in which independent work can be encouraged.
3. No matter how much rapport is established between the student and the supervising teacher, each must compromise her responses and reactions to classroom occurrences because of the dual nature of the roles they play.
4. My most successful teaching occurred in the areas in which I assumed full responsibility for the project or teaching unit and presented the lesson without help, in the method used or the preparation, from my supervising teacher.
5. The area in which I had most difficulty in establishing a satisfying . . . learning atmosphere was reading. . . .

6. I worked best with the children when I let their response to stimulation guide the pattern of teaching technique.
7. Group response is the most sensitive measure of acceptance of learning. I feel that much more could be done in analyzing the basic factors which cause group response. I felt like an actor when I had the group with me. I played on their interest, and they encouraged me to continue on a nonverbal, yet obviously visible, level. The ability of the group to bring a hostile or disinterested child into the acceptance range of interest amazes me. I think that somewhere in this area lies the key to successful schoolroom learning and discipline.
8. Being able to spend time every day discussing my reactions and impressions with my supervising teacher was the most important asset, and most valuable contribution, to my growth as a teacher in my student-teaching experience.

Another student teacher makes the following statements regarding interpersonal relations:

During my stay at Smithville Junior High School I followed the duties and responsibilities of my supervising teacher very closely. She controlled the physical comforts of the classroom as far as possible; she maintained a wholesome teacher-pupil and pupil-pupil relationship in all of her classes; she used varied teaching techniques; she has mastered her subject matter; she was successful in handling discipline problems. Mrs. Blank was a busy teacher and an enthusiastic one. Her fellow teachers sought her advice on many subjects.

As a student teacher, you will have a better opportunity to study students than you have had previously in connection with other professional courses and, quite likely, more than you will have when you get into a regular teaching position. It is important that you make use of this opportunity, since it will help you to become better acquainted with the students with whom you will be working.

Every group has its cliques, its popular and unpopular individuals, its network of likes and dislikes, prejudices, crushes, and hatreds. Understanding these characteristics in a particular group and the ability to correct unwholesome situations and use such knowledge in facilitating learning are essential to the success of the teacher. Thus, the diagnosis of interpersonal relations between members of a class, and the implications of such knowledge in improving instruction, are among the most important activities of the student teacher.

You should begin your study of individual students while you are observing the class. However, such study should continue throughout the time of your student teaching. In fact, many characteristics of your students will not become evident until you have actually guided their learning experiences over a period of time. You will probably have much more time for study of students during the time of your observation than you will have when you get into the more active phases of your work. Specimen case studies are given in Appendix E.

Two elementary student teachers make the following statements regarding the importance of their relationships with their pupils:

In the Blank Elementary School I had the opportunity to work with all types and classes of children—from the hesitant farmer's child of poor parents to the child of the professor who has had all possible opportunity. To draw their progressing interests together presented a challenge to . . . every plan to be made. Children have a way of living and do not know the harshness of self-seeking adults who have acquired the actions that so often inhibit free expression. The child is willing to satisfy your commands without question. His eagerness to "swallow" plans that you have made for him stirs a desire to give him every opportunity you are capable of presenting.

※   ※   ※

I have found it particularly helpful to become acquainted with each pupil's background and cumulative record. If I know more about a pupil, I am able to anticipate his needs and to see his limits and his possibilities.

One caution it is important to remember in making a study of students is to be careful about letting them know that you are making a special study of certain individuals, at least at the beginning of your student-teaching experience. Later, when you have been accepted as a more-or-less regular member of the teaching staff, you may be able to have formal and informal conferences with the students you are studying, provided such study is approved by your supervising teacher and the administrators of the school in which you are working.

Sometimes it is not considered best for the students and for the school if the student teacher makes detailed case studies of individual students. This is determined by the age of the students, the location of the school, and other factors which may vary from school to school and from time to time. Under such circumstances, it may be well for you to carry on a sociometric study of an entire class. This type of study will help you become better acquainted with your students, and as a rule it does not carry the dangerous possibilities that the individual case study may have. A specimen sociometric study is given in Appendix D.

You should always remember that systematic study of students by a student teacher should not be done without the approval of the supervising teacher and the administrators involved. It is sometimes true that school authorities do not approve of the student teacher's examination of cumulative records of students. Since the student teacher is not actually a licensed teacher, he has no legal authority with regard to school matters. Therefore, any opportunity that you may have to examine school records will depend upon the cooperation of the public-school officials involved.

The rule that should be kept in mind is that you should get as much experience as possible in making individual and group studies of students. The value of such studies is indicated in the following quotations from student teachers:

The range of pupil ability was wide in my room, which I feel has been a real asset to my teaching in helping me to learn how to deal and cope with all types of pupils.

o   o   o

I have had many experiences which have helped me to understand the student-teacher relationship. One of these was tutoring a girl who was frequently absent because of family duties. Another was the case studies which I did. These studies revealed to me the fact that we often do not understand what is behind the difficulty, what is causing students to react as they do.

Certain student teachers in junior and senior high schools make the following statements regarding their studies of the interpersonal relationships of students:

My case study was important in helping me to understand many of the problems and hindrances with which boys and girls of eighth-grade age are faced.

*   *   *

My students were very interesting because of the differences in their backgrounds. The effects of environment were shown very plainly.

*   *   *

Working on my case study made me conscious of people with a need. It also helped me to be more understanding and tolerant of the things I saw and heard.

The following report, which was made by a student teacher at the senior-high-school level, indicates the value of a sociometric study in helping the beginning teacher to become better acquainted with his students and to understand how to deal with them individually and collectively so as to provide the most effective teaching-learning situation:

Making a sociometric study of my class has given me a better understanding of the class in general and several new insights regarding particular interests. First, I was much impressed by the sound judgment most of the class displayed in selecting coworkers. It would seem that status in this group is achieved by intelligence and hard work. Those students who were not cooperative with my supervising teacher and me were rejected by the group. But, regarding these students, I can see more clearly how important it is for me to find activities in which they can experience success, so that they will not need to "show off" in order to gain the approval of their fellow students. I also feel a good deal more sympathetic with the shy student in this connection. I see a similar need for providing experiences that will aid the shy student in building self-confidence. Most important, I have begun to see more clearly the connection between satisfaction in social relationships and success in school.

If it does not seem advisable for you to carry on one or more detailed studies of students because of the type of school or an administrative regulation, or for any other reason, you may wish to do a series of sociometric studies, each one demonstrating one phase of interpersonal relations in the classroom. One student teacher obtained some very interesting and helpful results by asking his students a series of questions relating to recreation, scholarship, citizenship, and social affairs, and making a sociogram representing each phase of the interpersonal relations involved. Questions for such a study may include the following: With whom would you most like to play a game? With whom would you most like to study in preparation for an examination? Whom would you consider to be the best citizen in your class? With whom would you most like to attend a party? Analysis of sociograms produced as a result of such questioning may lead to definite indications regarding the attitude of various students toward their fellow classmates, and in this way may help the student teacher to better understand the interpersonal relations in his class which may be of importance in dealing with individual students and the class as a whole.

INDICATIONS REGARDING INTERPERSONAL RELATIONS

While you are observing the classes to which you have been assigned, you should take advantage of the opportunities afforded to determine evidences of strongly organized cliques and other interpersonal relations. Notice any harmful effects of cliques, such as interference with class work. Also, notice any good effects of strong friendships between members of classes and the ways in which your supervising teacher capitalizes on such friendships in making assignments and in motivating students to do improved work.

Notice indications regarding popularity ratings of various students. It is often possible to determine, without the use of a sociometric study or any case studies, the most popular student or students in a given class. Take notes on these indications while you are observing, and then determine through a more objective study how well your observations coincide with the actual situations.

Prejudices and intolerant feelings may often be shown by students as they participate in classroom activities. It will be interesting for you to try to determine such attitudes in the students you are observing, and then test your conclusions in a more scientific way through a sociometric study or through case studies.

It is well to notice methods used by your supervising teacher to reduce unwholesome feelings among students. It is often true that the way in which the teacher reacts to evidences of unwholesome feelings shown in a class will have much to do with the effects of these feelings on individual students and on the class as a whole. Your supervising teacher, because of past experience in these matters, is likely to have developed some methods and devices which are valuable in keeping proper relationships between the students in his classes. It may not be possible for you to use the same methods. However, you should get some ideas which will be useful when you get into an actual teaching situation.

THE SOCIOMETRIC TEST

A sociometric study will usually be more accurate and meaningful if it is conducted as a part of a definite phase of the students' work. It may be that your supervising teacher will wish to divide a class into small groups for a certain phase of the work in progress. If so, he may ask the students to write on a small piece of paper the names of the person with whom they would like best to work on a committee, the person with whom they would like next best to work, etc. It should be made plain to the students that their preferences will be honored, as far as possible, in setting up committees. In this way they will be likely to indicate their true preferences. You may then use these preferences in working out a sociometric study of the class.

In making a sociogram to represent the interpersonal relations in a class, the students should first be numbered so as to obscure the identity of the students involved. Boys and girls should be represented by different shapes; for example, girls may be indicated by circles and boys by triangles, thus making it easier to analyze the sociogram. Lines should be drawn between circles and triangles to indicate choices of students. Arrowheads on the ends of these lines will show the direction of the choice. A specimen sociometric study is given in Appendix B.

Conclusions regarding interpersonal relations between the members of a class may be drawn from the sociogram, and then comparisons may be made with previous observations. By locating students who are rejected by their classmates, or who are in any other way having difficulty in their interpersonal relations, it may be possible to arrange committee personnel in such a way as to help these individuals. Personal conferences may be helpful in determining ways in which certain students may become accepted members of the group and thus be aided in their school work as well as in their social relations.

CASE STUDIES OF STUDENTS

Every group of students includes some who suffer from a certain amount of maladjustment. Such a difficulty may be caused by hereditary characteristics, traumatic experiences in early childhood, unhappy home life, or other unfortunate circumstances. One of the most important problems for the beginning teacher is to be able to diagnose the difficulties of "problem students" and to provide remedial measures.

Diagnosis should precede teaching, and, as a student teacher, you have an excellent opportunity to carry on such diagnosis before starting your period of actual teaching. Thus you will be better able to understand the students with whom you will work and to apply remedial measures in connection with your teaching.

The first step in carrying on a case study is to obtain as much information as possible regarding the subject of your study. This may be done by searching cumulative records, through personal interviews, through informal contacts, and through any other feasible procedure. The methods to be used will, of course, depend upon the age of the students, the type of school involved, the rules of the school administration, and other factors. Before carrying on a case study, you must first consult your supervising teacher and perhaps the principal or vice-principal of the school in which you are doing your student teaching. All studies must have the wholehearted approval of all persons involved and must be carried on as expected.

After obtaining all the information that is available regarding the student or students under study, you should analyze the data in an attempt to determine the causes of any apparent difficulties. Through such analysis and through conferences with the student(s), the supervising teacher, and others, you should be able to determine the best procedures to be followed in correcting any difficulties that may be evident.

In order to gain as much experience as possible, it is well to make an analytical study of two students of the same age and sex, but with different social, emotional, and/or scholastic records. By making a comparative study, it will probably be possible to understand both students better than you would otherwise be able to do. In this way you will be able to help them more, and you will be better prepared for future studies of students. Specimen case studies are given in Appendix E to provide guides which you may follow in making your own studies.

In connection with sociometric studies and individual case studies of students, the same rule applies that was mentioned concerning other phases of the student-teaching experience—that is, the more satisfactory the experiences you can get, the better prepared you will be for teaching and other duties which you will encounter in your first teaching position. Therefore, through conferences with your supervising teacher and with school administrators, you should determine just what you will be permitted to do and then take advantage of every opportunity that is given you. In schools where the student teacher is not given access to cumulative records, your supervising teacher may cooperate by obtaining valuable information for you. In any case, one important thing to remember is the fact that all information obtained for studies of students must be kept in strict confidence. If your supervising teacher works with you on such studies, the information must be shared between the two individuals involved, but it should not be distributed any further.

It is well to use fictitious names in any written reports that may be made regarding students, thus making it more difficult for any improper use to be made of such reports. Should the students involved or any other students or their parents obtain copies of the studies that have been made, it might bring about repercussions which would cause trouble for all concerned. The use of fictitious names or a system of numbering that is understood only by the student teacher, and possibly by the supervising teacher, will help to prevent unsatisfactory results. The importance of care in such studies cannot be overemphasized.

One senior-high-school student teacher makes the following suggestions regarding interpersonal relations:

No person can be successful as a teacher unless he has a tremendous sense of humor. A teacher gets along not only by his capacity to render decisions in a constructive way, but also by his capacity to "look the other way." It is very important to get along with students. You must have patience. You have to be firm, once you are right. Firmness does not mean being dictatorial. You have to be fair and treat all students alike and be especially considerate of those whom you find trying. Homework should be given [only when it] can be accomplished in the time available to the students. Credit should be given when due, and, if at all possible, students should be scolded only in private. You must make certain that the work makes sense to the students and that they find it of some value.

QUESTIONS AND PROBLEMS

1. From your observation of a class, determine whether there are outstanding indications of strongly organized cliques. If so, cite specific examples.
2. What harmful effects of cliques do you notice?
3. What use does your supervising teacher make of the tendency of students to form cliques?

4. Choose students who, according to your observation, appear to be the most popular and the least popular in a given class. What reasons might be advanced for these differences in popularity?
5. What incidents do you observe which indicate the presence of prejudices and intolerant feelings between certain students? What does your supervising teacher do to reduce unwholesome feelings among students?
6. Cite incidents that indicate serious crushes or hatreds between individuals in your classes. What does your supervising teacher do to cope with unwholesome feelings in this regard?
7. Conduct a sociometric study of a class which you are observing.
8. Identify a student with an adjustment problem and conduct an individual case study of this student, obtaining all possible information that will help you in diagnosing the situation and determining possible remedial treatment.
9. Make an analytical study of two students of the same age and sex, but with different social, emotional, and/or scholastic records. Diagnose any problems involved, and make recommendations. Carry out the recommendations which you have made, and evaluate the results.

SELECTED REFERENCES

Burton, William H., *The Guidance of Learning Activities.* New York: Appleton-Century-Crofts, Inc., 1952. The construction and use of sociograms are presented on pages 258 through 267.

Cunningham, Ruth, et al., *Understanding the Group Behavior of Boys and Girls.* New York: Bureau of Publications, Teachers College, Columbia University, 1951. Chapter 5 gives a clear analysis of sociometric techniques.

Frank, M. H., and L. K. Frank, *Your Adolescent at Home and in School.* New York: The Viking Press, 1956. A book which is written for parents, but which will be illuminating and helpful to prospective teachers.

Gesell, A. L., et al., *Youth: From Ten to Sixteen.* New York: Harper and Brothers, 1956. This book is intended as a guide for parents, but is useful to prospective teachers as well.

Grambs, Jean D., William J. Iverson, and Franklin K. Patterson, *Modern Methods in Secondary Education*. New York: The Dryden Press, 1958 (Revised Edition). In Chapter 3 the authors give an excellent discussion of the high-school student as a person. An analysis of sociometric techniques and their interpretation is given on pages 568 through 581.

Jersild, Arthur T., *In Search of Self*. New York: Bureau of Publications, Teachers College, Columbia University, 1952. A research report which discusses implications of the adolescent's search for self in the secondary-school situation.

Kyte, George C., *The Elementary School Teacher at Work*. New York: The Dryden Press, Inc., 1957. Chapter 4 includes all personnel involved in the work of the elementary school.

Logan, Lillian M., and Virgil G. Logan, *Teaching the Elementary School Child*. Boston: Houghton Mifflin Company, 1961. Part One, "The Growing Child," gives an excellent explanation of the elementary-school child and the learning process.

Millard, Cecil V., and John W. M. Rothney, *The Elementary School Child. A Book of Cases*. New York: The Dryden Press, 1957. Case studies of various types of elementary-school pupils.

Ohlsen, Merle M., *Modern Methods in Elementary Education*. New York: Henry Holt and Company, Inc., 1959. The use of sociometric tests in analyzing peer relationships is presented on pages 56 through 63.

Prescott, Daniel A., *The Child in the Educative Process*. New York: McGraw-Hill Book Company, 1957. An analysis of the knowledge and skills that a teacher needs to understand pupils. Case-study materials are used wisely to make these six chapters in Part II very helpful to teachers.

Rothney, John W. M., *The High School Student. A Book of Cases*. New York: The Dryden Press, 1953. Case studies of various types of high-school students.

Seidman, Jerome M., *The Adolescent: A Book of Readings*, Second Edition. New York: The Dryden Press, Inc., 1954. Sixty-seven articles embracing characteristics of adolescents.

Taba, Hilda, et al., *Diagnosing Human Relations Needs*. The American Council on Education, Washington, D. C., 1951. Sociometric techniques are applied to actual group situations.

Wattenberg, William W., *The Adolescent Years.* New York: Harcourt, Brace and Company, 1955. The book stresses the developmental approach to the study of secondary-school students.

Wellington, C. Burleigh, and Jean Wellington, *Teaching for Critical Thinking.* New York: McGraw-Hill Book Company, Inc., 1960. Chapter 3 refers to "Adolescents and Adolescence," with special reference to needs and problems as related to education.

Wingo, G. Max, and Raleigh Schorling, *Elementary School Student Teaching.* New York: McGraw-Hill Book Company, Inc., 1955. Chapters 2 and 3 deal with the successful teacher at work, including consideration of individual differences in teaching.

8. Miscellaneous Classroom Duties

There are many classroom duties which may not be considered instructional activities but which are nevertheless important in preparing the atmosphere of the classroom for optimum learning conditions. As a student teacher, you should have excellent opportunities to assist in the performance of these duties before beginning the more difficult work of actual teaching. In this way you can provide excellent assistance for your supervising teacher and at the same time gradually work your way into the more difficult phases of the student-teaching experience.

Since your supervising teacher is an exceptionally busy person, the more assistance you can give him with routine duties, the more attention he will be able to give to the more difficult phases of teaching. Thus, you will prove your value near the beginning of your student-teaching experience and at the same time learn much which will be of inestimable value to you when you begin teaching.

Among classroom duties which may be assumed by the student teacher early in his student-teaching period are (1) bulletin-board work, (2) arrangement of display cases and other exhibits, (3) care of books, periodicals, and other instructional materials, and (4) arrangement of classroom decorations. The number and kinds of such duties that will be available will, of course, depend upon the type of subject matter being taught, the location (whether your supervising teacher has one room of his own, or whether he is a "floating teacher"), and other factors. Your supervising teacher should always be in charge of all such activities, and you should often consult with him, especially near the beginning of the student-teaching experience. As a matter of fact, there must always be cooperation between the student teacher and the supervising teacher. Since you are a visitor in the supervising teacher's domain, you should always conduct yourself accordingly. The amount of initiative which you can and should take in all activities connected with your student-teaching experience will depend upon your supervising teacher and upon many other factors related to the situation in which you are placed. As a rule, the more responsibility you can take in all classroom duties, the greater will be your progress in preparation for actual teaching.

PREPARING BULLETIN-BOARD DISPLAYS

The student teacher is often adept at arranging bulletin-board displays. In fact, it may be that you have had experience along this line during your previous school work. Whether or not you have had previous experience in bulletin-board arrangement, this is one activity which you should be able to learn with very little difficulty, even though you may not be artistically inclined.

Since bulletin-board displays should be, and usually are, related to the work which is in progress, it is necessary for the supervising teacher to guide the student teacher in the selection and arrangement of such materials. However, you should be permitted to use your own ingenuity and creativity in this work. With proper guidance and suggestion, you may be able to obtain display materials from industrial firms in the community or through the mail. The acquisition, use, and filing of such materials not only provides the student teacher with valuable experience, but can be very helpful to your supervising teacher.

The first step in the preparation of bulletin-board displays is to make a survey of materials that are on hand or readily available. List these materials, noting their location or how they may be obtained. Indicate the unit or block of work to which each is related and the approximate time when this work will be considered by the students. It may be that your supervising teacher will have bulletin-board materials collected which he has not yet been able to classify and file for easy access. If so, you can provide a valuable service by getting this work accomplished.

One student teacher in elementary art describes some of her activities as follows:

I spent time experimenting with media new to me, such as balloons, papier-mâché masks, and sawdust and paste objects. I supervised a study period, assisted in arranging bulletin-board displays, room decorations, and other displays for special units, holidays, and programs. I participated in all-school programs, and I was allowed to sit in on principal-student counseling. I set up and stored equipment and previewed books and films.

A regular elementary student teacher tells about activities that are almost as complicated as those described above:

It is amazing what the class accomplished in twelve weeks. Some of the highlights included preparing a rodeo for the spring festival; working with clay, using the kiln, and finally sending the finished objects to be filmed and put on exhibit for Blaine County schools; using the opaque projector to make six huge maps and preparing wheat flour and paste for the mountains and deserts; making a mural on spring; showing a motion picture; doing experiments for the unit on "sound"; and preparing a class newspaper.

It is probably true that the supervising teacher had much to do with the activities mentioned above, but the student teacher learned much by assisting with the projects.

The student teacher in a special subject-matter field, such as art, has some advantages over the one who is doing his work in a regular elementary class or in a subject-matter field of the more academic type. This fact is well illustrated by the following quotation:

Among the valuable things learned were the organization of an art class (bulletin boards, displays), preparation of a course of study for high-school art, and the importance of having a well-organized method of distributing and collecting supplies. I learned the importance of being flexible in approach to these factors. I also learned the active role an art teacher plays in a high school—that of advising other teachers, assisting with scenery construction and preparing place cards, as well as posters, for school affairs.

Many free or inexpensive materials are available from various business and industrial firms either in the community or at a distance which may require using the mails. You may be able to get two copies of many pictures or other bulletin-board materials and begin your own collection, as well as adding materials to your supervising teacher's collection. You may have started such a collection during your previous professional course work. If so, your student-teaching experience will provide you with many opportunities to add to your collection.

Make a survey of the bulletin-board space available in your room. Is it ample and well arranged? If you feel that certain changes might be made for the improvement of bulletin boards, confer with your supervising teacher and see if he is ready and willing to have changes made. It may be that he has some definite reasons for keeping them as they are. If so, this is his prerogative. When you get into a classroom of your own, you can try some things that you may not be able to do when you are under a supervising teacher.

After you have determined the materials available and the bulletin-board space that you are free to use, you should confer with your supervising teacher about the arrangement. It may be that your supervising teacher will have certain students designated to help with bulletin boards. If so, you can work with them and become better acquainted with them while arranging displays.

Since bulletin-board displays should be changed as often as necessary to maintain student interest and to conform to teaching procedures, you should have several opportunities to do this work during your student teaching. When you begin your actual student teaching, you will doubtless take even more initiative in arranging displays than you will when your supervising teacher is doing the teaching. However, you should still consult with your supervising teacher about this work, as well as about other plans that you make. The amount of individual initiative that you can take will depend to a great extent on your supervising teacher and on the situation in which you are placed.

Keep notes regarding various displays, with diagrams showing the arrangements. These notes will be very valuable to you when you get into a teaching position.

WORKING WITH DISPLAY CASES AND
OTHER EXHIBITS

Most types of subject matter lend themselves to display-case arrangement and other types of exhibit, as well as to the bulletin board. The work involved in arranging such exhibits is similar to that involved in the arrangement of bulletin-board displays, and the benefits derived by both the student teacher and the supervising teacher are similar to those mentioned above.

One housekeeping chore with which you may help is the cleaning of display cases and arranging exhibits for maximum usefulness and attractiveness. Students may also help with this work under the direction of the student teacher, thus giving him an opportunity to work with the students and get better acquainted with them before beginning his actual teaching.

As with bulletin-board displays, the first step in working with display cases and other exhibits is to make a survey of the space available and the use being made of it. It may be that you will be able to make some constructive suggestions for the improvement of displays that are already in place. However, you should remember that the supervising teacher may have definite reasons for keeping exhibits arranged as they are, and in this case, as has been previously mentioned, you should follow the directions of your supervising teacher while you are working under his supervision.

In science rooms and other rooms in which large amounts of apparatus or other materials are stored, the amount of cabinet space which is in need of attention may be quite large. It may be that student assistants are assigned the task of caring for storage and display cases. If so, you may supervise the students' work and perhaps assist with the work and make suggestions regarding arrangement of materials, etc. The more experience you can get in use and arrangement of apparatus and other curriculum materials, the better prepared you will be for your first full-time teaching assignment.

In many rooms, cases are provided for exhibits that are related to the subject matter being studied. For example, a history room may have a display of dolls representing costumes that were common during various historical periods in certain countries. In an English room there may be a display of Shakespearean stages or other articles typical of that age. Many of these exhibits have been developed over the years with models that have been contributed by students or faculty members, and they are often quite valuable from a monetary as well as aesthetic viewpoint. For this reason your supervising teacher may be reticent about permitting students or even a student teacher to handle the articles. However, you should have as much experience as possible with such displays.

CARE OF BOOKS, PERIODICALS, AND OTHER INSTRUCTIONAL MATERIALS

Almost all classrooms and laboratories have some reference books, periodicals, and other instructional materials which must be stored and kept available for use by students and teachers. Such materials require much care if they are to be kept in order and in proper condition. As a student teacher, you can assist your supervising teacher with this work and at the same time become acquainted with the materials.

The first step in your assistance with this work is to make or acquire a list of all books, periodicals, and other reference materials that are available in your classroom, noting their arrangement and location. Your supervising teacher will probably have such a list, a copy of which has been submitted to the administrative officers of the school system. If so, it may be well for you to use the prepared list, checking it with the materials. Thus, you may help your supervising teacher in determining whether any materials have been lost or added since the last report was made.

Notice the arrangement of these facilities. It may be that you will be able to suggest changes in the arrangement which will improve the situation. Under the direction of your supervising teacher, you may dust and arrange reference books and other materials for maximum usefulness and attractiveness. If your room is adequately equipped, you may have a specially made rack for periodicals and newspapers. However, as a rule, these materials must be kept on ordinary shelf space. Whatever the arrangement, you should assist your supervising teacher with the care of such materials.

Maps, charts, pictures, and other materials may be kept in the classroom. If so, their storage and arrangement concern both teacher and students. Notice the arrangements that have been made for the storage and display of such materials. Under the direction of your supervising teacher, you may clean and arrange all instructional materials.

HELPING WITH CLASSROOM DECORATIONS

Notice all pictures, calendars, and other decorative materials that are found in your classroom. Is the flag displayed in an attractive and useful position? Ask your supervising teacher about rules that affect the display of the flag, fire-drill instructions, etc.

Notice all aquaria, terraria, potted plants, or other decorative and useful articles that you find in the room. It may be that you will be able to offer suggestions for improving their arrangement. You should at least assist your supervising teacher and students in caring for such materials.

The following statements by student teachers illustrate the value which they received by participating in activities such as those mentioned in this chapter:

Mrs. Smith allowed me to help grade papers, set up bulletin-board displays, and aid her in many other ways. Since she was in charge of the school's films, I was permitted to observe the equipment and organization of the film crews. I led home-room opening exercises. Mrs. Smith also taught me to use the ditto machine.

❊   ❊   ❊

The completion of various projects, such as preparing displays for bulletin boards and show cases, attending faculty functions, and enrolling in a course on fashion, have all been most rewarding.

❊   ❊   ❊

Other activities in which I participated were also helpful to me. For example, I ordered movies from the library to show to my French classes. After showing them, I succeeded in organizing a lively discussion concerning them, in which the pupils were allowed to voice their reactions. I also supervised the home room during assembly programs.

✿   ✿   ✿

As a part of my participation, I was given the whole room to arrange in any way I thought proper. Since art is my hobby, Mr. Jones suggested that I do this as a special project. The students and I enjoyed this very much, and the room was always decorated with their work. Culminating all of our art activities, we made a large frieze which stretched across the front of the room.

✿   ✿   ✿

In selecting and using teaching materials for the classes which I taught, I came to realize more than ever how important it is to take every aspect of the situation (and the material) into consideration before actually deciding to use certain material, and how important it is that all materials be completely ready before starting the lesson. The importance of, and some good "pointers" [to be followed] in keeping the bulletin board up to date were made real to me, and I know this will be useful to me in the future.

If you are doing your student teaching in science or in any phase of work in which apparatus or tools may be used, you have an excellent opportunity to assist your supervising teacher with the arrangement, care, storage, and exhibition of these materials. You can set up and put away equipment used by your supervising teacher or by students in connection with regular class work or for special exhibits such as those prepared for open-house programs or back-to-school nights. This type of activity will help you overcome your fear in beginning your actual teaching. Any activity which gives you the opportunity to work with students, or to present demonstrations or other parts of lessons before a class, will be advantageous to you in preparing for the more difficult phases of student teaching.

Other secondary-school student teachers describe their miscellaneous classroom duties as follows:

Most of the interested students were wonderful to work with and did commendable work on science research projects and science-fair projects. I graded papers, recorded grades, checked books and supplies, and supervised study periods and bulletin-board displays. I attended assemblies and participated in home-room activities, devotionals, and lunchroom activities.

✻　✻　✻

I liked my supervising teacher, and as a result I learned a great deal and applied it to the principles of teaching that I have acquired during my college years. I found myself directing musical groups (something I had never done before), having authority, advising students, trying to work simple eighth-grade arithmetic problems and failing, directing plays, breaking up fights, and participating in countless other valuable, as well as amusing, learning situations.

The above quotation is from a student teacher in a small elementary-secondary school. This accounts for the wide variety of experiences he received. Another student teacher in a large senior high school, however, reports almost as wide a variety of activities as did the one in a small school.

To complete my evaluation, I can also state that I found that the teacher not only teaches classes, but also does many other jobs, such as hall duty, working with clubs, working on school projects . . . and finally, but most important, he does a great deal of clerical work connected with such things as grades, attendance, records, and other reports.

QUESTIONS AND PROBLEMS

1. Under the direction of your supervising teacher, make a survey of bulletin-board materials that are readily available. List materials that will be especially useful during the period of your student-teaching experience, indicating the unit or block of work to which each is related. Plan bulletin-board displays which you may use in connection with your teaching.
2. List all display materials that are found in your classroom. How may these materials be used in connection with your teaching?
3. List all reference books, periodicals, and other instructional materials that are readily available. How may these materials be used in connection with your teaching?
4. What changes may be made in the arrangement of classroom decorations, such as pictures, flags, aquaria, potted plants, etc., to make the room more attractively, as well as conveniently, arranged?
5. Draw a plan of your classroom indicating location of cabinets, tables, and other fixtures. Consider the possibility of making changes in the arrangement of such equipment to provide for attractiveness and convenience.

SELECTED REFERENCES

Dale, Edgar, *Audio-Visual Methods of Teaching*. New York: The Dryden Press, Inc., 1954. An excellent source of ideas for teaching.

Finn, James D., *The Audio-Visual Equipment Manual*. New York: The Dryden Press, Inc., 1957. A guide to the operation of all major types, models, and varieties of audio-visual equipment.

Klausmeier, Herbert J., and Katharine Dresden, *Teaching in the Elementary School*, Second Edition. New York: Harper and Brothers, 1962. Chapter 4 describes various patterns of instruction for use in the elementary school.

IV. ACTUAL TEACHING

9. *Guiding Learning Activities*

Undoubtedly the most important phase of the student-teaching experience is actual teaching. Observation and participation are both important in preparing the student teacher for this stage of his preservice preparation. However, it is only through actual teaching of students, either individually or in groups, that the prospective teacher really learns to teach.

This is the phase of your student-teaching experience to which you have looked forward with great anticipation but, perhaps, with a certain amount of fear. Such concern over the beginning of actual teaching is a natural sensation which affects every prospective teacher, to a greater or less degree, because of the fact that he is now facing new responsibilities and that there is always the possibility of failure. However, the great advantage of the student teacher over the beginning teacher who has not had student teaching is that he has an experienced teacher on whom he can rely for encouragement and suggestions. Your supervising teacher is just as interested in your success as you are, and he will be glad to give you all possible help to insure your success in this undertaking.

Experience has shown that the student teacher who is extremely overconfident in starting his actual teaching is more likely to encounter difficulty than is the one who is not so confident. This does not mean that you should begin teaching with a defeatist attitude. If you do this, you are almost certainly doomed to defeat before you start. Either extreme overconfidence or extreme underconfidence can be a detriment to you in beginning actual teaching, just as it may be in any other work you may undertake.

141

The best time for you to undertake the responsibility for teaching a student or a group of students can be determined only by you and your supervising teacher. Your supervising teacher will probably suggest a time for you to start teaching, and if you feel that you are reasonably well prepared, it is usually wise to follow his suggestion. However, this time can only be determined in conference with your supervising teacher.

The feelings of student teachers when beginning actual teaching are well illustrated by the following statements:

Mrs. Blank was most helpful before I started teaching my first class. She discussed ways to keep the class going and suggested that I have additional questions and illustrations prepared before each class. . . . I told her about my fear of teaching the class, and she encouraged me to forget the fear. "After all, John," she said, "I am here to help you, and don't be afraid to ask for help from me."

❂   ❂   ❂

From teaching the class, I learned that I must have the complete attention of the students before I can teach them anything. If someone cannot understand an assignment, I must have patience and help him to understand it, even if it means explaining it over and over again several days in a row. I also found that I must provide the class with enough work to keep all students busy. When planning my lessons, I must keep each child in mind. I had slow learners as well as fast learners in my class. Many of them needed much individual help. The most important thing that I learned is that I must have complete control of my class at all times (in order to have the best possible teaching-learning situation).

GRADUAL INDUCTION

In order to encourage the student teacher and to assure him of success in actual teaching, the supervising teacher usually provides some minor teaching responsibilities such as presenting one phase of a lesson, tutoring individual students, or some other activity which will enable you to get the feel of teaching before attempting to present a lesson to an entire class. The number and kinds of such activities will depend upon several factors: (1) the age and grade level of the students, (2) the type of class, (3) the subject-matter involved, and (4) the type of school. Your supervising teacher is the one who understands the situation and who can best determine the procedure which should be followed in introducing you to the more difficult phases of teaching.

The following statements of student teachers at the senior-high-school level indicate the importance of gradual induction into teaching:

Slowly I ventured, helping students prepare for their work, assisting in keeping them busy while the teacher was out of the room, keeping them in order, and talking to individual students concerning their work. More and more confidence was gained by taking attendance. This part [of the work] was valuable in helping me to get acquainted with the students. I was able to listen to my voice and to see if it were being projected so that each student could hear his name.

⬥   ⬥   ⬥

As I began giving individual attention to students, I began to know each one better. Some of their questions kept me on my toes, and, even though I hated to do it, many times my answer had to be "I don't know," or "Let's look that one up."

⬥   ⬥   ⬥

At the conclusion of my observation period, I was able to assist Mrs. Jones very gradually in various capacities. She thought this was a good idea—that it would help me get used to the pupils and help them to become accustomed to seeing and knowing me. I began by taking the roll. In this way I became familiar with the names of the pupils and associated their faces with their names. Then I began proctoring examinations which she gave. It wasn't long before my first big assignment came. I was to take over one of the seventh-grade groups the last half of the hour. I carefully planned my lesson before the class met. I had prepared a little quiz which I had written on the board. We answered these questions in class. Surprisingly enough, I wasn't too nervous before that large group. I certainly approve of Mrs. Jones' emphasis on my gradual induction to the conducting of a class.

⬥   ⬥   ⬥

The principal of Goodwin Elementary School and my supervising teacher were extremely helpful throughout my student teaching. Miss

Blank guided my program in a general way, while Mrs. Smith [supervising teacher] worked closely with me day by day. She began my program even before I arrived, by orienting the children to the idea of having a "second teacher." When I arrived, the children were as eager as I for this new experience. Mrs. Smith gradually gave me more and more responsibility, so that by the time I took charge of the whole class, I felt comfortable and reasonably capable of handling the situation. Each day Mrs. Smith discussed with me the lessons I had taught, and suggested ways of improving my teaching.

PRESENTING LESSON MATERIAL

One excellent way to get started in the process of actual teaching is to present parts of lessons. Your supervising teacher will probably be able to arrange for you to give an appropriate reading, a travel story, or an incident from your previous experience which will contribute to the lesson he is teaching. This will give you an opportunity to appear before the class for a relatively brief time, thus helping to break down any fear or feeling of tension which you may have at the thought of standing in front of such a group. The type of presentation which you can make will depend upon the subject matter being studied. For example, in a science class you might give a demonstration experiment. This should, of course, be something which you have done a number of times previously and in which you feel fairly secure.

Confer with your supervising teacher about possible contributions which you might make, and then prepare as well as possible so that you will feel relaxed and be able to do a good job. This will help to build your self-confidence and prepare the way for your future appearances before the classes.

Your supervising teacher may bring you into class discussions in a more informal way by asking your opinion on certain problems which are being discussed in class. It may be that he can foresee certain questions on which you can comment more as a member of the class than as a teacher. In this way you will be able to improve your relationships with the students. Any way in which you can help with the class work before actually taking over the teaching will prove to be beneficial to you and to the classes as well.

The following statement by a student teacher indicates the proper attitude in this matter:

At no time did I feel that I must sit back and remain a silent listener. Mr. Jones tried to bring me before the students from the first day by asking my opinion on certain questions. In this way they gradually became accustomed to my presence in the room, and I did not feel that I must hesitate to make decisions or refer the students to Mr. Jones when they asked me questions.

One student teacher in a junior high school gives the following account of her teaching activities previous to full-time teaching:

Mr. Blank encouraged me to participate in simple tasks from the first day. I began by recording test marks, grading tests, and checking attendance. By the end of the first week I had stood in front of a class! —with my knees shaking—to tell the students a little about some of the more important persons of the Civil War period. I shall never forget the warm sense of satisfaction I experienced at the end of that period—and also my surprise when I discovered I could still stand up!

One student teacher in music makes the following observation:

When I first arrived at Clay School, it was difficult for me to realize that I was actually beginning my student teaching. Miss Smith, however, didn't give me a chance to work myself into a case of stage fright. Almost immediately, I was walking around the room, listening to voices, testing parts, and checking individuals for words. It seems that I arrived just in time to help her prepare for a concert for an education convention.

A young man who did student teaching in English describes his experiences as follows:

My first teaching experience occurred during the first week of school. Mrs. Blank was anxious to get me started as soon as possible. One day the class discussion was centered around some speeches of Winston Churchill which related to their current study of literature. I came back the next day with these speeches and a recording of Beethoven's Fifth Symphony. I read some of Churchill's most famous speeches, gave the war background, and tied in the significance of Beethoven (V for Victory, . . . etc.). They were favorably impressed, and Mrs. Blank encouraged me to start a unit on American literature with her third-period group. We got the ball rolling from the second week on. Whether I liked it or not, teaching was my primary objective, and my supervising teacher was determined to shove me into it at full speed. As I look back on it from this point, [I feel that] she was very wise.

 ⚬   ⚬   ⚬

The second-grade teacher had a successful way of getting beneath the children's level and pushing them up in their thinking and doing. This is a very important technique, especially when teaching young children. After watching and imitating her several times, I was able to do the same, although not quite as naturally as she. However, I did feel that this technique became more a part of me each time I taught.

 ⚬   ⚬   ⚬

I also had the painful experience of running out of material before the class period was over, and I know now that this is one of the pitfalls to be avoided.

 ⚬   ⚬   ⚬

One of the most rewarding teaching experiences is working individually with pupils after school. These pupils are usually having trouble in mastering the subject matter. Much patience and clarity of explanation are required to help them achieve understanding. However, the personal satisfaction gained when a glimmer of understanding is reached makes every effort worthwhile. Then, too, when these pupils begin to show improvement in their work, because of this individual help, the teacher feels highly rewarded.

TUTORING STUDENTS

Another actual teaching experience which the student teacher can perform near the beginning of his period of student teaching is the tutoring of students who have been absent or who, for any reason, need extra help in order to get as much as possible out of their school work. Your supervising teacher will probably have a number of students who fall in this category, and your helping them will be of great assistance to both the students and the supervising teacher. The teacher's time is thus conserved for use with the class as a whole, and the student who needs extra attention receives it.

If there are a few slow-learning students in your classes, you may continue their special tutoring throughout the time of your student-teaching experience—at least until you begin your full-time teaching period. You may use one or two of these students for case-study purposes, and in this way you will be able to help them more than would otherwise be possible. You will have much more time for such activities while doing student teaching than you will have after you get into a teaching position, and all of the experience you can get in teaching slow learners will be helpful to you in your future work.

One student teacher at the elementary-school level mentions the following experiences in the tutoring of slow pupils:

In my actual teaching experiences I really gained much helpful information. I was learning right along with the pupils; only the subject matter was different. I tutored pupils with below-average I.Q.'s and enjoyed it very much, and since it made me very sad to observe [them], I tried to help them all the more. As a result of this effort, on the last spelling test I gave them before I left, one pupil [who had been] considered "hopeless" by all previous teachers, but not by Mrs. Smith and myself, received a satisfactory grade, only missing four words.

GUIDING SMALL GROUPS OF STUDENTS

It is quite probable that your supervising teacher will be permitting the students to form small groups or committees for the purpose of more detailed work on certain phases of the material they are studying. In this situation you will have an excellent opportunity to work gradually into the teaching of an entire class by working with a few students at a time. It may be that some of these committees or special-interest groups will be working on a project that is especially interesting to you or one on which you have done much previous work. If so, you will be in an especially fortunate situation to begin teaching.

In guiding small groups of students, a number of steps should be followed. The first is the planning stage. As is true in preparation for any special project, the success of the undertaking will depend largely on the amount and quality of planning that precedes the actual research involved. As a student teacher, you will have opportunities to assist small groups of students in the planning of their projects. Your past experience in college courses should prove to be very beneficial in this type of work. Make certain that the students really understand what it is that they are planning to do and how they are going about the research. This is one place where many students, especially teenagers, tend to be lax, and you will have an excellent opportunity to help them understand the importance of proper planning and to guide them in this stage of their work.

After the students have planned their projects—know what they are going to do and how they are going to do it—they must locate the materials to be used. You can be of great assistance to them in this regard and at the same time become better acquainted with the materials which you may use in connection with your teaching of an entire class. Textbooks, reference books, charts, maps, filmstrips, and many other materials may be used in carrying on a research project. These may be found in other places besides the classroom and the school. Your knowledge of the community and your past experience in locating research materials should help you in guiding your students in their work. One word of caution is necessary at this phase of your guidance. This is the importance of remembering that the students, and not yourself, are the ones who are doing the research. This does not mean that you cannot bring in materials which you feel will be helpful to your students. In fact, this is one way in which you can develop good rapport with your students, and this will be important when you begin your teaching of the entire class. However, you should permit the students to choose from any materials that you may contribute, instead of trying to force them to use the materials you choose.

The next step in developing a special project is the organization of the materials and the actual research that is necessary to accomplish the desired result. One important factor to remember in this step is the division of labor among members of the group. Too often, one person who is particularly interested in the project at hand will take over too much of the research. Your job is to help the committee to so organize the work that each member will have his share. You may have to provide some external motivation for certain members of the group in order to help them carry their part of the research to a proper conclusion. This is another common problem with teenagers and one with which you can be of great assistance.

After the researching stage of the project has been completed, it is necessary to plan the time and methods of reporting to the class. This may be done through a panel discussion, through individual reports, or through some other means which is applicable to the particular project involved. Posters or other materials may have been produced which will be valuable in reporting the research. A display of such materials may be prepared by the students under your direction, thus providing excellent experience for you as well as the students. Filmstrips, motion pictures, recordings, and other audio-visual materials may be used in connection with the reporting stage of the project, provided they are available and appropriate.

The last step in conducting a special project is the process of evaluating the success of the undertaking. This may be done by all of the students in the class, by your supervising teacher, and by you yourself. The methods used will depend upon the type of project involved and the purposes sought. It may be well to ask the students to list facts and skills that they have acquired through work on the project. Members of the class who were not working on this particular project may make criticisms, additional remarks, or suggestions. The final stage of the evaluation process may be a written test which will determine what all of the students have accomplished. You may prepare this test with the assistance of your supervising teacher. The use that is made of such test results will be determined by the nature of the project and the policy of your supervising teacher.

The value of work with small groups or committees is indicated in the following statements of student teachers:

By working with individuals and committees, I was introduced to actual teaching. This was an opportunity to further enhance my relationship with the students.

✿   ✿   ✿

It was on an assigned project in biology that I noted how a particular student tackled a problem. She was ready to give up on the project, an experiment in osmosis, when, with added help and encouragement, she continued her efforts. It was this bit of help which brought about a favorable change in this student's behavior. This was most gratifying to me.

✿   ✿   ✿

One of the most rewarding experiences in which I engaged was a project involving work with a small group of ten or twelve students. This project, a puppet show, consisted of such things as making the puppets, making the stage and curtains, selecting and organizing a topic for the show (we chose pioneer days as compared with modern days, to tie in with their social studies), assigning the characters, writing the script, and supervising rehearsals and final presentation of the show. This experience alone pointed out to me many problems and difficulties which take place when working with such a group.

✿   ✿   ✿

My first experiences in handling the children were with small groups. I took groups out to recess, to lunch, to the library, and out of the building when the school day ended.

Since the elementary teacher is usually expected to teach all subject-matter fields that are offered in the elementary grades, and since no teacher has equal interest and enthusiasm for every subject, it is quite probable that you will need to adjust to such

a situation. If you take the attitude that you are going to do the best possible job, you should be able to compensate for your lack of interest, and you may even be more successful in teaching a subject in which you have felt a lack of enthusiasm than you are in subjects that you enjoy. As you succeed in teaching material in which you have lacked interest, your enthusiasm for this subject matter will increase, thus increasing your success in teaching. Such a situation is well stated by a student teacher in the following way:

I enjoyed teaching every subject, even arithmetic, which has always been a subject for which I have lacked enthusiasm. I felt very proud when one day Frank, a very bright, well-rounded, and mature child, said to me, "Miss Jones, I think I know what your favorite subject is. I'll bet it is arithmetic, because you look as if you enjoy teaching it so much." I was overwhelmed that I had not given the impression that arithmetic was one of the subjects for which I had little enthusiasm. As our conversation continued, Frank said, "Now arithmetic is a lot more interesting to me."

"Success," I said to myself. "And now even I feel the same way."

TEACHING AN ENTIRE CLASS

As soon as you and your supervising teacher feel that you are ready, you should take over the work of teaching an entire class. You may start by teaching a part of a regular lesson. In this way you can become accustomed to appearing before the entire class without the necessity of preparing the work for a full class period. You will need to study your supervising teacher's plans and make definite plans of your own regarding questions, methods, devices, and procedures to be used.

After teaching parts of several lessons, you may be ready to take over the work of an entire class period. Your plans for such work should be carefully made ahead of time, and your supervising teacher should have an opportunity to check such plans closely and make suggestions for their improvement. It is said that "nothing succeeds like success." For this reason, it is important that your first experience in teaching an entire class be successful, and no amount of pre-planning and discussion with your supervising teacher can be considered as wasted time if you succeed in your first attempts at teaching a class.

One junior-high-school student teacher makes the following observation regarding the beginning of her actual teaching:

The greatest benefit that I received from my student teaching was self-confidence. I found that teaching a class was somewhat like playing a musical instrument for an audience: you have a little stage fright and a few doubts before you begin to play. However, as soon as you strike a few familiar chords and feel the instrument's response, your self-assurance returns. In this same manner, as soon as one develops a certain rapport between himself and his class, the self-assurance returns.

Another student teacher, in a senior high school, states her feelings this way:

One by one, Mrs. Jones let me try first one class and then another. I shall never forget my first class. It was the last period in the afternoon, and it was our largest class. I have always been, and to this day am, the sort of person who dislikes heartily getting up in front of a class or other gathering to give any sort of an oral report. I am usually almost sick from nervousness. Something happened to me that day that has never before happened. I was nervous before I got up to teach, but suddenly I felt so calm that I couldn't understand what was happening; all those young faces turned toward me, just waiting for what I had to offer. There was no question of not caring what I said. I was the teacher, and even though I was new at teaching and they knew it, the position of teacher gave me the authority and wisdom, in their eyes, to be their leader in their search for knowledge, help, advice, etc. I have never before experienced such a feeling, and, thanks to Mrs. Jones' gentleness in indoctrinating me, I never became so nervous or lost that I could not cope with the situation.

It may be added that the student teacher who is quoted above did an excellent job, and, undoubtedly, much of the credit for her success goes to her supervising teacher, who gave her opportunities to succeed in relatively easy teaching situations for short periods of time until her confidence had been developed to the place where she was prepared to take charge of a class for an entire period and finally for a whole day's teaching.

The value of actual teaching in preparing the prospective teacher for future activities is described in the following quotations:

I feel that my actual teaching was my most valuable experience. It gave me an opportunity to see my weak points. It gave me an opportunity to see more of what one really has to accomplish. I particularly appreciated Miss Blank's frankness with me in telling me my weaknesses. It made me see where I needed to improve. She gave me many valuable suggestions which gave me a greater desire to improve.

❋ ❋ ❋

I find actual teaching very challenging. The ability to present factual material, which in itself has a tendency to be boring, in such an interesting manner as to capture the interest and enthusiasm of the pupil is one of the fascinating aspects [of teaching]. What task could be more rewarding than the knowledge that we are helping to equip and prepare the youth of our nation to meet successfully the problems of life which will confront them in their tomorrows?

SUBSTITUTE TEACHING

It may be that you will have the opportunity to do some substitute teaching during the period of your student teaching. One student teacher gives the following account of such an experience:

The biggest day for me, however, was not my first day of actual teaching. It came three weeks later when, one Sunday evening, Mrs. Jones called me to say that she was ill and couldn't be in class the next day. I was to be her substitute. I was elated—and scared. Always before, her presence had given me self-confidence, for I knew I could always call on her for help if necessary. Now she wasn't even to be in the building.

The next day, after having made plans for all the classes, I arrived early and was sitting in the room when the first students began arriving. The day seemed to sail by. Thanks to the routine I had learned from Mrs. Jones, I had no problems and was ready to face the students for as long as she was ill. I was glad she was able to return the next day, but I had felt so independent that I hated to give back some of the classes.

*   *   *

The final test came in the last weeks when my supervising teacher went to the hospital and I was left in charge, with full responsibility and authority. It was only then that I was able to achieve a unified and individual approach in teaching my students, and able to bring about a balance in the organization of the amount of time given to each aspect: presentation of material, practice of students, and normal classroom duties, such as distributing materials and organizing the speaking order.

One of the difficulties of student teaching is that the student teacher often feels the full *responsibility* of the teacher but does not feel the full *authority* of the teacher. In the last few weeks, I was given the opportunity of feeling the authority as well as the responsibility. I found this to be a beneficial experience that I hope all student teachers can include in their student-teaching experience.

Since the student teacher is not actually a licensed teacher, it may be that the school authorities will require that a certified substitute be in the classroom whenever the regular teacher is absent. However, this does not prevent the student teacher from

getting the experience of conducting the classes. In fact, it is often true that the student teacher is able to carry forward the class work in a more satisfactory manner than the substitute would be able to do. The apparent inconsistency of the student teacher's doing the work and the substitute's being paid for it is not as bad as it seems, since the student teacher is gaining some very valuable experience that will help him immeasurably in his first teaching position. The regular substitute serves as a legally authorized person, thus protecting the student teacher in case of any difficulty.

Of course, the question of the student teacher's acting as a substitute teacher must be considered by the administrator or administrators in charge of the assignment of substitutes. However, if the supervising teacher recommends such procedure, the administrator will usually comply with the suggestion.

It is sometimes true that a student teacher will be given a position as a regular substitute after he completes his student teaching, when there is no vacancy for a teacher. Such a situation provides the prospective teacher with the opportunity for additional experience which will be useful to him at a later time. One student teacher makes the following observations regarding this type of work:

Mrs. Blank, the assistant principal, asked me to become a full-time substitute at Uptown Junior High School during the weeks that I faced before the next session. From November 1 to December 22, I "subbed" in English, history, speech, band and orchestra, physical education, mathematics, French, Spanish, library, art, shop, journalism, general education, and social studies. I have taught grades 7, 8, and 9 at Uptown and visited Downtown, John Smith, and Jones Junior High Schools as well. Dr. Mann (the principal at Uptown) asked me to make an application for next year. He seems interested in having me at Uptown. My substitute experience was not a part of my student teaching, of course, but to me it seems an extension of it because of the way things worked out.

You may not feel that you are as versatile as the student teacher quoted above. In fact, few people would want to tackle as many different subjects as he did. However, as a rule, the more substitute-teaching experience you can get, either during or following your student teaching, the better prepared you will probably be to start your first year as a regular teacher.

QUESTIONS AND PROBLEMS

1. Confer with your supervising teacher regarding possible contributions that you can make in line with the material being presented to a class. Make a list of such activities, and prepare several which you can present.
2. Confer with your supervising teacher regarding students whom you may tutor. Work with one or more of these students, helping them to get caught up with the rest of the class.
3. Determine any special methods, devices, and procedures which are useful in assisting slow learners.
4. What difficulties arise in connection with the tutoring of individual students? How may these difficulties be overcome?
5. Make a case study of one of the students being tutored (see Chapter 7 of this volume).
6. Work with one or more committees or special-interest groups, guiding them in their research activities.
7. Study your supervising teacher's plans for a lesson and/or a

unit which you may teach. Make definite plans of your own for use in teaching a lesson and/or a unit.

8. Keep a record of problems that arise during class periods, and discuss them with your supervising teacher.

9. Evaluate your teaching according to the following criteria:
   a. effectiveness—test students, either orally or by means of a written examination.
   b. motivation—note indications that students are interested in the work you have presented.
   c. ways of improving—consider possible ways in which the teaching-learning situation might be improved.

SELECTED REFERENCES

Association for Supervision and Curriculum Development, *Guidance in the Curriculum,* 1953 Yearbook. Chapters 3 and 4 discuss effects of pressure groups and mass-communication media on education.

Bond, Guy L., and Miles Tinker, *Reading Difficulties: Their Diagnosis and Correction.* New York: Appleton-Century-Crofts, Inc., 1957. An excellent guide to work with retarded readers.

Burton, W. H., *The Guidance of Learning Activities.* New York: Appleton-Century-Crofts, Inc., 1952. Chapters 7 and 8 emphasize the importance of understanding the learner and his relationships with his peer group.

Grambs, Jean D., William J. Iverson, and Franklin K. Patterson, *Modern Methods in Secondary Education.* New York: The Dryden Press, Inc., 1958. Individual differences and the communication skills are discussed in Chapters 13 and 14, with suggestions regarding methods of caring for the needs of all students.

Ingram, Christine P., *Education of the Slow-Learning Child.* New York: The Ronald Press Company, 1953. Provides excellent suggestions for the person who is working with slow learners.

Logan, Lillian M., and Virgil G. Logan, *Teaching the Elementary School Child.* Boston: Houghton Mifflin Company, 1961. An excellent discussion of the education of all types of exceptional children is given in Chapter 14.

National Society for the Study of Education, *The Education of Excep-*

tional Children, Forty-ninth Yearbook, Part II, 1950. This entire volume is a comprehensive treatise on the general problem involved in the education of exceptional children, with certain chapters devoted to discussions of specific types of handicapped pupils and the intellectually superior student.

Ragan, William B., *Modern Elementary Curriculum*. New York: Henry Holt and Company, Revised Edition, 1960. Methods of organizing a class for living and learning are discussed in Chapter 6.

Wellington, C. Burleigh, and Jean Wellington, *Teaching for Critical Thinking*. New York: McGraw-Hill Book Company, Inc., 1960. Chapters 4 and 5 include excellent descriptions of methods which may be used to develop critical thinking.

Wiles, Kimball, *Teaching for Better Schools*. New York: Prentice-Hall, Inc., 1952. An excellent discussion of the individualizing of instruction.

Witty, Paul (ed.), *The Gifted Child*. Boston: D. C. Heath and Company, 1951. Practices in the education of the gifted are suggested.

10. Methods, Devices, and Procedures of Instruction

The methods, devices, and procedures which you should use in stimulating your students' learning and in guiding their learning activities will be determined to a great extent by the subject-matter field in which you are teaching. However, certain general suggestions may be made to aid you in your choice of methods. You have doubtless received some help in this regard in your previous course work in general and special methods, and your supervising teacher will be eager to give you suggestions and criticisms.

One common difficulty of beginning teachers and student teachers, with regard to methods, is that they often try to use the same methods that were used by their professors in college. It has been said, and often truthfully, that "we teach as we are taught, and not as we are taught to teach." It is true that some methods, devices, and procedures that can be used with college students are also applicable at the secondary level. However, secondary-school students must not be taught entirely as college students.

The opportunities that you have had to observe the work of your supervising teacher should give you many ideas regarding the teaching of your students. By taking notes on these observations, reviewing your methods-course notes, and studying other materials having to do with education, you should be prepared for the work of guiding the learning experiences of your students. However, the only way in which you can increase your ability along this line is by actually working with a class. By making use of information which you have already obtained and through conferences with your supervising teacher regarding the methods, devices, and procedures that he uses, you should have little difficulty in your first actual teaching experience.

One student teacher expresses his problem with methods of teaching in the following words:

At first, my teaching had the nature of college lectures, but I soon learned that the students were not getting what I was trying to put across. Hence, I came down to their level of comprehension.

MOTIVATION

Since motivation is a necessary prerequisite to learning, it is important for the prospective teacher to understand how to stimulate the learner's desire to develop to the greatest possible degree at the greatest possible rate. Observation of the techniques of your supervising teacher can and should provide you with many ideas which you can use in motivating your students. This does not mean that you should mimic your supervising teacher. Each teacher is an individual, and what will work for one may not work for another. However, there are certain characteristics which you may observe in your supervising teacher which will give you ideas regarding procedures that may be valuable when you begin the process of instruction.

Your approach to the unit or block of work which you will be teaching will have much to do with your success in motivating your students. It is impossible for you to motivate students to accomplish work in which you are not interested. Enthusiasm is contagious, and lack of enthusiasm is also contagious. Plan with your supervising teacher to present, for your first lesson or unit, a phase of the work in which you are particularly interested and in which you feel reasonably well prepared. Determine all of the illustrative devices, such as pictures, charts, clippings, films, or other audio-visual materials, that you may use to introduce the block of work with the greatest possible motivational effect. Your supervising teacher will be glad to help you find materials for use in setting the stage for the lesson or unit which you are going to teach. The more successful you are in the motivational aspect of teaching, the less difficulty you will have with classroom management.

Suggestions for increasing motivation are given by student teachers in the following quotations:

I learned that the pupils must be treated as individuals and that they must be loved and praised. Children want acceptance from those they meet, and we as teachers must give them security and encouragement.

* * *

Keeping the classroom interest up is one important factor in successful teaching. It is necessary that children continue to be interested in their work and feel that they have a definite part in it. A time each morning for the sharing of experiences is very helpful in keeping the interest as it should be. I have learned that each individual child needs to feel that he is important, and all children respond freely to love and kindness.

* * *

I have learned many interesting ways to present art and music work, and I now realize that one doesn't have to be a great artist or an accomplished musician to do either. We learned songs to go along with our unit on weather, and we made Easter eggs. Even Zorro appeared in the Easter parade.

* * *

The teaching of my unit on "birds" showed me how much a unit can be related to various subject-matter fields. It was really interesting to see how the children responded to the teaching of the unit and the interest they showed in their work.

MAKING THE ASSIGNMENT

In the traditional school, and to far too great an extent in the modern school, the assignment is considered as consisting solely of a statement regarding the number of pages in a textbook and the number of problems to be solved or the story to be read or written. Each of these activities may be included as part of the assignment; however, the assignment includes more than any one of them. The assignment is a cooperative enterprise to be carried on by the students under the guidance and supervision of the teacher. It affords the greatest opportunity for motivating students to activities that will promote their growth and development. It is an integral part of instruction and thus an important phase of the teaching-learning situation, which should be understood by the prospective teacher. Your care in preparing assignments and your method of making assignments will determine, to a great extent, your success in teaching.

Your supervising teacher will be glad to help you in preparing for this phase of your teaching. Your previous observation of his teaching should give you some definite suggestions regarding the procedures which you may use. In the plans you developed before starting your actual teaching you should have some suggested activities for use in making assignments.

A necessary prerequisite for effective assignments is adequate pre-planning for the work to be assigned. This is especially true with the student teacher, since he does not have the background of experience which is so valuable in making clear assignments. This pre-planning should be done in cooperation with your supervising teacher so that you may be as well prepared as possible before attempting the duties involved in making the assignment.

The following statements of a junior-high-school student teacher illustrate the importance of pre-planning in preparation for the assignment and for other phases of teaching:

My actual teaching was what helped me most. . . . Planning and working with Miss Smith was very interesting and helpful. It was through her guidance that I learned to plan my work by days, weeks, and units or blocks of time. This planning gave me the feeling that the subject I was teaching was my own and not something that my supervising teacher gave me and told me to teach. It also helped me to know where I was going and what I wanted to accomplish.

The assignment usually grows out of work which the students have been doing. Therefore, it is necessary for you to study the plans of your supervising teacher and tie the unit or block of work that you will teach to that which has preceded it. It is well to provide optional and individualized activities which may be of particular interest to certain students or, at least, may arouse an interest which they already have.

The assignment should be definite, clear, and logical. You cannot blame your students for lack of interest or lack of understanding of the work involved if you do not make the assignment understandable. The assignment must not be too difficult or too simple. It should be within the ability range of your class. In order to make the best possible assignment, you must first determine the status of your class and make any preliminary explanations that you feel are necessary.

TEACHER-STUDENT PLANNING

In order to achieve optimum learning, students must be encouraged to take an active role in the planning of both curricular and extraclass activities. It is necessary for the teacher to make careful plans previous to the teaching of a unit or block of subject matter. However, such plans should be sufficiently flexible to make possible their revision and adaptation in accordance with the interests and aptitudes of the students to be taught. Such planning may well be carried on throughout the entire period of study, including the evaluation of student progress. However, it should not be overdone, since constant insistence on student choice can be just as frustrating to the learner as the denial of such choice.

Since the first step in planning any unit or block of class work is the setting up of objectives or aims, it is important that students be given opportunity to consider their own purposes in studying. These purposes should be similar to those which the teacher desires for his students; but unless they are actually the students' own purposes, the maximum learning will not take place. In order to guide your students in determining specific objectives, questions such as the following may be provided on slips of paper or written on the chalk board: What do I know about the proposed unit or block of work? What understandings, skills, and attitudes would I like to acquire through my study of this unit or block of work? Your stimulation and guidance in presenting the proposed topic through a motion picture, an article from a periodical, or any other means will help your students to answer such questions in a way that will make the work more interesting to them.

Students should be encouraged to suggest topics or problems, in line with the unit or block of work to be studied, which will help them to acquire the understandings, skills, and attitudes that are desired. These may be individual or group problems and should be used throughout the study of the unit. The greater the amount of activity on the part of your students, the greater the likelihood that they will be motivated to achieve the goals which you and they would like to have them achieve.

Your students may help in locating pictures, slides, reference books, and other materials that will be useful in their study of the subject matter involved. They may also make charts or construct models, figures, etc., that are appropriate. They may bring materials from their homes or obtain them in the community. Your supervising teacher will help you in locating materials that will be helpful in connection with the unit which you are directing.

Students should be encouraged to suggest ways in which the desired goals may be attained. They should then organize into committees and also work as individuals for the purpose of achieving the desired objectives. They should also help in planning the culminating activities for use in presenting their findings to the class as a whole. In evaluating their progress, your students may summarize the understandings, skills, and attitudes that they have acquired. They may be permitted to evaluate the work of one another, although this type of activity must be used judiciously in order not to cause any feelings of jealousy or ill will on the part of the students. Your supervising teacher will have some ideas on this point.

The final stage of teacher-student planning comes in the consideration of future work in line with the findings that have been obtained. Students should be encouraged to list new questions that have come to mind through the study that they have just completed and to consider ways in which answers to these questions may be obtained. Such activity may lead naturally into the next unit of work and thus provide a powerful continuing motivational factor to the students.

The following statements by student teachers illustrate the use of teacher-student planning and indicate the values which they observed in its use:

Student teaching helped me to learn many of the techniques used in teaching. One particular technique that I learned and used was teacher-student planning. I had read and studied about this procedure, but I did not understand it until I was given the opportunity to put it into practice. This was a very interesting part of my student teaching. I learned how a teacher must work with individual students and study the needs and abilities of each one.

* * *

I saw demonstrated something which I consider to be the exception rather than the rule in the modern classroom in America: a firmness without harshness, a kindness without sentimentality, and always a willingness to explain when a student was confused or slow to learn. All of this, in my opinion, created a constructive situation which greatly facilitated the learning process. . . . The teacher's recognition of individual differences and his ability to see and meet the needs of the bright and the less bright gave each one a sense of achievement.

The amount of teacher-student planning which you may use in your student teaching will depend upon a number of factors, including the age of the students, the subject matter involved, and the type of students in your classes. Your supervising teacher will also have something to say about such activity. There are some excellent teachers who do not feel that teacher-student planning has a very important place in the teaching-learning situation. Since you are working under the supervision of an experienced teacher, it is imperative that you consider his ideas and follow his suggestions, even though you may feel that you would like to use different procedures. You may take note of methods and devices which you cannot use in your student-teaching experience but which you would like to try when you get into a full-time teaching position. Remember that your supervising teacher is the one who is held responsible for the accomplishments of the students in his classes. Therefore, you must follow his suggestions in working with these students.

GROUP-PROCESS TECHNIQUES

Group work is an important technique for use in the classroom. It not only provides for many kinds of new learning experiences, but it is also unusually effective in deepening understanding. The use of this technique facilitates social interchange and at the same time utilizes cooperative problem-solving skills. Since one of the basic concepts underlying a democratic society is respect for the dignity and worth of every human being, group activities are essential to the training of citizens to carry on the work of such a society. Effective group dynamics can provide the learner with opportunities to participate in, and contribute to, the activities of a group and thus feel that he belongs to the group regardless of his ability, background, color, or religious creed.

In using group process, the first factor to be considered is the objectives to be obtained. If the desired objectives are more likely to be reached through group-process techniques than through other means, this is reason enough for their use. Your supervising teacher will be glad to help you in determining the techniques which you should use.

One problem which usually presents itself in preparing a class for group activities is the method of organizing the groups. Your supervising teacher will be able to help you in this procedure. The first step in organizing groups is to determine the previous experience of your students in this type of activity and their attitude toward previous group experiences. If they are not favorably inclined to such work, it may be better for you to use some other approach. If there is an indication that group process will be useful in a given situation, it will be necessary to list possible problems for group consideration. You should have some of these problems in mind before suggesting the procedure. However, it is well to give the students an opportunity to suggest possible problems.

The method of dividing the class into groups is another problem to be faced. Various devices involving interest, ability, special skill, sex, sociometric information, student choice, or arbitrary decision may be used. No one method can be considered best in every situation. You must determine, with the help of your supervising teacher, the method which is most likely to be successful with your students.

When the students get started on group activities, it is necessary to have a definite time schedule. Otherwise it is quite likely that certain groups will take more time than they should, while other groups may finish too soon. This matter should be discussed with the entire class at the beginning of the group work, so that everyone will have a definite idea of what is to be accomplished and of the time that is allotted for this activity. Space should be provided so that the members of each group can work together without interfering with the activities of another group. This may pose quite a problem if you have a large class in a relatively small room. However, it is not impossible to use group techniques even in a crowded situation.

The final phase of group process is reporting and evaluating. Proper reporting is necessary in order that all students in the class may benefit by the work of every other student. Evaluation should be accomplished by the members of the class as well as by the student teacher and possibly the supervising teacher. Rating forms may be developed for use by the members of each group and by the class as a whole in evaluating their work. You and your supervising teacher may work together in developing evaluation instruments which may be used. These should usually include a written examination over the material covered. Reporting and evaluating are most important in the use of group process. Probably the most common cause of failure and criticism of group activities is laxity in this regard. If students get the idea that group process is merely "an excellent way of wasting time," that is exactly what it will be.

The use of group process techniques in an elementary classroom situation is described by a student teacher as follows:

Mrs. Blank is a very capable teacher—both kind and talented. She has so much initiative, and she is wonderful in art work. She has so many good ideas for making new games, such as spelling and arithmetic ball games. . . .

In her room the students have a room-management plan, fashioned after that of city governments. A "mayor" and "assistant mayor" are elected, and a council is chosen to keep the room in order whether or not she is in the room. A "Good Citizen" chart is used, and the children are treated as citizens. In discipline she often says, "Do you think that a good citizen does . . . etc.?" The children respond well to this type of management.

INDIVIDUALIZED INSTRUCTION

One type of teaching which the student teacher has an excellent opportunity to perform is individualized instruction. It is possible for the student teacher to take one or two students into another room or into the corridor and give them individual instruction and help which would otherwise be impossible. This work is helpful to your supervising teacher and at the same time gives you opportunities to study different types of students and learn how best to work with them when you are in charge of the entire class.

One student teacher states his ideas about individual instruction as follows:

Student teaching helped me gain a keener insight into the problems of the "low achievers" or "science-shy" students, or those who plan to make science their life work, and also the "normal track" students.

It is often true that the better students may need some special instruction, either because of enforced absence or because they are working on a special problem. The more experience you can get in individual instruction, the better you will understand the problems of various types of students and how to guide their learning.

DRILL, REVIEW, AND SUMMARY

In all subjects taught in elementary and secondary schools there are phases and items involving acquisition of skills which cannot be effectively taught incidentally or accidentally. Well-planned drill is an important factor in developing skills. Review and summary are techniques which serve to deepen understanding of relationships. Such deepening is essential to maximum retention and application of important facts and principles.

In planning for drill, the teacher should consider two points: what phases of the work to be taught should become more or less automatic for the students, and what devices or methods may be used to help make these understandings and skills more automatic. In the first place, the understandings and skills on which drill should be given should be those which are most important for proper development of the students involved. One of the objections which has been raised in the past is that too much emphasis was placed on drill on unimportant details, instead of giving drill on important understandings and skills.

Review may be conducted as drill. Whatever the method used, the purpose of review is to help students remember important facts or skills that will be useful to them in later life either in the schoolroom or after graduation—preferably both. It is an established fact that much of the material which is learned in school is forgotten in a relatively short time. Therefore, it is important to choose carefully the understandings and skills to be re-emphasized during review.

Such questions as the following may help to emphasize learnings which are essential: What are the most important facts or skills that we have learned? Which of these facts or skills will be most significant to us in later life and why? In what ways does the material learned through the study of this unit or block of subject matter relate to that which was learned previously? Does our study of this material indicate possible subjects for future study? As these questions are discussed, the students should write them down for future reference. It may be well to ask them to hand in a list of the five new ideas or processes that they have learned. These may be summarized, mimeographed, and returned to all members of the class the next day.

A summary is usually given by the teacher. It may be in the form of duplicated material, or it may be oral. A concise summary will help to emphasize the essential concepts and skills which all students should remember. It may be well to ask certain students to summarize important sections of the material that has been studied, and then give opportunity for class discussion of these summaries. However, it is usually best for the teacher to make the final summary and bring together the most important concepts and skills for the benefit of the entire class.

The amount and type of drill, review, and summary that should be provided will vary with the subject matter and the type of students involved. Your supervising teacher will be glad to help you in planning this work.

One student teacher expresses her ideas regarding the importance of the student-teaching experience in the following words:

In brief, here was my chance to apply the principles, methods, and psychology of education which the college had so carefully furnished me. Here was a time to see theory become reality. Here was an opportunity to learn about students and to experiment (as all new teachers must do) under the practiced eye of my supervising teacher. Most of all, I believe, here was my chance to learn about myself and my relations with other people (particularly students), along with the impartial but critical aid and wise counsel of a supervising teacher.

Other student teachers summarize their observations regarding methods, devices, and procedures of instruction in the following words:

I learned, as I observed, that better order is kept when the teacher does not raise her voice. I was also interested to find in a conference period that it is very successful to counsel problem children rather than send them to the principal and thereby show them that you can't handle them.

Another thing I noticed that helped to get a child to cooperate was, when correcting him, the use of the term "let's" instead of "you." "Let's" makes him feel that he is not alone, while "you" is a command, and a child may rebel against it.

          ❈   ❈   ❈

As to methods of teaching, I have learned a lot. As I observed in Mr. Blank's room as well as in our own, I noticed that after a majority of the students understood a thing, it was best to let them go ahead while

the teacher individually assisted the slower students in a supervised study period. In this way, slower students get needed attention without making it evident, to them or to the rest of the class, that they need special attention. If some students do not understand problems or questions, it is good to let another student who is ahead help them.

* * *

In observing class instruction, I found that lessons [should be] . . . practical to the students. They decided why they needed to know what they were going to study. After it became practical to them, they were ready to learn. Mr. Blank let his class read their meters at home and figure their own light bills to make it practical, rather than merely using problems in the arithmetic book. Mr. Smith brought checks and deposit slips when teaching an arithmetic lesson on writing checks and making deposits.

I like the idea of one pencil and two sheets of paper (one to write on and one to cover with). This takes away the temptation to cheat. I observed that, before tests were given, the students had been well prepared by the teacher. When they were given a test . . . , instructions were plainly given. I like the discussion-type test because it helps the students to learn to think.

* * *

If children are talking too loudly, it is better for the teacher either to wait or to talk so softly that the children will have to quiet down if they want to hear what she is saying. If the teacher tries to talk loudly, she will only end up yelling. Also, a quiet atmosphere helps children do their work more quickly and with a more efficient and happy attitude than if the teacher is yelling.

One student teacher describes her feeling of inadequacy and need of help in regard to methods in the following way:

There are several large areas in which I feel I need help. (1) I am not able to present lessons without having to refer to written lesson plans. It was not ideal to have to refer constantly to something written . . . while I was teaching. (2) I need a great deal of background in subject matter, particularly in science and social studies. (3) The general idea behind grading puzzles me. The policy is to mark on achievement, and yet how does a teacher mark individual effort and take account of individual differences when achievement doesn't take these [factors] into consideration?

The first of the above inadequacies can be remedied to a great degree by teaching experience. It is probably true, however, that some reference to written plans will be necessary regardless of the amount of experience the teacher may have. The second inadequacy should be remedied by further study in the fields in which the inadequacy is felt. Much may be accomplished in this line by studying material on your own. Additional college or university work in academic subject-matter fields will also prove to be beneficial. The third problem is one which may never be solved to the satisfaction of the conscientious teacher. This is such an important phase of the teaching-learning process that Chapter 11 of this volume is given over to a discussion of the problems involved in evaluation of student progress.

The following discussion of the entire student-teaching experience indicates many of the benefits that should be gained through this work:

As I progressed into my student-teaching assignment, my duties became more complex. I planned lessons, graded papers, gave tests, helped children after school, planned bulletin boards, went to faculty meetings, and spoke to parents concerning their children. It was a marvelous opportunity to accept the full responsibility of a teacher. I learned that teaching was a full-time job, and I was never able to go home at 4:00 o'clock and forget my duties. Almost every evening there were children who came in to receive extra help, or there were parent-teacher conferences. The grading of papers and preparing of lessons was done after dinner until bedtime. The task was time-consuming, especially when I taught a writing unit, for then I was grading over 120 compositions a night. But, although there is much hard work in the teaching profession, I found it to be a very rewarding experience. The rewards include seeing your students respond to your teaching, seeing a fast child stimulated or a slow child progressing, and seeing the children both interested in your course and doing well. It was especially pleasing to find that I could get along with the groups so well and to find that certain individuals who were known as "problems" gave me no trouble. The children became important to me as individuals, and their problems became my problems. I tried to encourage them, praise them for work well done, and evaluate them with regard to their effort and individual progress. I was indeed sorry to see my student-teaching experience come to an end, and I decided to remain at Central Junior High an extra week because I had enjoyed my assignment so very much.

Student teaching has been a wonderful experience in which I have been able to apply the theoretical material learned to the classroom situation. Only through such an experience as this can one gain a realistic insight into the teaching profession and prepare oneself to become a capable teacher.

The student teacher quoted above illustrates in an excellent way the truly professional prospective teacher.

One essential point to remember is that your supervising teacher is there to help you in choosing methods and devices which are likely to be best for you to use in a given situation and with a certain group of students. If you make use of this valuable resource, you are not likely to have great difficulty.

QUESTIONS AND PROBLEMS

1. What devices and materials can you use in introducing a unit of work which you will be teaching, in order to provide the greatest possible motivational effect?
2. List ten characteristics that distinguish a good assignment from a poor one.
3. Mention five types of assignments, and give advantages and disadvantages of each.
4. Discuss the importance of determining the status of students,

with reference to the material to be studied, before making an assignment. How may the status of students be determined?

5. In what ways should teacher-student planning be used in connection with a unit or block of work which you will be teaching?

6. List materials such as pictures, slides, charts, constructions, reference books, etc., which may be contributed by your students in connection with a unit or block of class work which you will be teaching. Compare this list with the materials that are actually contributed by the students.

7. What objectives are more likely to be attained through the use of group-process techniques than through other methods? What specific objectives of the unit or block of work which you are preparing to teach may best be attained through group-process techniques?

8. List advantages and disadvantages of various methods of dividing your class into groups.

9. In what ways should drill be used in teaching a unit or block of class work? Give specific examples from a unit of work which you will be teaching.

10. Summarize a unit or block of work, and test your students to determine the value of such a procedure.

SELECTED REFERENCES

Barron, Nora M., et al., *Teaching with Groups*. Minneapolis: Burgess Publishing Company, 1955. This booklet contains many practical aids to beginning teachers.

Burton, William H., *The Guidance of Learning Activities*. New York: Appleton-Century-Crofts, Inc., 1952. Chapters 11, 15, 16, 17, and 18 give a comprehensive discussion of the organization of the setting for learning, including the assignment, recitation or discussion, providing for creative expression, and the use of instructional resources.

Butler, Frank A., *The Improvement of Teaching in Secondary Schools*. Chicago: The University of Chicago Press, 1946 (Revised Edition). Chapter 9 on the assignment, and Chapter 11 on the improvement of questions and questioning are worth thoughtful reading.

Flanders, Ned A., *Teaching with Groups*. Minneapolis: Burgess Publishing Company, 1954. A pamphlet which provides a guide for teachers who are working with small groups.

Grambs, Jean D., William J. Iverson, and Franklin K. Patterson, *Modern Methods in Secondary Education*. New York: The Dryden Press, 1958 (Revised Edition). Chapter 10 gives valuable suggestions for group techniques in the classroom.

Haas, Robert B. (ed.), *Psychodrama and Sociodrama in American Education*. Beacon, New York: Beacon House, 1949. This book offers many examples of classroom practices.

Klein, Alan F., *Role Playing in Leadership Training and Group Problem Solving*. New York: Association Press, 1956. This small volume provides practical and specific guides for use in role playing.

Lane, Howard, and Mary Beauchamp, *Human Relations in Teaching*. New York: Prentice-Hall, Inc., 1955. The effects of group work on human relations are considered in Chapters 16 and 17.

Lurry, Lucille L., and Elsie J. Alberty, *Developing a High School Core Program*. New York: The Macmillan Company, 1957. This book gives, in explicit detail, the procedures of core instruction.

Miel, Alice, and associates, *Cooperative Procedures in Learning*. New York: Bureau of Publications, Teachers College, Columbia University, 1952. Illustrations of group work at both elementary and secondary levels.

Ohlsen, Merle M., *Modern Methods in Elementary Education*. New York: Henry Holt and Company, Inc., 1959. Chapter 1 describes learner-centered teaching. Methods of teaching the various elementary fields are presented in Chapters 7 through 17.

Russell, David H., *Children's Thinking*. Boston: Ginn and Company, 1956. A summary of research on problem solving, critical thinking, and methods of improving the thinking process.

Wellington, C. Burleigh, and Jean Wellington, *Teaching for Critical Thinking*. New York: McGraw-Hill Book Company, Inc., 1960. Part III explains various techniques that may be used in developing critical thinking.

11. *Evaluation of Student Progress*

One important phase of the student-teaching experience includes the administration and scoring of evaluation instruments, a summary of the results of evaluation, and the use of the information thus gained in evaluating student progress and in determining ways of improving instruction. Too often, paper-and-pencil tests are thought of as the only means of evaluation. However, the prospective teacher should find as many other ways of appraising student progress as he can use. Of course, all types of instruments are not equally useful in evaluating the same types of work or the work of students at all grade levels. It is therefore necessary for the prospective teacher to decide on the instruments that are most useful for purposes of evaluation in the situations in which he is working.

Regardless of the amount of course work which you have had in the field of evaluation, the only way in which you can actually learn how to determine student progress is by working with a group of learners. During the time of your student teaching you should have opportunities to administer and score standardized tests as well as to construct, administer, and check all kinds of teacher-made evaluation instruments. The amount and kind of opportunity will, of course, be determined by the grade level, the type of subject matter being taught, the situation in which you are placed, the amount of responsibility that your supervising teacher is willing to give you in evaluating and reporting student progress, and other factors that vary from school to school. As a general rule, the more opportunity you have in this type of work, the better able you will be to carry on such duties when you are in a regular teaching situation.

Since this is such a difficult phase of the teacher's work and the one which is most often criticized by students and parents alike, it is necessary that your supervising teacher carefully check your work. Any errors in judgment, either real or fancied, that are made by the student teacher will reflect on his supervising teacher. This is true in all phases of the student teacher's work, but it is especially noticeable in connection with the evaluation of student progress.

Teachers and schools vary greatly in their philosophy of evaluation and in the methods used. Therefore, it is imperative that you discuss with your supervising teacher, as soon as possible after starting your work in the school, the philosophy of evaluation to which he subscribes and the methods that are recommended. It is true that you have (or should have) your own ideas regarding evaluation. However, you should understand and follow the philosophy and techniques of your supervising teacher and those which are recognized by the administrative officers of the school and the system in which you are working. On the other hand, you should not be made to feel bound or limited to such an extent that you will not use your own initiative.

The importance of evaluation and some of the problems involved are indicated in the following quotations from student teachers' reports:

Actual teaching has helped me to form some very wholesome attitudes toward young people. It is not enough to merely insure mastery of subject matter; one must also inspire confidence in the pupil, praise him . . . for his effort to improve, and evaluate his own abilities rather than evaluate him in relation to his classmates.

❖   ❖   ❖

I like the charts on growth and development. I think such teaching is a positive factor in the growth of children. It is important to learn to grow up—and, in talking together, the students learn to help each other solve their own problems.

❖   ❖   ❖

I was extremely interested in the method of evaluation used at Hill-crest School. Having each child present a conscientious evaluation of himself, and discussing that evaluation in the light of the teacher's evaluation, . . . is beneficial. In the first place, the student learns to evaluate his own worth, and second, he has a chance to bring his feelings into the open when a teacher-student conference is held. This causes the student to have a more healthy attitude toward grading. Parent conferences are very important also because, when a parent can discuss his child openly with the teacher and when he understands the problems which the teacher faces with that child, he is more likely to understand why a particular grade was given. These are methods that I plan to use when I begin my teaching, for I feel that they are worthwhile. They will prove to be much more difficult than merely putting a grade on a card, but I know that grading in this manner will pay big dividends.

PREPARING EVALUATION INSTRUMENTS

The first step in any program of evaluation is to consider the objectives of all concerned. As a teacher you should consider your own aims for your students—i.e., what you hope to have accomplished through the teaching of a given unit or block of work. However, since your students are the ones whose work is to be evaluated, it is necessary to determine the objectives or aims from their viewpoint. In your previous planning for the work which you will be teaching, you should have studied the objectives and evaluation devices and procedures which your supervising teacher has developed. You may also study the objectives that have been set up by other teachers for a similar unit or block of work. The degree of consistency between statements of objectives and the actual methods and materials used in evaluation will determine the validity of the devices that you use in measuring student progress.

After determining the objectives which your students should attain, it is necessary to define these objectives in terms of behavior and content. The three types of behavior which should be considered in evaluating student progress are (1) concepts or understandings, (2) skills or abilities, and (3) attitudes or ideals. One excellent way of defining objectives for the purpose of planning evaluation procedures is the two-dimensional chart, an example of which is provided below. This chart was developed by a student teacher for use in planning evaluation devices and procedures for a class which had studied a unit in solid geometry. However, the same ideas may be used in defining obejctives for any unit or block of work in either the elementary or the secondary school and in any type of subject matter. One advantage of this type of chart is that it indicates very clearly the behaviors that should have been developed through the unit or block of work that has been taught and the content or subject matter that has been provided to help the students in attaining these behavioral aspects. This provides the teacher with a basis for determining situations and devices which will most successfully measure behavioral changes in his students.

CHART 3

Basic Concepts of Solid Geometry

	Understanding of Important Facts and Principles	*Ability to Interpret Data*	*Ability to Apply Principles*	*Ability to Abstract Ideas from Content*	*Desire to Relate Content to Everyday Life*
CONTENT					
Relation Between Solid and Plane Geometrics	x	x		x	
Geometric Solids	x	x	x		x
Surfaces	x	x	x		x
Lines	x	x	x		x
Points	x	x	x		x
Analogy Between Solid and Plane Geometrics	x	x			
Proving Relationships	x	x		x	
Beginning Postulates and Corollaries	x		x		x
Preliminary Theorems 1, 2, and 3	x	x	x	x	x

The relationships between content and behavior indicated on a chart such as this must be determined by each individual teacher through consideration of the methods, devices, and procedures used in teaching the material as well as through attention to the subject matter itself.

The student teacher who devised the above chart evidently felt that each phase of the content studied in this unit should contribute to understanding of important facts and principles. On the other hand, only three phases would be expected to help develop the ability to abstract ideas from content. Two of these have to do with proving relationships, and the other indicates the proving of certain theorems. This is to be expected, since the only way in which a student can develop a skill is by actually practicing the activity involved. This principle also holds true at the elementary-school level. For example, skill in the use of numbers or in reading can be developed only through practice in activities in which the use of these abilities is required.

The development of attitudes, such as the "desire to relate content to everyday life," depends largely upon the methods, devices, and procedures used by the teacher. For example, the question of whether a study of geometric solids will contribute to the development of this attitude will be determined by the emphasis which the teacher places upon the relationship of such solids to actual objects and experiences encountered by the student in everyday life. At the elementary-school level, relating classroom activities involved in nature study to the plant and animal life in the child's own neighborhood will tend to relate school work with everyday life.

In order to develop a chart which will be as accurate as possible, it is suggested that a number of charts be made in conference with your supervising teacher. In this way you will gain a much more thorough understanding of the subject matter involved and greater skill in developing evaluation devices which will measure your students' progress toward desired objectives.

After defining the objectives in terms of content and behavior, the next step is to determine the type or types of items or devices which will best measure the progress of your students. In constructing paper-and-pencil tests, you will need to decide whether multiple-choice, completion, or other short-answer items may be used, or whether a more subjective type of item will be more satisfactory in determining student progress toward the desired goals. It may be that a combination of objective and subjective items will be the best arrangement. Your supervising teacher should be very helpful to you in the development of evaluation instruments that will be useful in measuring progress of students in the various desired behaviors. The most difficult type of behavior to evaluate is the attitude. In fact, this may require the most subjective type of evaluation instrument or method.

The experiences of a student teacher with evaluation in a senior high school are described as follows:

I learned to make my own evaluation of a test made by someone else, to make and evaluate my own tests, to grade all . . . types of papers and average grades, to find and utilize supplementary work, [to understand] the importance and effectiveness of attractive bulletin boards, to make out monthly reports . . . and many other things equally important but too numerous to mention.

THE PRE-TEST

In order to determine the progress that students make as a result of their study of a unit or block of work, it is necessary to administer one or more pre-tests at the beginning of the period of study. The type of pre-test will vary with the subject matter and the grade level. At the elementary-school level, standardized tests of the fundamentals may be used to determine the status of boys and girls and the type of work that they may be expected to do. In certain academic subjects the pre-test may consist of a set of oral questions or a brief written test covering the main concepts, skills, and values to be considered in the unit. In skill subjects, such as typewriting, it may be a brief speed test or a period of questioning regarding past experiences of students with the device in question. In shop courses the students may be asked to construct a simple article, thus demonstrating their skill and prospects for future accomplishment.

Pre-tests may be standardized tests that are provided by commercial test companies or by publishing companies which produce the textbooks used. They may also be made up by the teacher or the student teacher. It is usually well to use some of your own tests for this purpose, since you are the one who will be teaching the unit or block of work and the one who should know what is expected of the students.

As a result of the administration of a pre-test, you should be able to determine (1) the status of the class as a whole, (2) individual students who show signs of exceptional ability and interest in the content area to be studied, and (3) individual students who are evidently slow learners in the field or subject matter to be studied. By studying these results in conference with your supervising teacher, you can revise your plans so as to present the material in a way that will be best for the students.

MEASURING STUDENT ACHIEVEMENT

Evaluation should be a continuous process. Every day the teacher is determining the progress of his students in subjective, if not objective, ways. In some types of subject matter, and at certain grade levels, it may be valuable to both students and teacher to administer a brief test each day. In other types of work the daily evaluation may be of a subjective nature, and the more objective evaluation procedures may not come until the end of a longer unit or block of work. In art work, for example, there is a certain amount of day-to-day evaluation to measure student progress in connection with a given project. However, the final evaluation of the completed project will probably be the most objective phase and the one on which the grade will be largely determined.

If standard tests are available, it may be possible to use two forms of a given test, one at the beginning and the other at the end of one phase of classwork, thus measuring quite accurately the accomplishment of the students. If standard tests are not available, or if your supervising teacher does not wish you to use standard tests, you must devise your own evaluation instruments for use throughout the time you are teaching. It may be that your supervising teacher will recommend that you use evaluation devices and procedures that he has been using. If so, you should comply with his desires, but you may study the results with the idea of improving such devices when you are in your own classroom.

Since methods and devices will vary with the type of subject matter involved and the type and age of students with whom you are working, it is important for you to observe the ways in which your supervising teacher evaluates his students' progress, and to discuss these matters with him before planning your own evaluation instruments and procedures. As a student teacher, you should have as much experience as possible with all types of evaluation that are applicable to your subject-matter fields and grade level. In this way you may be able to determine advantages and disadvantages of each method and each device. The guidance of your supervising teacher is essential for proper understanding of the various evaluation procedures which he has developed. However, you should have some experience in developing your own devices and procedures. It is probably easier, for both student teacher and supervising teacher, if previously developed evaluation devices are used, but this procedure will not give you the experience that you should have for future work of an educational nature.

The following statements indicate the reactions of student teachers regarding their work in evaluating student progress:

Grading papers was a most profitable experience for me. I was able to see the results of my teaching—where I had succeeded and where there was still much work to be done. I also learned, through experience, to evaluate pupils' work in general rather than in too much detail—in other words, to make a general analysis of all the papers that I had graded.

                    ✿   ✿   ✿

I composed my tests without specific help from my supervisng teacher, and I was pleased to discover that the results were an accurate picture

of past performance of my students. I spent several hours analyzing the results of my tests, finding weaknesses in teaching as well as in test construction, and also finding students who indicated specific weaknesses by consistently missing certain types of questions, and others who were unable to arrange material in chronological sequence.

* * *

I enjoyed helping with achievement tests. It was interesting to note the pupils' progress by comparing the marks made on the tests given this quarter with the ones they had previously taken.

* * *

I graded papers and found that one cannot be too strict in evaluating the work that children do. Reading-readiness tests were very helpful in determining what the pupils could do.

MARKING

As a student teacher, you should have some experience in marking or grading the students with whom you are working. However, since your supervising teacher is the one who is actually responsible for this phase of the work, he should have the opportunity to make final decisions regarding the mark to be given an individual student. Most supervising teachers are very considerate in working with a student teacher, and they will usually give the student teacher opportunities to grade the students with whom he has been working, but it is always best for you to consult your supervising teacher before making any final decisions regarding the grading of students' work. If this plan is followed, there is less danger of complaint on the part of the student or his parents. The more responsiblity you can be given in connection wtih the grading of your students' work, the better prepared you will be when you get into your first teaching position.

One student teacher gives her thoughts regarding the marking of students in the following words:

Doing some of the grading of papers, keeping records, and making reports helped me to realize the importance of this work. I administered and corrected achievement tests and tabulated scores in the record book. . . . I had several conferences with my supervising teacher concerning the possible failing of certain students. . . . I learned that there are many factors to be considered before determining whether a child should be failed or passed to the next grade.

One excellent plan that is often followed is to ask students to grade their own work, if it is the type of work that lends itself to this procedure. After the students have graded their own work, you and your supervising teacher should always discuss the work with them and indicate all errors and ways in which the work might be improved.

QUESTIONS AND PROBLEMS

1. Construct and administer one or more pre-tests to determine status of students with reference to the unit or block of work which you will be teaching. Determine the status of the class as a whole. Determine students who show signs of exceptional interest and ability in the content area to be studied. Determine students who show evidence of being slow learners in the subject matter to be studied.
2. Administer one or more standard tests covering the content area to be taught. In what ways are these tests more or less satisfactory than teacher-made tests?
3. Ask your students to evaluate their own work. Then discuss their evaluation with them and with your supervising teacher.

4. Construct and administer one or more evaluation instruments to determine the progress of your students as a result of your teaching effort. Are there evidences that desired objectives have been achieved? What evidences are there that changes in materials and/or methods of instruction might increase achievement of students?

5. Determine the plan of marking which is used in the school where you are working. Discuss student marks with your supervising teacher to determine ways in which your ideas may be different from those of the faculty members with whom you are working.

SELECTED REFERENCES

Blair, Glenn M., R. Stewart Jones, and Ray H. Simpson, *Educational Psychology.* New York: The Macmillan Company, 1962. Chapters 15, 16, and 22 provide excellent suggestions for the promotion of personal and social development of pupils and of the teacher.

Bradfield, James M., and H. Stewart Moerdock, *Measurement and Evaluation in Education.* New York: The Macmillan Company, 1957. Provides excellent descriptions of available published tests.

Burton, William H., *The Guidance of Learning Activities.* New York: Appleton-Century-Crofts, Inc., 1944. Chapters 19, 20, and 21, on evaluation, diagnosis, and reporting, give excellent suggestions for the prospective teacher.

Cronbach, Lee J., *Educational Psychology*, Revised Edition. New York: Harcourt, Brace and World, Inc., 1963. Chapters 7 and 16 explain problems encountered by the teacher in appraising pupil progress, and ways in which such problems may be overcome.

Gerberich, J. R., *Specimen Objective Test Items.* New York: Longmans, Green and Company, 1956. Selected test items furnish good models for the construction of teacher-made tests.

Grambs, Jean D., William J. Iverson, and Franklin K. Patterson, *Modern Methods in Secondary Education.* New York: The Dryden Press, 1958. Evaluation, the construction of evaluation instruments, and reporting on student progress are discussed in Chapters 17 and 18.

Greene, Harry A., Albert N. Jorgensen, and J. Raymond Gerberich,

Measurement and Evaluation in the Secondary School. New York: Longmans, Green and Company, 1954. Concrete suggestions are given for the improvement of teacher-made tests.

Ohlsen, Merle M., *Modern Methods in Elementary Education*. New York: Henry Holt and Company, Inc., 1959. Methods of appraising personal adjustment, mental growth, and school achievement of elementary-school pupils are discussed in Chapters 3 and 4.

Ragan, William B., *Modern Elementary Curriculum*. New York: Henry Holt and Company, 1960. Chapters 14 and 15 give methods of evaluating pupil progress and the elementary-school program as a whole.

Torgerson, T. L., and Georgia S. Adams, *Measurement and Evaluation for the Elementary School Teacher*. New York: Dryden Press, 1954. An excellent discussion of the measurement of intelligence and development of elementary-school pupils.

V. YOU AND THE TEACHING PROFESSION

12. *Evaluating Your Student-Teaching Experiences*

Evaluation should be a continuous process, whether it is your evaluation of the work of your students, your supervising teacher's evaluation of your work, the evaluation of your work by the university or college supervisor, or your evaluation of your own work. However, when you approach the end of your period of student teaching, it is well for you to look back over the entire period and determine those experiences which have been most helpful to you and those which might have been improved. Regardless of the amount of experience that your supervising teacher has had, he is quite likely to make some mistakes in dealing with his students as well as with you. There is a wealth of common sense in the statement, "He who makes no mistakes does nothing." You should not criticize your supervising teacher (at least, openly) for such blunders, because you may make some more serious ones when you are placed in a similar situation. This does not mean that you should fail to profit by all mistakes that are observed, whether they be your own or those of another person.

Re-examine your log of student-teaching experiences, with the idea of determining ways in which you might be able to improve if you had the opportunity to begin again with another group of students and another supervising teacher. Discuss your experiences with your supervising teacher, soliciting his comments and criticisms. This is one of the best ways of profiting by past mistakes and capitalizing on your best experiences. The criticisms and suggestions of those with whom you are working are intended to help you develop into the best possible teacher, and they should be considered in that light.

One student teacher at the junior-high-school level expresses his reactions as follows:

My supervising teacher, Mrs. Blank, has been most helpful. She has given me advice out of her wealth of experiences. She has been most cooperative and friendly. When encouragement was needed, Mrs. Blank was always there. She was not one to dominate, but one who was interested in me and tried to show me and help me to understand things that will be most valuable in future teaching. She has definitely challenged me.

Student teachers sometimes feel a lack of constructive criticism on the part of their supervising teachers, as indicated by the following quotation from a student who did his work in a senior high school:

At times I felt that my supervising teacher did not criticize my work as much as she should have, but I always found her willing to help me in every situation.

One elementary-school student teacher gives the following evaluation of her supervising teacher:

Mrs. Jones was certainly a wonderful supervising teacher. . . . Her encouragement and constructive criticism was certainly appreciated, and her example as a teacher will follow me through many years to come.

A similar statement is made by a student teacher who did her work in a senior high school:

I found Miss Smith to be constantly friendly and helpful. She has helped me to understand my own abilities and potentialities as a future teacher. And above all, she has given me constructive advice and criticism about my teaching.

MEETING YOUR OWN PERSONAL PROBLEMS

Your personality characteristics which have been developed over the years will determine, to a significant extent, your personal problems in student teaching as well as in other interpersonal relations. The grade level of your students and the principal characteristics of your class or classes will also have some effect on the personal problems which you may encounter. Most important for your success in student teaching is the way in which you meet such problems. Your supervising teacher can be very helpful at such times, but it is you who must make as objective an examination as possible and you who must meet the problem rather than evade it.

You cannot, overnight, change personality characteristics that have taken years to develop. However, you must try to adapt such characteristics to the situation at hand in order to establish the best possible rapport with your students and all others with whom you are working. When you make a mistake and a difficult situation develops, it is useless to try to disregard the problem. If the mistake is not too serious, it is quite probable that, with the help of your supervising teacher, you will be able to redeem yourself in the eyes of your students and make satisfactory progress in overcoming the personality characteristic which precipitated the unpleasant situation. It is no disgrace to make an honest mistake, but the harm is in failing to face the difficulty in an objective manner and make the proper adjustment.

It is quite probable that your supervising teacher has met a similar difficulty and overcome it. If so, he may be more understanding and better able to help you face your problem. Regardless of the situation in which you are placed or the previous experience of your supervising teacher, one essential factor in your success as a student teacher and in your future success in an actual teaching position is your ability to objectively evaluate your strengths and weaknesses and solicit the assistance of your supervising teacher whenever you feel that such help is needed.

One student teacher at the senior-high-school level makes the following observations:

Regarding my weak points, I would say that they were my organization and my speaking voice. Through the help of Mrs. Blank, I was able to improve somewhat upon my weaknesses. She allowed me almost a free hand in the handling of classes. She gave me much valuable advice, but she did so when we were alone. She also allowed me to make my own mistakes, and this, in itself, is a good thing. In my opinion, teaching is a matter of sinking or swimming, and one does not learn to swim if he must continually have others move his arms and legs for him. In terms of teaching, this is true. You have to meet squarely every problem that comes before you.

Two elementary student teachers make similar statements:

My weaknesses were many when my teaching began. With Mrs. Smith's guidance and criticism, improvement has been evident. When entering a classroom, I feel I will be better qualified to teach the pupils than I would have been without this experience.

✿ ✿ ✿

Student teaching is an experience that every prospective teacher should have. It has helped me to improve, and has also shown me where I still need to improve.

YOUR PROBABLE SUCCESS AS A TEACHER

Many factors will enter into your success as a teacher. It is probable that the difficulties encountered in student teaching will be a fairly accurate indication of the difficulties that you will have in an actual teaching position. Your progress in overcoming weaknesses and capitalizing on your successes should indicate your ability to improve during your first years as a regular teacher.

During your first experience as a full-time teacher, you will not have the benefit of an experienced teacher who can give you constructive criticism and assistance when you need it. However, if you have made good use of the help that your supervising teacher has given you, the chances are excellent for your success in a teaching position. In many schools the supervising principal, supervisor, or some other school official will have the responsibility of working with new teachers and of helping them become oriented to the actual teaching situation. However, such a person usually has quite a number of beginning teachers with whom to work, and therefore he cannot spend as much time as he would like with any one teacher. In other words, you will be largely on your own when you are employed as a regular teacher.

In some ways this may make your work more satisfying, since you will be free to carry on the activities in the way you wish.

Two student teachers in secondary schools make the following predictions regarding the value of their student-teaching experiences in preparation for an actual teaching position:

The hardest part of teaching, for me, is in discipline. I have thought it over carefully and discussed my difficulty with Miss Blank. I see that it is necessary to keep the class busy all of the time doing work that will count, not just busy work. Also, a teacher needs to be firm from the first and to establish the fact that she really means business.

❊ ❊ ❊

As a whole, this quarter's work has been wonderful. I was elated at times; other times I was very much discouraged. Sometimes students loved me; other times they hated me. Discipline was no problem one day; another day students acted as if they owned the school. As a student teacher, I have met many of the problems with which I will be faced when I begin teaching on my own. These months of experience will help me to solve these same problems. I gained confidence and assurance as I taught more and more, and now I feel ready to begin a job of my own.

The following student teachers in elementary schools describe the values received from student teaching and their attitude toward the prospect of a full-time teaching experience:

I found out in my student teaching that . . . lots of common sense needs to be used. I learned that students expect fairness in all things and will speak up when they feel they are not being treated fairly. They can see through any pretense you may try to put up, and they respect you more if you are sincere.

❊ ❊ ❊

It is only when you have the opportunity to put into practice the . . . [learnings] that four years of education . . . [have provided] that you can "see" for the first time. You realize why you have learned what you have been taught, and wonder why you let the opportunity to learn more slip by. It has been said that education successfully applied reveals the opening to endless possibilities through knowledge, and that the educated person is one who knows how to use what he has learned to its fullest advantage.

❊ ❊ ❊

The most valuable experience I have had in these past four years of college is student teaching. Life is a continuous process of learning, and if we are exposed to the highest educational circumstances, our learning is the most natural process and will cease to be the dread experience too many of us make it, at least in our mind's eye. The teacher learns along with the students. She feels herself with their feelings, she sees through their eyes, hears through their ears, speaks with their mouths, and understands through their minds. Each child senses her every whim and her every ambition, and this evidence challenges perfection to her ideals that she hopes to establish as the days fly by.

One elementary student teacher gives the following "helpful hints" which were gleaned during her student teaching and which should prove to be valuable to her in her first teaching position:

1. Let a child be successful in front of the group.
2. Be able to be flexible in well-planned lessons.
3. Be especially friendly with unpopular children. Other children often mimic the teacher.
4. Do not let children interrupt you continuously with their unimportant concerns.
5. Don't ever "bawl out" a person; only criticize what he does.
6. Do nothing to lower the self-esteem or self-respect of a child.
7. Setting the stage for a lesson is important.
8. Talk on the grade level of the children, not above or below. Write directions on their grade level, also.
9. When going around the room giving help to individual children, just give one suggestion at a time, so that you can cover the whole class; then come back and start over.
10. In discipline, just notice the important things. Don't call down for every little thing.
11. A good way to quiet a class is to talk in a soft voice.
12. The more the teacher talks, the more the children will talk.
13. Never let parents think you don't know your job. They are sometimes indefinite, but they expect the teacher to be definite and authoritative.
14. Lessons and plans should be "tight."
15. Always stand up straight and speak to the *whole* class.
16. Children appreciate it if the teacher is consistent in the punishment she uses—i.e., punish everyone equally, and punish for the same thing done wrong all the time.

17. Be specific in assignments. Don't say, "Do page eight and, if you can, page nine."
18. The more concrete experiences children can have, especially in arithmetic, the quicker the concepts will be learned.

REACTIONS OF YOUR STUDENTS

One of the best indications of your success as a student teacher and your probable future success as a regular teacher is the way in which your students have reacted toward you. This does not mean that student teaching is a popularity contest. As a matter of fact, if you overemphasize your attempts to be popular with your students, the chances are that you will become less popular the longer you stay in the school, and you may even lose the respect of your students. This is one mistake which student teachers and beginning teachers often make. As you evaluate your experiences, you should determine whether your students' reactions were, on the whole, proper and wholesome, or whether there are indications that you have spoken or acted in ways that have caused your students to react in an unwholesome way toward you. If you have made some mistakes in this regard, you should make the necessary corrections in your own mind so that you will not make the same mistakes again. It might be valuable for you to make written notes regarding the situations that you have encountered, with suggestions for the correction of mistakes.

The reactions of your students toward you will be determined, to a certain extent, by your supervising teacher. It is sometimes true that students will be partial toward the student teacher, even though the supervising teacher is excellent. This can lead to grave consequences if it is carried to the extreme. If you realize that such a situation is developing, you should do everything possible to make the necessary corrections. It may be that the principal cause of such an attitude is the fact that you are nearer in age to your students than your supervising teacher is; or it may be due to some particular personality characteristics of your supervising teacher or yourself. Whatever the reasons, it is unwise for you to foster attitudes toward yourself that will tend to alienate your students from their regular teacher.

The experiences of one student teacher with a fifth-grade class illustrate some of the mistakes that have been mentioned:

My real aim from the start was to try to stay on the good side of the pupils, and to do this I often joked and "cut up" too much. Then, at times, I began to notice that when it was time for serious business, it was difficult to handle the class. Through the advice and instruction of my supervising teacher, I realized my mistake and found that although you may use a firm hand, you can have the love and respect of the pupils at the same time. This was one of the greatest thrills that I had—when I was able to handle a class of fifth-graders all by myself.

The reactions of students toward a student teacher vary with the age and grade of the students, the socioeconomic area in which the school is located, and other factors. Students are likely to wish to give the student teacher a going-away party if they have reacted favorably toward his work with them. One student teacher in a primary grade relates the following experience:

I have gained a new outlook on teaching. It has made me realize just how important the teacher is to the child, especially in the primary grades. To illustrate this, my pupils gave me a party on the last day. They brought little gifts, but the one I liked best was the nickel that one little boy gave me, because it was all he had.

A student teacher in a junior high school relates the following experience:

At the end of my last week, the students in my third-period English class threw a party and brought in a specially made cake for the occasion. The frosted coloring on top read, "Good-bye, Mr. Davidson." That gesture meant to me more assurance, more encouragement, than thousands of dull words in any textbook. These are the moments that make teaching more than a [means of] livelihood, more than a pastime, more than a humanitarian interest. It is a living experience.

Of course, the type of activity that the students may carry on will depend on the location of the school and the rules of the school system. Some school systems have a regulation that students are not to present gifts to their teachers, and, of course, this rule would apply to student teachers. However, a question always arises: what is one to do when the students surprise the teacher or student teacher with a party and present gifts? Obviously, the only gracious thing to do is to accept the gifts and enter into the festivities with appreciation for the kind thoughts that prompt the occasion. Even junior- and senior-high-school students may wish to do something to express their appreciation for the student teacher's work with them, although their methods will be somewhat different from those of elementary-school pupils. One type of expression of appreciation that is often used by secondary-school students is the letter. This may be in the form of one letter which is signed by all of the students in a class, or it may be a collection of individual letters. Such mementos are valuable to the beginning teacher, especially when he is not certain of his ability 'as an instructor. Words of encouragement from a class of secondary-school students can do much to make a good teacher.

EVALUATION BY YOUR SUPERVISORS

You may be able to determine the amount of progress that you have made in overcoming weaknesses and capitalizing on your strengths during the period of your student teaching by re-examining the comments made by your supervising teacher on written reports that have been submitted to your university or college supervisor. It is expected that your supervising teacher will discuss these reports with you as they are produced. However, it is well to re-examine all of them in conference with your supervising teacher near the close of your period of student teaching.

The following comments, which were gleaned by a university supervisor from student-teaching and conference reports submitted by his student teachers, illustrate the type of reactions that may be valuable to you in evaluating your work as a student teacher. Some of these comments were made near the beginning of the student-teaching period, others near the close of the time of student teaching.

TABLE 1

Comments of Supervising Teachers Regarding
Their Student Teachers *

Favorable Comments	Weaknesses Indicated
1. Excellent lesson plan and lesson preparation.	1. Difficulty in responding to questions and in giving clear and explicit answers to students.
2. Good discipline—class well in hand.	2. Weak in conducting discussions where all participate.
3. Good rapport with students.	3. Lesson plans not mastered.
4. Good detail in lesson planning.	4. Timing of lesson is a problem: does not fit the lesson to the class time. Loose ends.
5. Good evaluation of students' work.	5. Amenities of written and spoken language need strengthening.
6. Invites questions from students.	6. Eye contact poor: looks at ceiling and floor.
7. Helps students formulate problems that will challenge them beyond the scope of the lesson being taught.	7. Needs to be aware of nervous mannerisms.
8. Provides supplementary reading assignments.	8. Should bring all students into group discussion.
9. Inspires students to learn.	9. Class is not challenged to its fullest capacity.
10. Shows special interest in individual students.	10. Irrelevant material interrupts attention span of class.
11. Constructs effective, thought-provoking questions and tests.	11. Stronger discipline needed at times.
12. Forceful voice.	12. Needs to learn to adjust pace of teaching to the learning pace of the class.
13. Expresses thoughts forcefully and well.	13. Corrects papers with too much haste; misses some errors. Needs to learn thoroughness.

TABLE 1—CONTINUED

Comments of Supervising Teachers Regarding Their Student Teachers *

Favorable Comments	*Weaknesses Indicated*
14. Student teacher is punctual.	14. Assumes *all* understand when only a *few* understand.
15. Student teacher is dependable.	15. Insufficient drill material.
16. Student teacher is cooperative.	16. Must strive to keep all interested while answering individual questions.
17. Excellent use of chalk board.	17. Feels insecure because she does not know her subject matter thoroughly. Students know this.
18. Interested in *individual* student.	18. Needs to be more forceful in handling less mature students.
19. Superb motivation of students.	19. Needs to see that students take notes—and do so *neatly*.
20. Takes suggestions and criticism well.	20. Needs to refrain from using "O.K."
21. Is well groomed; neat appearance.	21. No enthusiasm: takes teaching as a chore.
22. Excellent speech habits.	22. Needs to give more explicit instructions for assignments and home work: students do not know exactly what to do or what is expected of them.
23. Spends much time in planning work.	23. Does not use chalk board effectively.
24. Gives extra time to students although it involves self-sacrifice on her part.	24. Does not enlist student cooperation: tells rather than teaches.
25. Explanations are explicit and definite.	25. Fails to show the grace, courtesy and consideration which should be the mark of an educated person.

TABLE 1—CONTINUED

Comments of Supervising Teachers Regarding
Their Student Teachers *

Favorable Comments	*Weaknesses Indicated*
26. Encourages comments from students.	26. Is absent without letting supervising teacher know about the emergency.
27. Conducts well-ordered discussion.	27. Is not open and "above board."
28. Time awareness not apparent, but always ends class period exactly on time.	28. Sits on desk, dangles feet, slumps and shows no zest for teaching.

* Paul D. Leedy, *Comments of Supervising Teachers Regarding Their Student Teachers* (unpublished material).

It would be well for you to make a similar list of favorable and unfavorable comments that have been made by your supervising teacher and by others who have had opportunities to observe your work. You might arrange these comments in order, according to the time in your student-teaching experience when they were made, thus making it possible for you to determine indications of improvement and possible ways in which you can further improve in your teaching ability.

You may feel that some of the unfavorable comments are unwarranted. However, if you approach this re-evaluation process with an open mind, it is quite probable that you will be able to improve in some characteristics in which you feel you are already good. No one, regardless of his ability, ever gets to the place where he cannot improve. In fact, if he does get to such a place in his own mind, he is likely to find himself in a position of failure in his undertakings. It is much better to accept unwarranted criticism, with the idea of making improvements, than to disregard such comments through a process of rationalization and, perhaps, lose the value that you might otherwise receive.

It is recommended that your college or university supervisor arrange for a conference, preferably with you and your supervising teacher, after every visit that he makes to your classes (if you have been actively engaged in the teaching-learning situation). Thus you may receive his comments and suggestions and be able to profit by his observations as well as those of your supervising teacher. If it is impossible to arrange such a conference after some visits of your supervisor, he will probably leave some written notes and suggestions which you may consider with him at a later time.

The following statements by student teachers at the secondary-school level indicate their reactions to the suggestions and criticisms of their supervisors:

If I could dedicate this paper, I would do so to Mr. Blank. He was a wonderful supervising teacher, giving me constructive criticism and inspiring me to keep trying when the going got rough.

✿   ✿   ✿

My supervising teacher was especially good for me because she was best where I am weakest. She is a master at persuading the slow student to learn. My observation of her teaching in the classes I later taught and in other classes, coupled with her acute and most helpful critique of my teaching, pointed out techniques and attitudes that I lacked.

✿   ✿   ✿

My supervising teacher had a tremendous influence on me. . . . Our conferences many times brought me from "dark to light." His pleasing personality often brought me out of the shadows when I was discouraged, and his "That was a good job" kept me on the top because I felt I had accomplished something.

✿   ✿   ✿

My supervising teacher made it a point to discuss with me each lesson that I taught as soon as possible after it was taught, often during the next period if we had free time, and certainly no later than the end of the school day. In this way we could analyze what had happened during the lesson while the incidents were still fresh in our minds. Often in the course of the day, if I were teaching the same material to three classes, I could profit from his criticism of the first period and correct my mistakes in the second or third periods.

Elementary student teachers make similar statements regarding their supervising teachers:

Through Mrs. Smith I learned that two can work as a team and come out with better results. When you are a member of a team, you are more willing to help. Mrs. Smith put me at ease the first day I met her. I was made to feel as one of the faculty, and nobody tried to show off for my benefit. Mrs. Smith criticized me, but in such a way that I would try my best to correct it. She treated me as if my ideas were good, and she didn't expect me to accept all she said as fact. She was very frank in everything, and she is an excellent teacher in the true sense of the word.

◊   ◊   ◊

I was very fortunate to have Mrs. Jones as my supervising teacher, for she has been most understanding and helpful to me when I'm sure I have appeared quite ignorant. She gave me advice and showed me how to improve my teaching. By her excellent example she taught me many constructive methods in teaching elementary curriculum. She was always patient with me, as she is with her pupils, and [she] inspired me to make of myself the best teacher possible.

QUESTIONS AND PROBLEMS

1. Make a list of the experiences that you have had, during the period of your student teaching, which you feel have been most helpful to you in preparing for your first year as a regular teacher.
2. Make a list of the experiences which you feel might have been improved. What can you do during your first year as a regular teacher to compensate for experiences that you feel were inadequate in your student teaching?
3. Re-examine your log of student-teaching experiences with the idea of determining ways in which you might be able to improve if you had the opportunity to begin again with another group of students and another supervising teacher.
4. Solicit comments and criticisms from your supervising teacher and your college or university supervisor regarding your strengths and weaknesses as a prospective teacher.

5. Arrange for a conference with the principal of the school in which you did your student teaching to discuss your strengths and weaknesses as a teacher. (If the responsibility for student teaching is delegated to an official other than the principal, this person would be the logical one with whom to confer.)
6. Make a list of your strengths as a prospective teacher.
7. Make a list of your weaknesses as a prospective teacher. What may you do to improve yourself in regard to your weaknesses?
8. What indications are there that your students have been favorably inclined toward you and your work as a student teacher?
9. What indications are there that your students have an unfavorable attitude toward you as a prospective teacher? How might this attitude be overcome?
10. Make a list of favorable and unfavorable comments that have been made by your supervising teacher or by other persons who have had opportunities to observe your work as a student teacher. Arrange these comments in chronological order for the purpose of identifying possible indications of improvement during the period of your student teaching and possible ways in which you can further improve your teaching ability.
11. Compose a concise but complete report to your college or university supervisor of student teachers, giving your own evaluation of your student-teaching experience. Include in this report situations and experiences which you feel might have been improved and ways in which such improvement might be accomplished, as well as the better experiences you have had.

SELECTED REFERENCES

Association for Student Teaching, *The Evaluation of Student Teaching*, Twenty-eighth Yearbook. Lock Haven, Pa.: The Association, 1949. Chapter 8 contains student-teacher diaries which emphasize self-appraisal.

Byers, Loretta, and Elizabeth Irish, *Success in Student Teaching*. Boston: D. C. Heath and Company, 1961. Comprehensive Forms are provided in Chapter 12 for use by the student teacher in evaluating his work.

Lindsey, Margaret, and William T. Gruhn, *Student Teaching in the Elementary School.* New York: Ronald Press Company, 1957. Chapter 9 gives suggestions for self-evaluation.

McGuire, Vincent, Robert B. Myers, and Charles L. Durrance, *Your Student Teaching in the Secondary School.* Boston: Allyn and Bacon, Inc., 1959. Excellent checklists are provided for self-evaluation by the student teacher.

13. *Your First Year of Teaching*

Regardless of the quality of your student-teaching experience and the excellence of your supervising teacher, you will probably not be in your first full-time teaching position very long before you will encounter problems that you never anticipated. In fact, your first week with your own class or classes is quite likely to present a number of problems and situations that you never thought of experiencing. This is almost invariably true in any new situation, regardless of the type of work an individual is doing. However, it is probably more often noticeable in a position such as teaching, in which one is working with children or youth.

Your ability to cope with difficult situations that you have not previously experienced will be largely determined by your own personality characteristics and the facility with which you are able to adapt to new situations. However, experiences that you have had in your student teaching, which were similar to those that you will face as a regular teacher, should be helpful to you in solving new problems.

PROBABLE DIFFICULTIES

One of the most common difficulties with which student teachers and beginning teachers are faced is classroom management or discipline. Without proper order in the classroom, or in any situation in which the teacher is dealing with a group of students, it is impossible to have a really profitable teaching-learning situation. Your principal, vice-principal, supervisor, or other immediate superior will be able to give you some assistance in this matter, as well as in many other ways. However, it is largely up to you to work out your own plans and solve your own problems. Do not become discouraged if you seem to have more difficulties in classroom control than do other beginning teachers. It is probably true that they feel the same way about themselves. Even the experienced teacher will quite likely have some times when he feels that he is "losing" his class. The proper procedure in such a situation is to re-evaluate, as objectively as possible, your own actions and to try to determine whether you have made a mistake and, if so, how you can remedy it.

The following quotations from student teachers' reports typify the reactions of both student teachers and beginning teachers to the problems involved in classroom management or discipline:

Discipline was one of the primary things with which I was concerned in teaching. I have learned much concerning this, and I feel that to understand the student as an individual is a basis for successful discipline. A teacher's reputation also seems to mean very much in discipline in the high school. I have observed that Miss Blank has no discipline problems with students who are problems with other teachers. This, according to her, is true because of her reputation of demanding good discipline among the students.

✿   ✿   ✿

I had to learn one thing the hard way: that it is important to maintain firm discipline with a class from the start. Because I was unsure of myself when I began participating and teaching, I tended to be too lenient with my students. I paid for this later, when I tried to strengthen my discipline. The students had become accustomed to having such a good time in English class that they sometimes forgot they were there to learn. The situation never got really bad, mostly because my supervising teacher is a good disciplinarian; but I . . . now know . . . [that I must] meet my first real class on a more businesslike basis.

✿   ✿   ✿

Besides noting the various techniques used by Mrs. Smith to foster learning, I also made use of several of her methods of discipline. It is true that the junior-high-school group is a difficult one, because the individuals are neither children nor adults and must be treated as semi-adults. Because of their excess energy and loquaciousness, it is often difficult to keep them quiet, and thus a certain amount of discipline is necessary. Waiting a limited amount of time for them to be silent, marking "X's" (against conduct) in the record book, having specific individuals stay for detention, or keeping the entire class for detention were all methods that I learned to use at various times. I took into consideration the fact that the pupils knew I was learning a new profession, and thus they would try to give me a hard time. As time went on, the discipline problems became less and less difficult. I was learning how to handle them, and they were learning to respect my requests.

*　　*　　*

What I needed was not so much practice in planning and presenting material, but experience in classroom management and discipline. In my past experience (girl's college and Army Specialized Training Program) I had never encountered disciplinary problems. Now, for the first time, I met the indifferent students (both the passively and the actively indifferent), the capable and the incapable, the student of high ability who devoted his best efforts to troublemaking, and also, unfortunately, the dishonest students. I was encouraged to devise my own methods for dealing with all of these, and toward the end I felt that I was making some progress with a surer touch.

One technique which is helpful in preventing discipline problems is mentioned by a student teacher at the junior-high-school level, as follows:

I consider it easier to be in the classroom when the pupils arrive and prevent any possible disturbance, rather than to go into the classroom after the class has arrived and the pupils are "having a ball."

Your difficulty may be increased by the type of students with whom you are dealing. It may be that your student-teaching experience was obtained in a more-or-less ideal situation, with students of high quality who had been with an excellent teacher for some time, while your first teaching position may be in the opposite type of situation. The author's experience in the early part of his teaching career is an excellent example of such a change. After having taught for four years in small rural high schools, in which the students were largely well behaved, coming entirely from a rural and small-town environment, the author accepted a teaching position in a large city school system. To make matters worse, the school in which he was placed had the reputation of being one of the most difficult schools in the city in which to teach. The students were largely from broken homes, and those who were living with both parents came from the more underprivileged class socially and economically. Needless to say, the author had some difficulty in adjusting to this drastic change. This was true even though he had had four years of previous teaching experience. It would doubtless have been much more difficult if this had been his first year of teaching experience.

It is hoped that you will not be placed in a very difficult situation for your first years as a regular teacher. However, you cannot be certain that this will not be the case. In fact, it is often true that experienced teachers, who have been teaching in a given school system for a number of years, have the preference in the assignment of teaching positions. This is even true within a given school. The teachers who have been in the school and have proved their worth are given the better classes. It has been said that the beginning teacher is "at the bottom of the pecking order," as far as choice of classes is concerned. This is not to say that such an arrangement is best for the beginning teacher, but it is one of the "facts of life" which must often be met and solved if you are to be successful in the teaching profession.

There is also the possibility that you may encounter difficulties in your dealings with experienced teachers, especially if they get the idea that you have a superiority complex regarding your ability as a teacher. It is natural for experienced teachers to feel that they know more about teaching than a young teacher whose only experience has been in connection with student teaching. Some of your ideas regarding methods and classroom management may be excellent, but if you give your fellow teachers reason to conclude that you consider their methods to be old-fashioned or inferior to your own, you are likely to have difficulty with your colleagues. Of course, you should use the methods that are best for yourself. However, it is not well to talk about them or give your colleagues any reason to think that you consider your methods to be better than theirs.

Another difficulty that may be encountered at the secondary-school level is the fact that you may be asked to teach one or more courses in which your preparation may not be as adequate as you would like. This is another situation in which the "pecking order" usually applies. However, your principal or other immediate superior will be likely to consider your wishes and make a last-minute change of courses if such an arrangement is possible. If such a change is impossible, the only alternative is to do your best with the classes that have been assigned to you, unless you wish to resign your position or request a transfer to another school.

A difficulty that is quite common at the elementary-school level is the assignment to a different grade from the one for which you may be best prepared. If the difference is not too great, you will be able to adjust to such a change with little difficulty. If you did your student teaching in one of the primary grades, you should be able to teach in one of the other grades at the primary level. The same is true with the intermediate or upper grades.

One problem which is often faced by the beginning teacher— and, in fact, by the experienced teacher—is lack of desirable equipment. This is especially true in a small school system. Such a situation tests the ingenuity and creativeness of the teacher. Often a suggestion on the part of the teacher will encourage a capable student to make equipment for use in the classroom. Such a practice gives the student greater interest in class work as well as in helping the teacher. One student teacher makes the following statement regarding the problem of inadequate equipment:

Of course, a small system cannot afford the equipment of a large system, and one of the qualifications of a good teacher is the ability to make do with what one has.

The following statements of student teachers summarize their conclusions regarding the value of their preservice preparation in equipping them for their first teaching positions:

I am sure I would have been a very poor teacher without my theory, but I have come to realize that theory is only the beginning, and the teacher must go on from there using imagination, originality, and skill. . . .

I have learned that one's vocabulary must be suited to the knowledge of the child. I believe that a positive attitude is best when problems arise, including discipline problems. The special teacher (art, music, etc.) must gain the confidence and friendship of the regular teacher in order to be successful. The child must be approached according to his age level. . . .

I realize that there are many things yet to be learned and problems to be faced in the experience of actual independent teaching. However, student teaching has given the confidence and knowledge, . . . to tackle this consuming but worthwhile job of teaching.

❖   ❖   ❖

My future outlook in the teaching field has become more optimistic due to my experience at Smithville. I learned that the teacher should do his best and not be unduly upset about the results. This helps, I believe, to build a philosophy of teaching that will prevent the teacher from becoming negative and pessimistic in response to frustrating situations.

I am anxious to get "into the harness" of a sixth grade this fall to see for myself the results of the things I learned in student teaching.

❖   ❖   ❖

First by observation, then by actual teaching of the children, I have learned many things which I believe are most important for every prospective teacher to know: (1) that rapport between teacher and children is necessary for successful learning, (2) that detailed lesson plans are a must for effective teaching of any subject or learning activity, (3) that nondirective motivation makes the learning experiences of both teacher and student more meaningful, (4) that knowing each child as an individual—his background, cumulative records, etc.—is most important in bringing out the potentialities of all learning processes (in this instance, the studying and writing of case studies was of utmost importance in helping me to fully understand the above premise), and (5) that the teacher must be an enthusiastic, open-minded, well-integrated person, with an honest, healthy attitude toward the possibilities of our educational system in building future American citizens.

❖   ❖   ❖

I am certain that I learned much more than my students, but I trust I did not let them down in any way. To mention all of the things I learned, even if they could all be written, would be much too large a task. A few, however, were: be patient, prepared, understanding, reliable (both to students and administration), flexible, original, open-minded, alert, and above all, keep up to date and work.

ATTITUDE TOWARD SUPERIORS

Regardless of the difficulty that is encountered in your work as a beginning teacher, you should never fail to approach your immediate superior with a problem that you cannot adequately solve on your own. This is the place where some beginning teachers make a mistake that may cause their failure in the teaching profession. Your principal, vice-principal, or supervisor is just as interested in your success as you are. Therefore, if you go to one of these superiors with your problem, he will try to help you solve it. Of course, there is the possibility that if you go to your superiors too often with minor problems, they will get the impression that you are overdependent. Either over-confidence or overdependence may work to your disadvantage.

Your attitude toward your superiors should not be one of fear. It is true that such individuals may sometimes unintentionally give the beginning teacher reason to have such an attitude. However, if you are not oversensitive in this regard, you will usually find that your superiors are interested in your success and will do everything in their power to contribute to it. Otherwise they would not have been promoted to positions of greater responsibility.

When one of your superiors comes to your room to visit a class, do not become overanxious about making a good impression. If you do this, the chances are that you will not do as good a job or make as good an impression as you would if you were to go ahead with your work in the same way you do when there is not an observer in the room. This is a difficult thing to do, and it will undoubtedly be true that you will be tense and not do your best work the first time or two that you have a superior in your room. However, the superior will understand this and will probably try to make his visit as painless as possible by giving you encouragement for those things that you do well.

Always remember that the superior official is interested in your success, and anything that he does or says is done or said with this in mind. Do not be afraid to ask for suggestions and criticisms, and when your superior makes suggestions or criticizes your work, take it in the proper spirit and try to remedy the fault or correct the mistake. If you keep the attitude of a learner, you will not encounter the difficulties that you would if you should resent criticisms and suggestions.

WHAT ABOUT PROFESSIONAL ORGANIZATIONS?

Professional organizations of educators are intended to be helpful to the teacher or school official. They are organized by educators, and their programs are usually presented by educators. Since the number of professional organizations is so great, it will be necessary for you to choose the ones that you believe will be most interesting and helpful for you.

Local, state, and national education associations which include all professional educators will probably be the first ones that you should join. As a matter of fact, some school systems take it for granted that all teachers in the system will belong to these organizations, and dues will be deducted from your first paycheck. Such a clause may be included in your contract with the local board of education. In any case, your interest and activity in professional organizations will be beneficial to you as a teacher.

It is probably true that you have already had experience with the Future Teachers of America in high school and with the Student N.E.A. in college. If so, you will probably realize the value of such organizations.

In addition to the organizations previously mentioned, there are associations based on special interests. For example, the secondary-school teacher will probably have an organization composed of teachers of the same subject-matter area as his. The elementary teacher may be especially interested in the Association for Childhood Education International or the Association for

Supervision and Curriculum Development. This is the place where you must pick and choose the organizations that you wish to join and support. You cannot be expected to belong to all of them, and it is much better to choose a few in which you are particularly interested than to be a "professional joiner," who is impelled to become affiliated with every organization available and then probably does not participate in any of them to the extent that he should. You will receive from professional organizations the same amount that you contribute. Therefore, since your time will be limited, it will be better to belong to a few organizations and contribute as much as possible to their activities than to join too many organizations and contribute nothing to any of them.

In many school systems the Parent-Teacher Association is a very active and valuable organization and one in which the teacher must participate if he is to be successful. This is true to a greater degree at the elementary level than at the secondary level. However, there are some secondary schools which have extremely active parent-teacher organizations. Participation in the meetings of this group will give you splendid opportunities to meet the parents of your students and work with them for the improvement of the school.

YOU AND THE TEACHING PROFESSION

As you complete your student-teaching experience and, perhaps, your formal education (for the time being) and accept a regular teaching position, you are entering one of the great and important professions. The teacher holds a unique place as the molder of young lives in preparation for all of the other occupations and professions. The quality of education that the child and adolescent receives will determine to a great extent the quality of work which he will perform as an adult.

The question is sometimes asked, "Is teaching a profession?" The answer is that it is not as well organized as are some of the other professions, but it is going in the right direction to become a full-fledged profession. The efforts of the National Education

Association and the National Commission on Teacher Education and Professional Standards, as well as other professional organizations of educators, are doing much to contribute to the development of a teaching profession. This is one reason why the teacher should participate in these organizations, thus providing his support to the teaching profession as a whole.

The following expressions of student teachers, in anticipation of entering the teaching profession, illustrate the truly professional attitude:

Looking back over my weeks of student teaching I realize that a teacher of primary children must be a teacher, a mother, a nurse, and an encyclopedia of information! She should be familiar with her subject matter and have it prepared to present in an interesting manner. She should know her pupils and show an interest in their problems and joys, even seeing how loose a tooth is. Last of all, the teacher should realize that subject matter is important, but that the child's development in all aspects is just as important as reading from a book. My experience of "learning by doing" and practicing the methods I learned in my college courses was very profitable to me, and I know I shall often recall the memories of my student-teaching days.

                          ❖   ❖   ❖

More than anything else that I have [received] from student teaching is a sound professional background. I have gained an appreciation and knowledge of children. I have been made to realize that my training and learning is not to end merely because I have finished student teaching. I realize that a teacher grows continually. I must read to keep abreast with the newest teaching methods and techniques and must work constantly to improve my teaching.

                          ❖   ❖   ❖

Student teaching has been an interesting experience, and I am sure that I have learned a great deal more than my students. I only hope they have learned a fourth of what I have learned.

                          ❖   ❖   ❖

All in all, I think I learned a lot this quarter. Not only have I learned to be a better teacher, but I also have learned to be a better person. I have learned to appreciate people more and to work better with them.

I have learned to be more self-confident. Now I am sure I want to be a teacher.

✿   ✿   ✿

Now I have a good idea of how the educational system in Blankville works and how my job as an elementary-school art teacher will fit into the program. I have seen professional people at work, and I have seen that it takes continuous research, professional educational training, and self-evaluation. In January, when I call myself a professional teacher, my work will have just begun!

✿   ✿   ✿

After this tantalizing experience of student teaching, I am looking forward to teaching on a credential in the fall. This experience has proved to me that the profession offers a challenging career and one that warrants one's best efforts.

✿   ✿   ✿

I believe that my student teaching has been very profitable for me under the supervision of Miss Smith. She has greatly increased my knowledge and enthusiasm for the teaching profession.

WHAT BEGINNING TEACHERS SAY

In response to a questionnaire regarding the effectiveness of the student-teaching experience, as viewed by first- and second-year teachers, the following statements and recommendations were given:

1. The phases of the student-teaching experience which had proved to be most helpful to the respondents as beginning teachers were:
   a. the time spent in actually taking over the classwork, especially the time when the student teacher was required to teach for the entire day—all groups;
   b. the organization and planning of daily schedules; and
   c. the development of unit and lesson plans under the supervision of an experienced teacher.
2. The phases of the student-teaching experience which, in certain situations, were considered to have been inadequate were:

a. lack of opportunity to have student-teaching experience at more than one grade level (elementary);
b. lack of practical help in preparing daily and weekly plans, hints regarding methods, tips on flexibility of program and timing;
c. too much time spent in correcting papers, running off stencils, and other busy work, thus not providing enough time for thoughtful observation of the supervising teacher's work;
d. lack of opportunity to have student teaching in the type of school in which a teaching position was obtained; and
e. insufficient time spent in student teaching.

The following "recipe for successful teaching," which was submitted by a student teacher in senior-high-school English, is a concise statement of characteristics which should be valuable to the beginning teacher:

Add one cup of firmness, with politeness stirred in;
A dash of satire;
Heaping tablespoons of humor (any amount needed); and
Gallons of cheer (not the detergent!).
Stir and mix well, with
A peck or two of knowledge, horse sense, and luck.
Bake—in the classroom daily.
Serve—as a philosophy of life.

SELECTED REFERENCES

Brembeck, Cole S., *The Discovery of Teaching*. Englewood Cliffs, New Jersey: Prentice-Hall, Inc., 1962. Chapter 18 discusses the personal and professional phases of teaching.

Grambs, Jean D., William J. Iverson, and Franklin K. Patterson, *Modern Methods in Secondary Education*. New York: The Dryden Press, 1958. Chapters 22 and 23 give excellent suggestions for beginning teachers.

Holman, Mary V., *How It Feels to be A Teacher*. New York: Bureau of Publications, Teachers College, Columbia University, 1950. A pamphlet which furnishes insight into the feeling tones of teaching.

Jersild, Arthur T., *When Teachers Face Themselves*. New York: Bureau of Publications, Teachers College, Columbia University, 1955. A book especially recommended for new teachers.

Kyte, George C., *The Elementary School Teacher at Work*. New York: The Dryden Press, Inc., 1957. Excellent suggestions for the beginning teacher.

Logan, Lillian M., and Virgil G. Logan, *Teaching the Elementary School Child*. Boston: Houghton Mifflin Company, 1961. A good look at the professional responsibilities of the teacher is given in Chapter 16.

Mehl, Marie A., Hubert H. Mills, and Harl R. Douglass, *Teaching in the Elementary School*. New York: The Ronald Press Company, 1950. Chapter 23, on in-service education of teachers, emphasizes the importance of community and professional relationships.

Yauch, Wilbur, et al., *The Beginning Teacher*. New York: Henry Holt and Company, 1955. An excellent book for all beginning teachers.

APPENDICES

A. Student-Teaching Activities: Classification

The following is a fairly comprehensive list of activities for student teaching. Student teachers will not be expected to practice all of these activities, but they should have as wide a variety as possible. Some apply to the secondary school only, while others apply only to the elementary school. This information is designed to give supervising teachers and student teachers some specific idea regarding the activities which may be classified as observation, participation, and actual teaching.

I. Observation

1. Observing regular class activities
   a. Taking notes for later discussion with supervising teacher
   b. Observing methods, materials, and techniques of teaching
   c. Determining or evaluating the effectiveness of teaching
2. Observing classes other than the ones specifically assigned
3. Observing individual pupils
   a. Noting individual differences
   b. Making profile charts of application and distraction
4. Attending school programs
   a. Assemblies
   b. Parent-Teacher meetings
   c. Faculty meetings
   d. Athletic events
   e. Musical programs, etc.
   f. Professional meetings
      (1) City or local

(2) County
(3) State

II. Participation

1. Making case studies of individual pupils
   a. Keeping anecdotal records
2. Clerical work
   a. Grading papers and recording marks
   b. Checking attendance
   c. Assisting in making period reports
   d. Multigraphing materials of instruction
3. Making a class seating chart, and studying the seating arrangement
4. Caring for the physical conditions of the room
   a. Heating
   b. Lighting
   c. Ventilation
5. Supervising seat work (may be actual teaching)
6. Supervising study hall (may be actual teaching)
7. Preparing and arranging bulletin board displays, room decorations, and display cases or other exhibits
8. Constructing tests or other evaluation devices
9. Presenting a reading, story, descriptive account, or other contribution to class work
10. Outlining a learning unit or other plan for use in teaching
11. Working with student committees in planning extracurricular activities
12. Assisting with home-room activities (may be actual teaching)
13. Assisting with school publications (may be actual teaching)
14. Assisting with pep rallies
15. Refereeing or umpiring athletic events
16. Assisting with ticket sales and collections
17. Participating in school programs
18. Assisting with school projects

19. Assisting with civic activities in the community
    a. Scouts
    b. Recreational activities
    c. Sunday School, church, etc.
20. Counseling students (may be actual teaching)
21. Setting up and putting away supplies and equipment
22. Making and keeping progress charts
23. Assisting with library work
    a. School library
    b. Room library
24. Alphabetizing and filing materials
25. Evaluating textbooks and reference books
26. Conferences with supervisors

III. Actual Teaching

1. Actual instruction
    a. Individual instruction
       (1) Tutoring pupils who have been absent
       (2) Remedial teaching with slow learners or retarded children
    b. Group instruction
       (1) Using instructional daily lesson plans
2. Planning and presenting demonstrations in the various tool subjects over a period of time
    a. Reading
    b. Spelling and writing
    c. Language
    d. Arithmetic
    e. Social studies
    f. Science and health
3. Presenting one phase of regular classwork
4. Assisting pupils with supplementary projects
5. Planning and teaching a unit or block of class work
    a. Taking children on field trips and excursions
    b. Giving programs or parties, and inviting parents
    c. Arranging an exhibit based on unit, and inviting parents

B. Record of Student-Teaching Experiences

A JOURNAL

of My Student-Teaching Experiences

by
JOHN Q. DAVIDSON

in cooperation with
Mrs. Elinor Jones
Bruce Junior High School
Bethesda, Maryland

for
DR. CHARLES A. DIRECTOR

in
21.445—*Student Teaching: Secondary Schools* (9)
Elmwood University,
Hometown, Virginia
Fall, 1959

RECORD OF STUDENT-TEACHING HOURS

Date		Obser-vation	Partici-pation	Teaching	Total	Number of Conferences
Sep.	1	2	1		3	1
	2	2	1		3	1
	3	2	1		3	1
	4	2	4	1	7	2
	8	2	5		7	2
	9		7		7	2
	10		7		7	2
	11		7		7	1
	14		6	1	7	1
	15		6	1	7	2
	16		5	2	7	2
	17	1	4	2	7	2
	18	1	4	2	7	2
	21	1	4	2	7	1
	22	1	3	3	7	
	23	1	4	2	7	1
	24	2	3	2	7	2
	25	3	3	1	7	1
	28	2	3	2	7	1
	29	1	4	2	7	
	30	1	3	3	7	
Oct.	1		4	3	7	
	2		4	3	7	1
	5		4	3	7	1
	6	1	3	3	7	1
	7		3	4	7	1
	8		3	4	7	1
	9		6	1	7	1
	12		5	2	7	
	13		4	3	7	1
	14		3	4	7	1
	15		3	4	7	2
	16		4	4	8	2
	19		4	4	8	1
	20		4	4	8	1
	21		4	4	8	1
	22		4	4	8	1
	23		4	4	8	
	26		4	4	8	2
	27		4	4	8	3
	28		4	4	8	2
	29		4	4	8	
	30		8		8	
Days: 43		25	175	100	300	50 (*Totals*)

Tuesday, September 1

> Before School—met Mrs. Jones, talked
> Home-Room Period—observed first class
> After School—private conference

Observation Notes on Home-Room Group

The students reluctantly and confusedly pile into the room
to find a favorite seat, flinging chairs about as they slowly settle
themselves. Some humorously mock the greeting on the wall—
"Welcome Back"—with a musical twang. There is much whispering, giggling, and hurried conversation with buddies. The children answer questions in an unconcerned manner, sometimes
rather vague and indirect. Some slouch in their seats; most of the
boys sit on their spines. The general appearance is one of emotional confusion. Few dress sloppily, perhaps because it's the
first day; I don't see any dungarees, at any rate.

If this group is alert, it is because it is eager to stir up trouble.
The boys are huddled together over there by the door in a unified
expectation of the first opportunity to revolt. The girls giggle and
whisper a lot, but they remain complacently lost most of the
time. The boys' ringleaders seem to be John Small, Brad Carp, and
Don Jackson.

The children "test" the teacher with contradictions, wise-
cracks, and frequent outbursts of disorder. A continual murmur
pervades the atmosphere, but Mrs. Jones squelches this appro-
priately and abruptly shows the class that it is here to work. They
reluctantly resign themselves to the fact that further testing is
a waste of time and that they are doomed to a dull life of classroom English for another long year.

The seating arrangement, which is by personal choice, reveals
a disturbing group of male agitators by the door, but this may
have good leadership outcomes eventually. On the other hand,
the quiet ones on the opposite side of the room suffer from lack
of attention.

Routine matters are handled effectively after much direction
by the teacher; the signing and passing of cards was aided by the
selection of two people who collected them at the front—obvi-

ously not troublemakers. As soon as the routines were finished, the children saw another opportunity for disorder, but the rapid pacing caught them off guard. The matter of changing schedules caused some confusion, but the teacher offered a concrete solution to the problem.

Although the first day was set aside for "unnecessary" administrative matters, Mrs. Jones began an English lesson immediately to fill in the gap of time and to let the children know that they would have to get down to business. The purpose of the lesson was to establish motivation for learning and goals for future achievement. Questioning and imaginative ideas or "gimmicks" were two techniques used to hold interest. The children learned incidentally from their own questions and ideas. Don Jackson aroused group interest with his questions about the importance of formal English in getting a job. If there were any improvisation by the teacher, it was unnoticeable because of the rapid pace which she set for class activity.

At the end of today's lesson, I felt that most of the children were troublemakers. After reading their papers, however, I found that the majority of them are serious about the work. Their ideas about goals reflected this, at any rate. It seems to me that there are some worth saving, and that the few male agitators might successfully spoil it for the honest souls if they receive too much importance in the group. The insignificant, quiet ones need just as much attention and more encouragement than the more obvious, outspoken individuals.

Wednesday, September 2

> Home Room—opening exercises, roll
> 1st Period—filled out locator cards
> 2nd Period—conference
> 3rd Period—observed second class

Observation Notes on Third-Period Group

Today's third-period class is the antithesis of yesterday's first-period class. These students are reserved, relaxed, and quiet. The degree of attention is remarkable. Even the seating arrangement is neater, because they prefer to sit in orderly rows. I think I shall like working with these children very much.

The lesson began directly with a review of grammar and language mechanics, reading, and creative writing. It ended with an assignment for tomorrow and a future project in relation to the "course requirements."

Notes on Second-Period Conference

Mrs. Jones pointed out that it is a good idea that each class period be divided into three periods of about twenty minutes each; this will add variety and relieve boredom if each period is devoted to a different activity.

We spoke briefly on the possibility of starting a literary magazine with the third-period class.

Some questions to consider: Who are the leaders in the third-period class? the academically minded? (should be encouraged) seekers of recognition? (eliminate) the socially minded? (minimize).

Thursday, September 3

> Home Room—opening exercises, roll
> 1st Period—revised seating arrangement
> 2nd Period—conference with Mrs. Jones
> 3rd Period—worked on locator cards
> After School—conference with Dr. Director

Notes on First-Period Activities

Worked on locator cards; reseated children according to a new seating chart. Returned and commented on their compositions; took four boys to the library to choose books for a report, and specified the form for them. Observation: concept formation; leading toward the concept, "there are many dialects of English. English varies greatly in its form according to occupational group, regional group, and purpose of the user."

Friday, September 4

Home Room—opening exercises, roll
1st Period—observed grammar lesson
2nd Period—conference with Dr. Director
3rd Period—presented Churchill's speeches
4th Period—observed Miss Smith
5th Period—private planning period
6th Period—conference with Mrs. Jones

Notes on Daily Activities

During the second period, Dr. Director, Dr. Blank, Mrs. Jones, and I had a summit in regard to longer student-teaching hours.

I read Winston Churchill's war speeches to the third-period and fourth-period classes, with Beethoven blaring in the background. I was unprepared and ridiculously sloppy about the whole thing, but the kids seemed to like it.

At the end of the first week, I feel very much like an office boy. Of course, I realize the necessity of administrative details, but it leaves me very little time for observation. I am looking forward to the time when this will be behind me and I will actually get into the swing of teaching.

Tuesday, September 8

Home Room—opening exercises, roll
1st Period—locator cards finished
2nd Period—conference
3rd Period—observed spelling test
4th Period—observed grammar lesson
5th Period—planning
6th Period—conference

Notes on Daily Activities

Finished the locator cards, only to find that they were incomplete and could not be turned in until all the information had been obtained from the pupils. The public-law cards and clinic cards were inadequate in many cases. Mrs. Jones asked me to watch the spelling lesson during the third period, but I was so preoccupied with clerical work that I absorbed very little of what was going on around me. She insists that I am "out of it" because I have trouble thinking of more than one thing at a time. I don't think that is the case, however; it isn't that I can't think of more than one thing at once, but that I always have to direct 100% of my capacities toward adjusting to any strange or new situation. Right now I definitely feel strange and new in relation to my environment! In the afternoon I went through the confidential files in the guidance office. Besides obtaining test scores on section 9–1, I did some very interesting reading.

Wednesday, September 9

> Home Room—opening exercises, roll
> 1st Period—new bulletin-board display
> 2nd Period—planning
> 3rd Period—worked on bulletin board
> 4th Period—planning
> 5th Period—conference with Dr. Director
> 6th Period—conference with Dr. Director

Notes on Daily Activities

I finished the locator cards for good today and turned them into the office. The rest of the time was spent preparing a new bulletin board on the "teenage book club" (first period). I went to see Dr. Director about the pace of my activities: I feel that Mrs. Jones is pushing me faster than I can run on my own feet, but perhaps I will catch up soon. I have many new responsibilities this week.

Thursday, September 10

> Home Room—opening exercises, roll
> 1st Period—Morrison-McCall Spelling Scale
> 2nd Period—conference

3rd Period—introduced new bulletin board
4th Period—Morrison-McCall Spelling Scale
5th Period—gathered psychological test data
6th Period—conference

Friday, September 11

Home Room—opening exercises, roll
1st Period—assisted with lesson
2nd Period—conference
3rd Period—gathered test data
4th Period—assisted with lesson
5th Period—assisted Mrs. Matthews
6th Period—assisted Mrs. Matthews
After School—faculty meeting

Monday, September 14

Home Room—opening exercises, roll
1st Period—supervised reading period
2nd Period—planning
3rd Period—returned spelling papers
4th Period—gathered test data
5th Period—planning
6th Period—conference

Student-Teaching Activities—First Report Period

1. Observed students on first day of school.
2. Aided with ventilation.
3. Rearranged and improved physical arrangement of seats.
4. Made seating chart and conducted reseating of pupils.
5. Conducted opening exercises.
6. Assumed responsibility for taking roll in home room
7. Took small group of children to the library.
8. Prepared and completed bulletin-board display.
9. Assumed responsibility for completing locator cards; followed through completely without help.

10. Assumed responsibility for taking roll in home room.
11. Gathered test data for one group from guidance files.
12. Grouped students for reading.
13. Checked with reading teacher for teaching materials.
14. Assisted reading teacher with inventory of materials.
15. Presented Churchill's speeches to two classes.
16. Corrected initial sets of papers; recorded grades.
17. Taught lesson on sentence structure to two groups.
18. Gave and scored Morrison-McCall Spelling Scale.
19. Supervised spelling lessons and reading periods.
20. Attended faculty meeting.
21. Followed up on absent students—gave test to them.
22. Introduced a second bulletin-board display.

Comments by Supervising Teacher—First Report Period

"John shows lots of initiative and enthusiasm. He does excellent work in correcting papers and makes excellent comments. He adopts suggestions quickly and shows visible progress.

"John's feeling of disorganization (too much all at once) results in a dispersion of energy. He needs more systematic work habits. He needs to be in firmer control at transition periods. He needs to remain in active supervision during study time."

Tuesday, September 15

> Home Room—opening exercises, roll
> 1st Period—test on grammar
> 2nd Period—conference
> 3rd Period—returned graded papers
> 4th Period—planning
> 5th Period—planning
> 6th Period—conference

Wednesday, September 16

> Home Room—opening exercises, roll
> 1st Period—grammar lesson

2nd Period—conference
3rd Period—initiated new unit on American Literature
4th Period—typed spelling stencil
5th Period—learned to use ditto machine
6th Period—conference

Notes on First-Period Grammar Lesson

After opening exercises and the roll check, I explained the spelling scale used in scoring the Morrison-McCall test, filed the tests, and administered a new check test on adjectives and adverbs. Mrs. Jones criticized that my "voice was weak," that I "should have omitted the statement about commas," and that I "should have used a challenge approach." She had to interrupt me several times to bring the class back to order.

Mrs. Jones' Criticism of Third-Period Unit Introduction

"Your initial questions did not lead to discussion; therefore you had to answer them yourself. Could you have had a more stimulating question? 'What is literature?' leaves them no thoughts to express. The concepts are not thoroughly developed. You have excellent material in your introduction. The only problem is to be *sure* that the concepts get across: do not remain too abstract. This is beautifully prepared—my congratulations on your work. The vocabulary on Paine is too difficult for them. It would be better to have them read as you read aloud, interpreting as you go. When you ask for 'emotion,' you have not first checked to see that they get all the *meaning*. It is a good idea to ask for a listing of his *ideas* in material this difficult. So far, you have not tied it in to Churchill's speeches. When you get *one* answer, ask students if they agree. Are there other ideas? Don't supply the answers *yourself* once you have asked a question. Look up the pronunciation of 'formidable.' You are walking up and down a lot! Do I do that? I have a feeling I do—and it is distracting. Good development of dates, comparison to first battle; helps make it vivid. Metaphor is a complex idea. It needs *far* more development. You are doing too much talking. Look at your boys. Are they bored? Too *many* ideas—nationalism, for example. Exactly *what* concepts did you want to develop? Cutting out the distracting ones will help. Here comes Churchill! Excellent background on Paine. The whole period is devoted to the same *kind* of activity—some reading, mostly listening. The children are getting restless. We should plan a definite change of *type* of activity every twenty to thirty minutes. Why don't you construct a test covering the ideas you *thought* you got across and give it to them tomorrow to see how much you really *did* succeed in teaching? You may want to do some reteaching, and it will help them learn to listen. They would have listened better had the questions been on the board first. You ran out of time. Your questions are excellent. The last one would have been enough; they should have had twenty minutes to work on it."

Self-Criticism of Third-Period Unit Introduction

Assets: enthusiasm for literature, preparation, ability to comment spontaneously, directed questioning, dramatic reading, chronological sequence of material.

Weaknesses: failure to challenge, too much lecturing, too much material and not enough time, failure to give assignment, elevated language, no motivation provided, failure to respond to pupils.

Thursday, September 17

> Home Room—opening exercises, roll
> 1st Period—observed grammar lesson
> 2nd Period—planning
> 3rd Period—Amerindian poetry lesson
> 4th Period—Amerindian poetry lesson
> 5th Period—planning
> 6th Period—conference
> After School—faculty meeting: SCAT & STEP

Self-Criticism of Third-Period Poetry Lesson

Assets: firm control of class, imagination in planning lesson, extended explanation of metaphors.

Weaknesses: failure to let students participate, failure to give assignment, failure to respond to students.

Mrs. Jones' Criticism of Third-Period Poetry Lesson

"Mr. Davidson had the responsibility for beginning the class. I was not in the room. When I came in, he was in firm control and seemed quite assured. Students who were supposed to be working on a bulletin board in the hall were doing so. Students were quietly answering a written assignment. The lesson is imaginatively planned. The visual material on American Indian poetry is excellent. When papers have been collected, you completely bypass the opportunity to have students pick out the ideas. *Now is* the time—their interest is high—but you gave them no opportunity to state *either* the ideals of the Preamble or the ideals of Paine. You will find from their papers that they are extremely vague. Their thinking needs firming up, and you have to lead them to it. Can you use the seating chart to call students by name? The point about 'information' did not need belaboring. Only develop the things they do *not* know. Don't develop things they already know. How will you know? By their responses, or *lack* of it! With the term 'universal,' stress the fact that there are other meanings. Insist upon their listening to each other and upon their speaking loudly enough to be heard. There are too many private conversations going on. Your handling of the discussion of metaphors and similes was *excellent*—getting them to explain, and referring back to Emerson. Excellent! On Paine, you are *commenting* to their questions. Reflect it back to the class—'What do *you* think?' Defend yourself! Anyone disagree? What did you direct Stein and Roy to do? They are behaving as if nothing you are talking about is related to them. Individually explain to them what *has* been done and what *they* are to get out of it. On the dialect, translate as you go, line by line! Watch your time!! They are fascinated by the symbols and the lines. Have them draw comparisons with the Bible story—*specific* comparisons. Tomorrow you might even put the symbols up again to show the comparisons."

Friday, September 18

       Home Room—opening exercises, roll
       1st Period—taught grammar lesson
       2nd Period—conference
       3rd Period—lesson on literature, tastes
       4th Period—observed grammar lesson
       5th Period—planning
       6th Period—conference

Self-Criticism of Third-Period Lesson

Assets: used challenge approach, good classroom management, well-prepared lesson.

Weaknesses: questions too advanced, failure to keep interest, assignment too difficult.

Mrs. Jones' Criticism of Third-Period Lesson

"Excellent management of class at beginning of period in teacher's absence. Challenging approach to routine. Follow-through on yesterday's work on metaphor is excellent. Your question on 'good literature' was good, but the discussion was more of a murmur. There was no need for them to listen to each other because you repeated their comments. They didn't need to speak up because your voice supplied the volume. I think your material is a little advanced. This really belongs in the eleventh grade. Introducing some for stimulation is fine, but these children need to discuss characters in stories and relate them to their own lives. They are too young and their reading skills are not adequate for the authors you list. An assignment more on their level might be: 'Write an explanation of what makes literature *good*. What appeals to you? What makes writing good for you? Discuss your favorite authors and explain *why* they are good. Are they also universal? What makes literature good.'"

Monday, September 21

> Home Room—opening exercises, roll
> 1st Period—STEP (reading test)
> 2nd Period—STEP (reading & writing)
> 3rd Period—STEP (writing test)
> 4th Period—took kids outside for exercise
> 5th Period—observed Mr. Hulec
> 6th Period—conference
> After School—art film

Tuesday, September 22

> Home Room—opening exercises, roll
> 1st Period—STEP (listening)
> 2nd Period—STEP (listening & math)
> 3rd Period—STEP (mathematics)
> 4th Period—planning
> 5th Period—planning
> 6th Period—observed Mr. Hulec

Wednesday, September 23

> Home Room—opening exercises, roll
> 1st Period—STEP (science test)
> 2nd Period—STEP (science & social studies)
> 3rd Period—STEP (social-studies test)
> 4th Period—conference with Mr. Person
> 5th Period—observed Mr. Hulec
> 6th Period—conference
> After School—faculty meeting

Notes on Testing Activities

Mrs. Jones left a note which said that she wouldn't be in until later in the morning and that I was to handle everything. From the beginning of home room through the end of the first test, the kids "baited" me to see what they could get away with. I was terrified and near the breaking point when—*Deus ex Machina!*—Mrs. Jones came to the rescue. I spent the rest of the day visiting other teachers to see how they took care of discipline. Mr. Person was helpful and Miss Smith was sympathetic. Most were reluctant to give any specific advice; I was determined to find my own solutions.

Thursday, September 24

> Home Room—opening exercises
> 1st Period—taught grammar lesson
> 2nd Period—conference
> 3rd Period—taught lesson on "good literature"
> 4th Period—observed Mr. Adams
> 5th Period—conference
> 6th Period—observed Mr. Boyd
> 7th Period—pep rally

Mr. Adams' Discipline Techniques (Fourth Period)

1. Has a unique sense of humor.
2. Uses imaginative ideas.
3. Talks loudly at all times.
4. Stares firmly into the eyes of his students.
5. Pulls key ideas from his class by pausing in the middle of a statement to let them fill in the blank—a very effective and simultaneous response.
6. Waits silently and stares impatiently while the class settles down.
7. Thinks and moves through the material swiftly.
8. Everything is clear, precise, vivid, and entertaining.
9. Performs dramatic and humorous tricks to capture their attention momentarily.
10. Compliments kids on their learning.
11. Is a very fast thinker on his feet.
12. Asks Bill if he understands an abstract idea.

13. "Let's not talk out," he says in a quiet tone with an intent look—the contrast here of something softly spoken is very effective.

14. "You know what's happening?" he says in the middle of a private conversation, with his eyes still on the person with whom he was originally talking and slowly shifting his eyes without moving his head, "There's a lot of conversation going on up front that's going to stop MUY PRONTO! SIT UP! TURN AROUND!" The kids respond like a squad of cadets.

15. To cure the restlessness at the end of the period, he orders: "STAND UP! SIT DOWN! SHHHHHHH!"—repeats this several times, while they respond in a military fashion, until all movements cease.

16. "Where's your excuse? Do you have one? You're going to be really sick if you don't bring it in!" says Mr. Adams in a deadly serious mood.

17. Holds class absolutely still after the bell rings until he is ready to dismiss them.

18. Mr. Adams' control of his class is maintained through the class' intense respect for his military tactics and a fear for his grave temperament. Of course, the kids also enjoy a suppressed chuckle over his delightfully comic antics now and then; it is apparent that he likes to show off before them, but he seems to know how to do it at just the right time and for a good reason. His sense of humor is a technique for holding attention, providing vivid exemplification of abstract ideas, and for giving his students a peek at his more pleasant side. It serves as a balance to the fear he often arouses.

Notes on Daily Activities

During first period, I observed Mrs. Jones conducting student-council elections, and distributed and collected the seating-preference questionnaires for my sociometric study. Second period: Talked with Mrs. Jones and Miss Smith on techniques of classroom management; no definite conclusions, but I expressed my desire to follow the 9–1's around to their classes and observe them for one full day (maybe Monday). Third period: Gave new directions for homework, and assisted individuals in expressing their ideas on the question, "What do you consider good literature?" Listened to some readings of their essays. Mrs. Jones was pleased. Gave assignment: "Read Poe's *Tell-Tale Heart*." I observed Mr. Adams' fourth-period class; very entertaining! They are similar to the 9–1's. I dropped by room 134 to see Mr. Boyd during sixth period; the 9–1's were making "pompons" for the pep rally: it was interesting to see them working for a change, and it gave me an opportunity to talk and get acquainted with them. I make miserable pompons! We had a pep rally during the seventh period; I spent the hour sitting and joking with Joe Hart and Dave Crouse —both good boys, but they were obviously interested in bringing me down to their level of behavior. I decided that such a relationship could be dangerous unless I checked it quickly.

Mrs. Jones' Suggestions from Second-Period Conference

1. Cultivate friendship (before home room and at lunch).
2. Give directions in class firmly and immediately.
3. Give directions about *every little move*.

Friday, September 25

> Home Room—opening exercises, roll
> 1st Period—observed Mrs. Jones
> 2nd Period—observed Miss Smith
> 3rd Period—taught literature lesson
> 4th Period—planning
> 5th Period—observed Mr. Adams
> 6th Period—conference
> After School—attended student-teachers' meeting

Mrs. Jones' Criticism of Third-Period Lesson

"Excellent control of group. Excellent pacing of returning papers. Excellent explanation of grading scale and errors. Use of challenge approach to questions is excellent—but you still occasionally answer, yourself. Your command of the situation is impressive. Good reteaching on metaphors and similes. You need to have other examples besides the snake—perhaps have a drill changing different metaphors into similes by using 'like' or 'as.' George has *got* it, but the others don't have the insight. Good response to 'But she didn't say to write them down.' You should have said, 'Didn't you list them down for your own information?' As a routine, have the papers passed to your filing secretary. Teach her to keep a check on missing papers and hound students for them. Your discussion on *Tell-Tale Heart* metaphors is disintegrating. A good technique might be to make a board list with the group, listing in columns metaphors and similes; and giving pages would focus the group on one point. There *is* a sharp line on the similes. Look up the pronunciation of *vehemently*. I'm leaving: excellent control (11:22); return: relaxed appearance (11:35). Good interpretation of *Legend of Sleepy Hollow:* excellent explanation of meaning. Students' reaction is good, except boys are getting restless. Now your question, 'You remember what happened at the end?'—excellent timing. Your position is awkward—back to some students. How about taking a chair at the head of the circle? Your back is to four boys and three girls. Good question: 'How does this story compare with Poe's ending?' But you didn't let the discussion develop. You took one response and went on. They should have developed similarities and differences in the two endings. Period ending disconcertingly confused. Better planning will avoid that."

Mr. Adams' Observation Questionnaire (Fifth Period)

1. Indicate and discuss five methods of control employed by either the students or the teacher.
2. What difficulty did Richard Bays have in presenting his part of the report, and what can the teacher do to help him overcome this?
3. Discuss the audio-visual aids employed.
4. What are your comments concerning the bedlam that existed between the beginning of class and the actual committee reports?

5. What professional mistake did the teacher make, and how did the teacher overcome it?

6. What skills, attitudes, understandings, and information were communicated to the students?

Observation Notes on Mr. Adams' Fifth-Period Group

1. Five methods of control:
   a. Predetermined committee routine.
   b. Responsibility of pupils to take notes during committee reports.
   c. Responsibility of individuals who were giving committee reports.
   d. Teacher's evaluation of reports.
   e. Teacher's evaluation of pupils' ability to profit from notes.

2. Richard Bays has an obvious speech defect and is self-conscious about it. It would be beneficial for him to obtain as much practice as possible in speaking informally before a group. If he can learn to relax in such a classroom situation, he will certainly build more self-confidence.

3. The most noticeable audio-visual item was the solar machine—that gimmick with the sun, earth, and moon orbiting by means of belt-driven devices—which was borrowed from the science department. This was excellent. The display of the earth's progression through time, on the rear bulletin board, was also vivid. Photographs, in science texts, of the planets were large and colorful. Individual drawings of the Milky Way were too small and too difficult to read from a distance of ten feet.

4. The confusion of moving desks and chairs around was necessary to the situation and quite permissible, because the students came back to order easily when they were finished. The disturbance was not prolonged beyond the necessary minute that it required to arrange the desks in a semicircle.

5. The teacher made a serious professional mistake in reprimanding the boy who failed to comment on each of the planets, their relation to the sun, etc. It was obvious that this was an extremely difficult demand—even for an adult—and that the

boy was extremely uneasy about the pressure being exerted upon him by the teacher. The teacher realized his mistake and immediately tried to reassure the boy by admitting that it was too difficult a task. He was perspiring noticeably, but seemed determined not to let himself fall into such a trap again.

6. The students were skilled in gathering and presenting research materials; their attitudes were those of wholesome curiosity, intellectual honesty, and scientific accuracy. Their understanding of how the universe functions is remarkable.

Student-Teaching Activities—Second Report Period

1. Observed and participated in first-period grammar lessons.
2. Began new unit on American literature in third period.
3. Administered national standardized tests (SCAT & STEP).
4. Studied problems of discipline with other teachers.
5. Learned to operate the ditto machine.
6. Learned the challenge approach to questioning in class.
7. Improved the timing of transitional periods in study.
8. Established firm control of the third-period group.
9. Attended a second faculty meeting.
10. Made a special effort to become better acquainted with my home-room group during lunch.
11. Observed Mr. Adams' "fast" group, and answered a specially prepared questionnaire.
12. Attended a student-teachers' meeting at the university.

Comments by Supervising Teacher—Second Report Period

"Mr. Davidson has grown immensely in his ability to control a group. He is beginning to identify specific teaching techniques. Once he has identified a method, he is very quick in his ability to use it. He has brought some interesting and stimulating material to the third-period class. He is sincere and dedicated to his job.

"Mr. Davidson needs to be more careful about being on *time*. He needs to be thoroughly prepared daily. His approach to material is more suited to an eleventh- or twelfth-grade class than a ninth-grade group."

Monday, September 28

>Home Room—opening exercises, roll
>1st Period—observed grammar lesson
>2nd Period—planning
>3rd Period—Edgar Allan Poe readings
>4th Period—spelling test
>5th Period—observed Mr. Hulec
>6th Period—conference

Mrs. Jones' Criticism of Third-Period Lesson

"Nice control when I entered. Good, clear directions. I question the value of your assignment for bright youngsters. *Writing* answers to the questions is a waste of time unless you are planning to teach something specific about the nature of writing good answers to questions. It is far better to use them as a springboard to discussion. Why have them write an essay on Twain? Except for the critical appraisal, the information is all written on page 233. The assignment does not challenge them to research, but simply insists that they paraphrase. Is paraphrasing what you want to teach? Why not make it an assignment for the week to read at least one other work by Twain and write a critical appraisal *based on more than one work.* Most of what you are aiming for here could be handled better by intelligent discussion and perhaps a check test on listening. Another approach, after 'satire' had been discussed, might be to choose four good students to take four American humorists and present readings and a panel discussion. You are getting some wasted effort in here. See page 69 of *The Supervising Teacher* for a checklist to use to evaluate your assignments. Congratulations for having reached the point where you can evaluate *assignments* rather than *control* methods! Plan to do some follow-through on the spelling and private spelling list we started. Have you read the Guidebook on how to handle the *Bluejay Yarn?* See page 158. A list of metaphors you might have capitalized on is given on pages 159–160. The Guidebook gives a great amount of help in planning discussions. *Use* it! How much are the youngsters getting out of your reading? How can you check? How about asking them what *happened* in the story?"

Tuesday, September 29

> Before School—faculty meeting
> Home Room—opening exercises
> 1st Period—grammar lesson
> 2nd Period—planning
> 3rd Period—Mark Twain
> 4th Period—worked on bulletin board
> 5th Period—observed Mr. Adams
> 6th Period—delivered reports to Dr. Director

Mrs. Jones' Criticism of Third-Period Lesson

"Good, rapid handling of administrative details. Your discussion is enthusiastic, but degenerating—everyone speaks at once. Insist that the children speak out, and don't engage in a private conversation yourself. Excellently planned questions—the youngsters are doing very good thinking. *Look up* as you read! Your question on human weaknesses goes over poorly. When that happens, rephrase to suggest ideas. They are having trouble with metaphors. A good idea here is to assign them to pick and write them down in a brief study period. Good background on Calaveras. *Look up when you read. Cut* the story. Tell part of it. The vocabulary is throwing them. Get more expression in your voice; make them *see* it. Stop occasionally to check their interpretation with questions. You are still not reading fluently. Did you read it *aloud?* Good expression 'm-o-o-o-ore racket.' Very *good* reading on the race itself. Dialect at end is much improved. Good clear direction on Thurber. How about a bit of background on Thurber before they read him? Excellent lesson, over-all. An assignment on 'study . . . spelling . . . we'll test in a couple of days' is too indefinite; that's why I clarified it."

Mrs. Jones' Criticism of Fourth-Period Lesson

"You are growing in clarity of directions and ability to control the group. *Always* give a sentence with each spelling word. Your review of method on the reading charts was very good. 'x = 3' is a good illustration for a fast group, but way above this crowd. Save it for the time when you are *teaching* verbs of being, not

for a quick review. Now just *cover* parts of speech with definitions
they can copy. Your grammar presentation is *very* confusing. You
are telling them things they already know, but offering no chance
of practice. Improvisation doesn't work here for you. Plan tomorrow's lesson carefully—lots of *practice*. Review what I do with
the first period."

Personal Note on the Secret of "Professionalism"

1. Keep your mouth shut.
2. Keep your eyes and ears open.
3. Keep your mind on your job.

Wednesday, September 30

> Before School—faculty meeting
> Home Room—opening exercises, roll
> 1st Period—grammar lesson
> 2nd Period—planning
> 3rd Period—James Thurber
> 4th Period—grammar lesson
> 5th Period—ran off ditto sheets
> 6th Period—observed Mr. Boyd

Mrs. Jones' Criticism of Third-Period Lesson

"Insist that everyone speak loudly enough to be heard. Charles
is particularly soft-spoken. Enjoyable discussion on dogs. Children
are enjoying it. Well-planned questions. Good report on Thurber.
I hope you will mention his new book, *The Years with Ross*. It is
a Book-of-the-Month-Club selection. I also hope you will read
some *Fables for Our Times*. Good choice of reading on the lawn
dog. The students are enjoying the cartoons. Good use of Sawyer's
contribution. Good reading of *The Night the Bed Fell*."

Thursday, October 1

> Home Room—opening exercises, roll
> 1st Period—grammar lesson

2nd Period—planning
3rd Period—O. Henry
4th Period—grammar lesson
5th Period—ran off ditto sheets
6th Period—planning

Friday, October 2

Home Room—opening exercises, roll
1st Period—grammar, reading, spelling
2nd Period—planning
3rd Period—James Thurber
4th Period—grammar, reading, spelling
5th Period—planning
6th Period—conference

Mrs. Jones' Criticism of First-Period Flop

"Whoops! Unprepared—'no plans, no lesson!' But don't feel badly; my lesson was terrible! Did you notice? Too noisy; wasted time. I should have managed fifteen minutes of grammar, but I started too late in grading the reading. I let the spelling get out of hand. I think perhaps we should start planning twenty-four hours ahead. . . . It will be hard on *both* of us—because I myself have *general* rather than *firm* plans two days ahead—but it will avoid this business of being unprepared."

Mrs. Jones' Criticism of Third-Period Lesson

"You are feeling tense. Your voice is too loud. Theirs are rising in response. I myself did that this morning. Also, it is the day. All classes seem restless. What could you *do?* Did you notice what I did? (1) 'Your voices are too loud—everyone try to keep his voice down.' (2) 'Remember to raise your hand.' There is one more thing which *you* could do. What is it? For your next spelling lesson, take the words which have been missed on these two tests and reteach them. What grouping might you do? Then plan to retest again the entire list once you have retaught. Grades as low as they made yesterday are just evidence that they don't yet know the words. Are we trying to take too much at once? Is it a good policy to give a weekend assignment? When is it justified? Where are they to find the materials for Whitman?"

Personal Notes on Today's Goofs

I do feel badly about the first period, and I should, but not because of the quality of improvisation; I could kick myself for not staying up all night preparing. Mrs. Jones had to come to the rescue again when my ship was listing. That was first period. I guess I was not aware of the tenseness in the atmosphere because it was so contagious. If I had made a conscious effort to keep a level head, the kids would have followed. I gave the weekend assignment without really considering. It would be a good policy to go by: no weekend assignments. I must learn to think out the consequences of my planning before it goes into effect. Think a h e
a
d.

Monday, October 5

> Home Room—opening exercises, roll
> 1st Period—revised seating chart
> 2nd Period—planning
> 3rd Period—spelling test
> 4th Period—grammar lesson
> 5th Period—planning
> 6th Period—conference

Mrs. Jones' Criticism of First-Period Lesson

"Your seating chart was well planned and well received. Too much confusion on the spelling. No learning in this period. You should take the opportunity to teach a few words on the board— and insist on attention *or* direct study procedure. They get little out of a free study period without having a method supplied. Make me a new copy of the seating chart, please."

Mrs. Jones' Criticism of Third-Period Lesson

"Too slow-moving; your fast people could be working on literature while you gave the spelling test. It is now time for the bell, and all that has been accomplished is spelling, payment of money, and collecting money!!!!—which should have taken no more than fifteen minutes. Remember, I said two *well-planned* fifteen-minute spelling periods. Consider your time used for this week, and plan to come back to it next week. That will leave you free to concentrate on major goals."

Personal Note

The seating chart was based on the sociometric study which I have yet to finish. But since a "seating-preference questionnaire" was required for this, the kids were entitled to have their choices. Whether they remain where they have been seated depends upon their subsequent behavior. This business of collecting money, etc., still throws me off track, but I am beginning to be able to do more things at once—I hope. It is desirable to maintain a firmly established conception of *time*.

Tuesday, October 6

        Home Room—opening exercises, roll
        1st Period—reading, spelling, d. o. drill
        2nd Period—planning
        3rd Period—short-story discussion
        4th Period—adverb drill and spelling
        5th Period—observed Mrs. Jones
        6th Period—conference

Wednesday, October 7

        Home Room—opening exercises, roll
        1st Period—reading, grammar lesson
        2nd Period—planning
        3rd Period—Poe's *Tell-Tale Heart*

4th Period—reading, grammar
5th Period—spelling test
6th Period—conference

Mrs. Jones' Criticism of Third-Period Lesson

"Your drill is excellent. I suddenly realize that you have been collecting scads of homework papers without *immediately* correcting and returning them. Papers lose their value if they are held after the teaching passes. *Always* return them the next day, if possible—certainly no later than the following day. You *teach* from the papers once they've been graded. There is no point in piling on assignment after assignment unless you know how well they understand what you have just taught. It is one of the major errors of poor teachers—letting papers disappear into the teachers' hands with never a murmur. You are *again* hastily preparing just before class. Now, lesson plans for each class on my desk before school starts, or *no* teaching. I am going to have to insist on seeing them twenty-four hours in advance, if this kind of preparation continues. The *best* thing for you to do is take some stencils home and *cut* the stencil at home. It takes very little time to run them off in the morning, and if you arrive before eight, no one will be using the mimeograph. Remember, written plans and *all* materials at 8:30 in the morning, or *no* teaching. No more last-minute rush! They are doing excellent work on metaphors. You are really following through nicely. Your lesson is obviously well planned; I just haven't *seen* it! Use graph paper and keep your *own* grade book. Then the grades can be transferred to mine, and you won't have to wait to record them. The third period *must* have more grades recorded. We have *nothing* to grade them on. If we send home C's for these fast students, there will be considerable kickback. You have *lots* of papers. Where are the grades? I forgot to mention the guidance meetings—one yesterday afternoon. . . . These materials are from the meetings. They deal with methods of holding conferences and writing them up. Good grouping. Your review assignment is excellent. Go to the library and check on available poetry sources. Have the librarian set them on reserve."

Personal Note

I think the point from third period is not that I am not capable of planning effective lessons at the last moment, but that it just isn't a good idea to put planning off until then. At least there is time to sleep on it if the lesson is planned the night before. Don't count on free time in school—it doesn't always exist.

Thursday, October 8

> Home Room—opening exercises, roll
> 1st Period—routine class activities
> 2nd Period—planning
> 3rd Period—library research
> 4th Period—routine class activities
> 5th Period—spelling test
> 6th Period—conference
> After School—faculty meeting

Mrs. Jones' Criticism of Third-Period Research Assignment

"The beginning was awkward—your back to students, writing a lengthy list on the board. What should you have done? Assignment, 'read pp. 207–212,' needs more motivation. How are you going to check on the other two poems? Why not make your assignment both written and oral? Paraphrase two poems—written. Biographical sketch—written. Deliver one poem—oral. This assignment lacks *depth*. Everything I have suggested was designed to give *depth* and *scope* to individual research. Not all they do for *written* research needs to be included in the oral report. But fast students need assignments which give them *room* to learn. Your basic assignment, as narrowed down, seems too easy."

Personal Note

Mrs. Jones' decision to have *daily* homework assignments for the third period has prompted me to make up assignments for the sake of making assignments. This is not realistic! Sure, I feel that the children should have work to do every night, but I also feel that assignments should *grow* out of a motivational need for learning. It's my fault for letting the values become lopsided.

Friday, October 9

> Home Room—opening exercises, roll
> 1st Period—graded papers
> 2nd Period—planning
> 3rd Period—poetry unit
> 4th Period—graded papers
> 5th Period—graded papers
> 6th Period—conference

Personal Note

I have finally caught up with my stack of ungraded papers. Never again! *Carpe Diem.*

Student-Teaching Activities—Third Report Period

1. Revised seating chart from the sociometric study.
2. Taught grammar drills to first-period group.
3. Completed one unit with the third-period group.
4. Began to take over two other groups: #4 and #5.
5. Learned to speed up transition periods.
6. Retaught unlearned material.
7. Attained considerably more success in discussion.
8. Learned to prepare lesson plans twenty-four hours in advance.
9. Learned to grade and return papers promptly.
10. Attended three faculty meetings.

Supervising Teacher's Comments—Third Report Period

"John has developed effective methods of control. He has developed a sense of 'teaching' rather than 'covering' the material. He has learned to manage small groups for reteaching. He has learned to reteach abstract ideas and make them more meaningful. He is learning to be flexible in adapting lesson plans to the exigencies of the situation. He has learned to plan assignments on the correct level for his group. He has learned to construct grammar drills which isolate the material to be taught and do not confuse the students. He is strong in leading group discussion to develop a concept. He is not yet able to lead a group in which students react to each other and come to a group conclusion. He's beginning to be able to find out, during work period, which students need help. John is developing excellent techniques of classroom management. He is always prompt and is professional about responsibilities.

"Still disorganized. John has difficulty in planning far enough in advance. Once or twice he was unprepared, both in plans and materials. He has not learned to return papers promptly and use them as a teaching tool. As a result, he was forced to spend a period straightening out students on back assignments. John gets frustrated and confused if he doesn't accomplish what he planned in the way he planned it. He understands the principle of flexibility, however, and is trying to apply it."

Monday, October 12

      Home Room—opening exercises, roll
      1st Period—ran off ditto sheets
      2nd Period—planning
      3rd Period—oral poetry readings
      4th Period—previewed films
      5th Period—initiated new unit
      6th Period—previewed films

Tuesday, October 13

      Home Room—opening exercises, roll
      1st Period—discussion
      2nd Period—set up projector
      3rd Period—film on poetry
      4th Period—planning
      5th Period—discussion and spelling

6th Period—conference
After School—faculty meeting

Mrs. Jones' Criticism of Third-Period Lesson

"It is unrealistic to expect them to fulfill tonight's assignment. They don't *understand* the elements. You never *discussed* the assignment from the book on reading poetry. That assignment should have been returned and discussed *today*. You should always return and finish up one assignment before going on to the next. *Turn back each assignment the day after it is turned in*— or don't make another one! How can they learn if you don't discuss the assignments? You saw today in first period how I used the stories they wrote to *teach* them. Assignments are to be *used*, not filed away in the teacher's notebook. You are still trying to stick to preconceived plans. It would be more flexible to have moved the poetry-writing assignment to Friday, when you could have retaught the elements of poetry and had the class compare a poem on the board, suggest a list of subjects for poems, and begin to write in class, where you could help them. They could read their poems aloud on Monday. The film is excellent, and your guide questions were superb. Your only problem is that you are trying to do too much in one hour. When will you finish the oral reports? Notice how much simpler the film is than you are: 'comparison . . . contrast . . . sounds of words,' not 'simile, metaphor, alliteration, harmony, dissonance.' Your discussion of the film is excellent. This is one of your *best* lessons. The youngsters are really impressed."

Wednesday, October 14

Home Room—opening exercises, roll
1st Period—routine class activities
2nd Period—set up film
3rd Period—film on Walt Whitman
4th Period—grammar lesson
5th Period—discussion of literature
6th Period—conference

Personal Note

First period was a flop discipline-wise. Third period was a hit! Fourth period was so-so. Fifth period was a little rowdy but lots of fun. Assignment for tonight: go home and find as many resources for discipline control as possible.

Thursday, October 15

> Before School—conference
> Home Room—*no* opening exercises; roll only
> 1st Period—library
> 2nd Period—conference
> 3rd Period—American literature exam
> 4th Period—library
> 5th Period—introduction to short story
> 6th Period—conference with Brad Carp

Personal Note

The elimination of opening exercises during home room was in response to the farce which the kids made out of the Lord's Prayer and flag salute yesterday. I told them that since they displayed no respect for their God or for their country, we would forget the whole thing for a day. It worked. I think they felt some shame. Dr. Director came in during third period—about tied up our unit on American literature by that time and were having a test on it. Brad Carp asked permission to go to the library during first period to get a book (should never have given permission to him); he never returned. I cornered him at lunch and told him to stay after school. We talked it over.

Mrs. Jones' Criticism of Third-Period Lesson

"Good test. You might have had them exchange and correct the papers, since the test was short. They would have learned from the correction and discussion. You brought them back into line, after too much conversation, very nicely. For the poor readers, emphasis on 'what he did well' is a good idea. Then give *one* suggestion the poor reader can use for the next time. Pick up the discussion. Move it along. What was Joe reading? And Frank Miller?"

Methods of Enforcing Discipline (Assigned Yesterday)

1. Eliminate cause of trouble before it occurs.
2. Wait impatiently for attention.
3. Reseating of entire group.
4. Private conference or detention.
5. Isolation of individuals.
6. Under-react rather than over-react to provocative situations to show that you still have your wits.
7. See that what is demanded is carried out.
8. Be discriminating with individual behavior.
9. Remain aloof; keep a superior attitude.
10. Be cheerful.
11. Repeat the properly executed activity.
12. Eliminate the improperly executed activity.
13. Don't threaten meaninglessly.
14. Assume that students are capable of reasonable responses to reasonable requests.
15. Accept the feeling of the class.
16. Introduce a greater variety of activity into the classroom.
17. Dismissal, office, detention, etc. (last chance).

Friday, October 16

Before School—filled out report cards
Home Room—opening exercises resumed successfully
1st Period—routine class work
2nd Period—filled out report cards
3rd Period—finished literature unit
4th Period—routine class work
5th Period—discussion of literature
6th Period—conference
After School—conference

Personal Note

After I had finished filling out the report cards for third period, Mrs. Jones checked them over with me; they were due in the home-room teachers' boxes Monday morning, but we decided that it was better to get them out of the way early. I learned that it is just as important to consider individual capabilities, attitudes, and outcomes as it is to stick to a mathematical standard of evaluation. We are not grading machines. It was my responsibility, but Mrs. Jones corrected any errors I had overlooked. This report-card business is tricky! You really have to be careful about each minute detail.

Monday, October 19

    Before School—filed graded papers
    Home Room—opening exercises, roll
    1st Period—routine class activities
    2nd Period—planning
    3rd Period—creative-writing unit
    4th Period—routine class activities
    5th Period—review of short stories
    6th Period—conference
    After School—ditto sheets

Tuesday, October 20

    Before School—ran off ditto copies
    Home Room—opening exercises, roll
    1st Period—lesson on helper verbs
    2nd Period—planning
    3rd Period—Beowulf lesson
    4th Period—lesson on direct objects
    5th Period—promoting word perception
    6th Period—conference
    After School—planning

Mrs. Jones' Evaluation of Daily Lessons

"*First period:* Excellent handling of group. Improved discipline. On correcting homework—move it faster. I stepped in to show you a technique of correcting diagramming. You needed to plan one more activity. The period dragged a little. *Be sure to check and return homework papers tomorrow, since we are making a big deal out of homework.*

"*Third period:* Much better lesson than yesterday. Beowulf is *excellent.* Children were fascinated. Your work on poetry was well taught. I hope there will be a challenging homework assignment. Rhyming work excellent. Your examples of 'fish' and 'hitch' were good.

"*Fourth period:* I interfered too much! *You* are doing fine. This is dragging—on the timing of work. Congratulate me: I'm not saying anything.

"*Fifth period:* Don't let Tony dominate a review. You are not drawing discussion out of everyone—just a few. This is dragging —after you put things on the board. Awfully uninspired homework assignment. Very poor planning!"

Wednesday, October 21

> Before School—ran off dittos
> Home Room—opening exercises, roll
> 1st Period—grammar lesson
> 2nd Period—planning
> 3rd Period—organized committees for magazine
> 4th Period—grammar lesson
> 5th Period—word perception
> 6th Period—conference
> After School—planning

Thursday, October 22

> Before School—ran off dittos
> Home Room—opening exercises, roll
> 1st Period—grammar lesson

2nd Period—planning
3rd Period—library project
4th Period—grammar lesson
5th Period—library project
6th Period—conference
After School—received complaints on report cards

Personal Note

Sarah Davis and Frank Miller came in after school to inquire about their "low" grades. Sarah received a B because she had not worked up to capacity and her average grade for the six weeks divided out to a meager B-plus; this does not constitute a solid A. I told her so, but she had to put up an argument, thinking she could sway me. I let her know that she didn't have a leg to stand on. Frank Miller had the nerve to come in and complain about his E; he was just plain lazy—no assignments turned in.

Friday, October 23

Before School—ran off dittos
Home Room—opening exercises, roll
1st Period—grammar lesson
2nd Period—planning
3rd Period—creative writing
4th Period—grammar lesson
5th Period—word perception
6th Period—planning
After School—filed graded papers

Monday, October 26

Before School—planning
Home Room—opening exercises, roll
1st Period—routine class activities
2nd Period—conference
3rd Period—literary magazine
4th Period—routine class activities

5th Period—discussion of literature
6th Period—conference
After School—planning

Student-Teaching Activities—Fourth Report Period

1. Taught a full day of classes alone October 23.
2. Achieved a more stable control discipline.
3. Supervised the organization of a literary magazine.
4. Carried on two weeks of classes independently.
5. Directed committees and creative-writing projects.
6. Learned to tailor lessons to the needs of the group.
7. Accepted the responsibility of grading report cards.
8. Learned to operate the motion-picture projector.
9. Previewed and presented two films to the third period.
10. Began a new unit with the fifth-period class.

Supervising Teacher's Comments—Fourth Report Period

"John has developed control techniques, and is now, I feel, ready to teach on his own. He is overcoming his difficulty in handling papers, and learning to get them back promptly. For a week he has had almost complete responsibility for the classes and has done well.

"Occasionally a poorly planned or poorly motivated lesson will get John into trouble in controlling his group. He has difficulty in regaining control or in identifying his trouble spots. He still tends to simply make and collect assignments rather than use the assignment as a springboard for teaching."

Tuesday, October 27

Before School—conference
Home Room—opening exercises, roll
1st Period—routine class activities
2nd Period—planning
3rd Period—literary magazine

    4th Period—routine class activities
    5th Period—word perception
    6th Period—conference
    After School—conference

Wednesday, October 28

    Before School—conference
    Home Room—opening exercises, roll
    1st Period—routine class activities
    2nd Period—conference
    3rd Period—literary magazine
    4th Period—routine class activities
    5th Period—Beowulf reading
    6th Period—planning
    After School—filed graded papers

Personal Note

Mrs. Jones has been leaving me alone for over a week now in order to prepare me for the big shock: she left for Richmond at noon today to attend professional meetings. I had little trouble with the other classes, but fourth period was nasty. Fred Burgess and George Eberhardt asked to go to the library to check out books; like a fool, I let them (I seem to have a weakness for saying yes). They were gone for twenty minutes. I sent a boy to get them. He came back with this reply: "We're not coming back, and if you want us, you can come and get us!" I went to get them. In the room again I gave them an assignment: "Write a two-page essay on the uses of the reference materials in the library—due this period." Both refused. I demanded that they get busy immediately and stated that I expected to see their papers before lunch. Fred countered, "Do You?" "Yes, I do!" "Well, we're not going to do it!" I said, "Very well, then, you can see Mr. Mitchell about it." "Fine," said Burgess, "he won't do anything about it." As they both marched out the door rather proudly, George turned back to proclaim over his shoulder, "See ya later, Sarge!" I saw

Mr. Mitchell during lunch. He had sent them both home on a conditional basis: they had to bring in those essays if they wanted to come back to school. Fifth period was a hit.

Thursday, October 29

> Before School—planning
> Home Room—opening exercises
> 1st Period—library
> 2nd Period—finished printing magazine
> 3rd Period—special lesson for Dr. Director
> 4th Period—library
> 5th Period—Chaucer reading
> 6th Period—planning
> After School—farewell party

Personal Note

Mrs. Jones wasn't here at all; I had the whole day to myself. First period was good as gold. During second period, while we were assembling the literary magazine, Dr. Director entered. He got a copy hot off the press and sat in on a discussion of one of the readings in our literature book. He seemed to enjoy the lesson and said, "It is very interesting," then left. Fourth period gave me absolutely no trouble after yesterday's episode. I saw Fred Burgess in Mr. Mitchell's office during lunch. He had brought the essay, although it was only one page and was on the subject of transportation (he said he couldn't remember what the assignment was). However, he seemed to be reasonably humiliated by the embarrassing situation, and I thought he was sincerely sorry. That was all that mattered, so I accepted the essay and told him that this was a very uncomfortable experience, but that my actions were necessitated by his and George's defiance, and that I hoped it would never occur again, for his sake. George Eberhardt never returned. Fifth period was a little out of hand, but loads of fun, as always. After school, Sarah Davis, Barbara Burke, the Wright twins, and some other female admirers from the third-period class dropped in to surprise me with a farewell cake. They had ordered it specially from the bakery. It was white with green decorations. On top it read, "Goodbye, Mr. Davidson." If I only had a picture of it! I didn't deserve it, but the gesture was deeply touching. Wish Mrs. Jones could have been there.

Friday, October 30

> 12:00 noon–8:00 P.M.: Grading papers, recording the marks in Mrs. Jones' roll book, and filing papers away.

A Proverb for the Prevention of Head-Swelling

> "So long as you know you're green,
>   You grow—
> But just when you think you're ripe,
>   Then you begin to get rotten."

To Mrs. Jones

An insufficient "thank you" for everything!!!!

C. Specimen Plans

The plans which are included in this section were developed and used by student teachers under the direction of their supervising teachers. They represent three grade levels of work: elementary, junior high school, and senior high school. All of the plans follow the general format recommended for plan construction, including (1) the aims or objectives which the teacher hopes to have his students attain as a result of the study involved, (2) the activities or learning experiences to be provided to help the students in attaining the desired objectives, (3) evaluation devices and procedures which may be used to determine the progress of the students toward the desired objectives, and (4) a list of curriculum materials to be used.

These plans are presented as specimens to assist the student teacher in developing his own plans for the work which he is expected to teach. It is hoped that you will be able to improve on the plans which are presented. The type of plan which will be needed will depend upon the type of subject matter to be taught. Those which were chosen for presentation in this section are fairly general in character. More specific plans must be developed in the field in which you will be teaching.

The complexity of the plans, the types of learning experiences to be provided, and the types of evaluation instruments and procedures to be used will depend upon the grade level of the students involved and other factors that are peculiar to the situation in which you are placed. The skill which you demonstrate in developing and using plans appropriate to your specific situation will determine, to a great degree, your success in teaching.

SPECIMEN PLAN I

Third Grade

Travel

I. Objectives

A. General Understandings Increased
  1. Man first traveled by walking.
  2. Pack animals lightened the load.
  3. The skid and wheel were an improvement over the use of animals alone.
  4. The wheel helped in the development of bicycles, cars, trains, and airplanes.
  5. We must obey rules to prevent accidents.
  6. Transportation has an important place in our lives.

B. Habits Practiced and Improved
  1. The asking and answering of questions about travel.
  2. Listening attentively when others are reading or speaking.
  3. Doing work neatly and quietly.
  4. Following directions.
  5. Improving reading and writing ability.

C. Skills Developed
  1. Ability to read more fluently and comprehensibly.
  2. Increased vocabulary and word usage.
  3. Ability to express self through drawing and coloring.
  4. Improved writing ability.
  5. Ability to tell the class interesting stories about travel experiences and books read.

D. Appreciations and Attitudes Developed
  1. Appreciation of stories, poems, songs, and pictures about transportation.
  2. Appreciation of work of policemen, bus drivers, ticket salesmen, and patrol boys.
  3. Greater understanding and appreciation of safety rules.

II. Approaches

A. Preferred Approach
   1. Ask the children if they traveled during the spring vacation.
   2. List on the board their different ways of traveling.
   3. Turn to Unit 4, "How We Travel," in the book *Working Together,* by Alta McIntire and Wilhelmina Hill, and name other ways of travel.
      a. How many of those ways have you ever traveled?
      b. How many of those ways would you like to travel?
   4. Are there any other questions you would like to ask about traveling? Let's list them on the board.

B. Possible Approaches
   1. Listen to the conversation of the children about trips they have taken.
   2. Encourage them to read stories and poems about travel in other lands as well as at home.
   3. Display pictures of different ways of travel.
   4. Ask the children to mention places they would like to see and how they could get there.

III. Possible Learning Activities

A. Activity No. 1—Make a travel log
   1. For the cover, the children may make any kind of a design they choose with crayons on folded construction paper. Drawing paper and writing paper with lines are then stapled inside to make the book.
   2. Inside the book
      a. Make a list of safety rules for walking.
      b. Make a list of safety rules for bicycle riding.
      c. Copy the words to the song, "Riding My Bike."
      d. List things that you have seen trucks carrying.
      e. Draw a picture of some way you would like to travel.

B. Activity No. 2—Make a pop-up in the travel log
   1. Ask the children to draw a picture representing some mode of travel.

2. They fold the drawings in the center.

3. They then paste each picture on a slant so that it will stand up when the page is turned.

C. Activity No. 3—Write stories and poems about travel

   1. Write a story about "My First Bicycle Ride."

   2. Write a story or poem about a trip taken.

D. Activity No. 4—Make a travel mural

   1. Start a big travel mural on the bulletin board in your room. Paint in a background of sky, homes, and buildings. Each child adds his drawing of a bicycle, motorcycle, or scooter to the street.

   2. As the study of cars is made, each child draws a car, truck, or bus to add to the mural.

   3. Draw the different cars of the train and add them to a track, after the study of trains.

   4. Fill the sky with planes drawn by the children.

   5. Add ships and boats to the water.

E. Activity No. 5—Bring pictures for a travel scrapbook

   1. Label a scrapbook, "Ways of Travel."

   2. Children may look through old magazines for pictures of cars, trucks, planes, buses, trains, etc.

   3. They then paste these pictures on pages marked for each mode of transportation.

   4. Besides having a collection of ways to travel, the children may look through the scrapbook to be sure just how something looks when they are drawing.

F. Activity No. 6—Study road maps

   1. Each child is given a map of the community around the school.

   2. He is then taught that north is at the top, south is at the bottom, east is right, and west is left.

   3. Each child is then asked to find his street and show the class where it is.

   4. As the teacher pretends she is taking a trip, different children are asked to tell what street they are approaching next.

G. Activity No. 7—Toys in an exhibit
   1. Children are asked to bring toy trucks, cars, boats, airplanes, and animals to school.
   2. These are then arranged in a travel exhibit.

H. Activity No. 8—Make trucks and cars
   1. Construction paper is cut into strips of equal size.
   2. Each child is given two strips.
   3. One strip is gently rolled on each end to make the wheels.
   4. Then the radiator is pasted to the first construction.
   5. The paper is then bent to make the hood, windshield, top, and back of the car, and then pasted down.

I. Activity No. 9—Make a paper train
   1. Each child folds a long strip of paper to look like an accordion.
   2. With crayons they draw an engine on the first section.
   3. Then they draw the different kinds of cars on the other section.

J. Activity No. 10—Present a television program about trains
   1. An announcer is chosen.
   2. Each child is given a picture of something about trains.
   3. Before a toy microphone, each child tells about his picture.

K. Activity No. 11—Read stories about travel
   1. Books pertaining to the particular mode of transportation being studied are checked from the library.
   2. These books are placed on the reading table in the classroom.
   3. During a sharing period set aside for storytelling, each child tells the others about the book he has read.

L. Activity No. 12—Build a small lighthouse
   1. A box of the appropriate size is covered with paper and painted.
   2. The top is cut for the windows, and a light is placed there.
   3. The lighthouse is placed in the exhibit of toy cars, boats, etc., in a section made to look like water.

M. Activity No. 13—Keep a daily weather chart
   1. Make a chart for each day of the week.

     2. Show which days are sunny or cloudy by adding the sun for pretty days and clouds for cloudy weather.

     3. Add an umbrella for rainy days, or a snowman for snowy days.

     4. Correlate this chart with airplane travel.

N. Activity No. 14—Visit the airport and bus terminal

     1. Make a list of things to look for.

        a. Ticket window

        b. Information window

        c. Doors through which to enter the bus or plane

        d. Taxis

        e. Hangar

        f. Different kinds of planes

     2. Make a list of good manners for the trip.

        a. Stay together in a group.

        b. Listen carefully.

        c. Be quiet.

        d. Be an alert person.

        e. Remember what you see and hear.

O. Activity No. 15—Culminating activity

     1. Display posters, travel logs, collections, scrapbooks, travel mural, and car exhibit.

     2. Have a program to tell what has been learned.

        a. Sing "Riding My Bike."

        b. Do some choral reading of poems about travel.

        c. Have a television program about all the different ways of travel.

IV. *Evaluation*

The teacher may evaluate the results of the unit in many different ways. She may have formal tests in the form of a word game. On a chart she may keep a record of each child's ability to obey the safety rules on the school bus or on the trip to the airport.

She will observe the children's attitudes and behavior. She may ask herself:

1. Have they accomplished the objectives that were set up?

2. Are they able to obtain information by themselves and use it?

3. Are they learning to live, work, and play together?
4. Is each child a better citizen?
5. Is each child a better-adjusted individual?

BIBLIOGRAPHY

Beauchamp, Wilbur L., Gertrude Crampton, William S. Gray, *How Do We Know?* Chicago: Scott, Foresman and Company, 1947.

Elting, Alta, and Wilhelmina Hill, *Working Together*. Chicago: Follett Publishing Company, 1954.

Peattie, Donald Culross, *The Story of the New Lands*. New York: Grossett and Dunlap, 1937.

Petersham, Maude and Miska, *The Story Books of Ships*. Wisconsin: E. M. Hale and Company, 1935.

Pitts, Lilla Belle, Mabelle Glenn, Lorraine E. Watters, *Singing On Our Way*. Boston: Ginn and Company, 1949.

Tatham, Campbell, *The First Book of Boats*. New York: Franklin Watts, Inc., 1945.

Tatham, Campbell, and Jeanne Bendick, *The First Book of Trains*. New York: Franklin Watts, Inc., 1948.

Dudley, Lavinia P. (ed.), *The Encyclopedia Americana*. New York, Chicago: Americana Corporation, 1953.

Child Training Association, Inc., *Children's Activities*. June, 1954; page 45.

Pete, The Policeman. Indianapolis: General Motors, 1950.

Association of American Railroads, *Railroads at Work*. Washington, D. C., 1954.

SPECIMEN PLAN II

Third Grade

Lesson Plan

Topic: Reading   Date: May 9, 1956

Student Teacher: Julia Scott

Supervising Teacher: Mrs. Mabel Blank

Aims:

    To correlate subject matter with everyday experiences.

    To teach the children new words.

    To improve both silent and oral reading.

    To check comprehension of what is read.

Assignment:

    Scott, Foresman and Company Basic Series, New Friends and Neighbors, pages 60–64, *A Funny Telephone.*

Subject Matter	Method
1. Introduction of new words	1. Flash cards with "telephone," "line," "tie," "pull," "clothes," "use," until all the children know all the words.
2. Silent reading	2. After reading silently, each child makes up two good questions about the story that cannot be answered by "yes" or "no."
3. Demonstration of telephone used in the story	3. Telephone was a pulley clothesline between two buildings. Demonstrate by placing two chairs, back to back, about three feet apart. Loop a continuous piece of string from the top of one chair-back to the other.
4. Questions asked over the telephone	4. Have a child fasten his question to the line with a paper clip and pull the string until it reaches the other chair. The child he chooses must correctly answer it before he can ask one.
5. Story read orally	5. Check to see if all questions were answered correctly.

SPECIMEN PLAN III
Third Grade

Phonics Lesson

Sounds: <u>an, it, at</u>

Student Teacher: <u>Julia Scott</u>

Supervising Teacher: <u>Mrs. Mabel Blank</u>

Write these words at the top of your paper and draw a line under each. Like this:

<u>   an   </u>   <u> it </u>   <u> at </u>

Pretend they are the names of three baseball teams.

Now, under each one write as many words as you can find that have these small words in them. All the words with <u>an</u> go in the row under that team's name. Those with <u>it</u> go under <u>it,</u> and so on.

Here are all the consonants except 'x':

b c d f g h j k l m n p q r s t v w y z

Try one after the other, in front of the baseball team's name, and when you get to one that will make a real word, sound it. If it makes a word, write it down with the team name behind it.

f-an   fan

(sound it)   (write it)

For baseball, you should have nine players. Can you get a whole team for each?

SPECIMEN PLAN IV

Core Curriculum: A Resource Unit for Seventh Grade

Living in Our Community

I. Objectives

A. To gain a broader understanding of our community
B. To learn to become better citizens of our community
C. To have greater respect for the community
    1. Greater appreciation of institutions
    2. Greater appreciation of officials
    3. Greater appreciation of people in general

II. Problems

A. What do we want to study about our community?
B. How shall we go about studying our community?
C. Where will we find the information to answer our questions?
D. How shall we evaluate our work?
E. What outcomes or improvements have been made as a result of our study?

III. Activities

A. Making an all-day tour of Jonesboro
B. Keeping a spelling list
C. Making written and oral reports
D. Conducting interviews
E. Conducting panel discussions
F. Writing letters
G. Inviting speakers
H. Making bulletin-board displays
 I. Making a frieze
 J. Making a booklet
K. Performing dramatizations
L. Making graphs
M. Visiting the weather bureau

N. Learning to read meters
O. Making out checks, money orders, deposit slips, and order blanks
P. Recording earnings and expenses
Q. Charting history dates
R. Making scale drawings
S. Making wage scales
T. Learning percentages
U. Making "peep boxes"
V. Making a study of housing
W. Learning about the Community Chest
X. Conducting a spelling bee
Y. Showing films
Z. Showing filmstrips

IV. Materials

A. Textbooks
   1. *A World View*—Clarence Woodrow Sorenson
   2. *Junior English One*—Stoddard, Bailey, Lewis
   3. *Mathematics We Use*, Book I—Brueckner, Grossnickle
   4. *Reading Literature*—Eberhart, Swearingen, Leary
   5. *The Story of Kentucky*—Thomas Crittenden Cherry
   6. *Understanding our Environment*—Franklin B. Carroll
B. Other Books
   1. English
      a. *American English*—Goddard, Camp, Lucan, Stockwell
      b. *English in Action*, Course II—J. C. Tressler
      c. *Junior English in Action*, Book III—J. C. Tressler
      d. *Language Skills*—Ruth H. Teuscher
      e. *The English We Need*, Book I—Bell, Johnson, Godman
   2. Mathematics
      a. *Child Life Arithmetic*—Breed, Overman, Woody
      b. *Daily Life Arithmetic*, Books 7 and 8—Buswell, Brownell
      c. *Fundamental Mathematics*—Schorling, Clark, Smith
      d. *Home Run Hitters*—Osborn, Riefling, Raflin

    e. *How to Make Arithmetic Meaningful*—Brueckner, Grossnickle

    f. *Junior Mathematics for Today*—Betz

    g. *Mathematics and Life*—Ruch, Knight, Studebaker

    h. *The New Curriculum Arithmetics*, Grades 5, 6, 7—Brueckner, Anderson, Banting, Merton

3. Science

    a. *Discovering Our World*—Beauchamp, Williams, Blough

    b. *Everybody's Weather*—Joseph Gaer

    c. *Everyday Weather and How it Works*—Herman Schneider

    d. *How and Why Experiments*—Frasier, Dolman, Shoemaker, Van Noy

    e. *Picture Books of the Weather*—Jerome S. Meyer

    f. *Science Problems*, Book II—Beauchamp, Mayfield, West

    g. *The Sky is Blue*—W. Maxwell Reed

    h. *The Wonderworld of Science*, Book 7—Meister, Keirstad, Shoemaker

4. Science UniText—Row, Peterson and Company

    a. *Ask The Weather Man*

    b. *Electricity*

    c. *Light*

    d. *Our Ocean of Air*

    e. *Soil*

    f. *Sound*

    g. *The Air About Us*

    h. *Water*

    i. *Water Supply*

5. Little Wonder Books

    a. *Agriculture*

    b. *Air*

    c. *America's Opportunities*

    d. *America's Transportation*

    e. *Electricity and Magnets*

    f. *Our Land of Cities*

    g. *Our Land of Farms*

h. *Our Land of Plenty*
i. *Pioneering in Agriculture*
j. *Pioneering in Communication*
k. *Pioneering in Industry*
l. *Pioneering in Ways of Travel*

C. Films
1. Community Government
2. How Weather is Forecast
3. Metropolis
4. Our Community
5. River in the Way
6. The Junior Citizen

D. Filmstrip
1. Our Homes and Our Communities

E. Miscellaneous
1. Maps of Jonesboro
2. Pictures for bulletin board
3. Graphs for bulletin board
4. Newspapers
5. Magazines
6. Radio programs
7. Television programs
8. Cardboard meters (gas and electric)
9. Electric meter
10. Checkbooks
11. Deposit slips
12. Order Blanks
13. Post Office money orders
14. Graph paper

V. *Procedure*

A. Make an all-day tour of Jonesboro.
B. Put maps of Jonesboro on bulletin board.
C. Display pictures on bulletin board.
D. Students make a list of things they want to find out about Jonesboro.

E. Students list ways in which to find the information.

F. Students list ways of presenting the information to the class.

G. Appoint committees.
   1. Students decide committee on which they wish to work.
   2. Committees appointed
      a. Horse and Stock Farms
      b. Police and Fire Departments
      c. Vital Statistics
      d. Education and Religion
      e. Population and Size
      f. Communication and Transportation

H. Each committee makes a list of questions concerning its particular topic.

I. Committees plan to conduct interviews with certain business people of the community.

J. Subjects studied
   1. Geography
      a. Study "A Living in Town and City" in textbook.
         1) How towns and cities grew
         2) Rural and urban
         3) Kinds and types of manufacturing
         4) The world's urban areas
         5) Kinds of trade
         6) Transportation
         7) Special services
            a) Education
            b) Government
            c) Health
            d) Religion
            e) Communication
         8) Cities of tomorrow
      b. Give tests covering the material studied.
   2. Spelling
      a. Students keep spelling lists of difficult words studied in all subjects.
      b. Teacher compiles spelling lists for students from these words.

  c. Tests are given over words that have been studied.
  d. Conduct a spelling bee covering all spelling lists.
3. English
  a. Study how to conduct interviews.
  b. Study how to write good business letters.
  c. Discuss telephoning and telephone manners.
  d. How to give good oral reports
  e. How to give good written reports
    1) Outlining
    2) Capitalization
    3) Punctuation
  f. Study stories with urban and rural backgrounds in literature book.
4. Science
  a. Air
    1) Use introduction to the unit on air to stimulate thought and discussion.
    2) Where the Air Is˘and What It Is—Chapter 16
      a) Where is the air?
      b) Does air have weight?
      c) Why does the wind blow?
      d) What is air?
    3) How Oxygen Behaves—Chapter 17
      a) What makes a candle burn?
      b) Air that disappeared
      c) Making new substances
      d) Oxygen alone is inactive
      e) Oxygen in action
      f) Joining with oxygen
      g) The fire within you
      h) Carbon dioxide
    4) Bad Air and Good Air—Chapter 18
      a) Many kinds of dust
      b) Examining dust
      c) Breathing dust
      d) Dusty, dangerous jobs
      e) Taking care of the air

      f) Poisonous gases in our homes

      g) Stagnant air

      h) Let in fresh air

      i) Get the air into your lungs

      j) How to avoid colds

   5) Use questions and vocabulary list in discussing the above chapters.

   6) Continue the discussion of air by relating it to the weather, which is to be discussed in some detail.

   7) Prepare a list of terms used in a study of weather.

   8) Secure library books on weather, and distribute to class in order that youngsters may find definitions in various books.

   9) Use film, "How Weather is Forecast."

  10) Use various materials in the geography book on weather.

  11) Have a committee prepare a large graph on which may be kept Jonesboro's high, low, and normal temperatures over a period of several weeks.

  12) Relate the importance of air and weather to the on-going life of the community.

5. Mathematics

  a. Meters

    1) Electric

      a) Learn the meaning of words and symbols involved in reading meters and computing bills.

        (1) Kilowatt hour

        (2) Cubic feet

        (3) Clockwise

        (4) Counterclockwise

        (5) Dial

        (6) Unit

      b) Learn to read meters.

        (1) Read electric meters at home.

      c) Learn to compute bills.

        (1) Use Jonesboro rates.

        (2) Bring bills and receipts from home.

2) Gas
   a) Repeat from electric meters.
3) Water
   a) Bonus work.
b. Graphs
   1) Reading graphs
      a) Collect graphs from newspapers and magazines.
      b) Display on bulletin board.
   2) Construct graphs
      a) Picture
      b) Bar
         (1) Make graphs, using county and city school enrollment.
         (2) Make graphs comparing county school enrollment, city school enrollment, and those enrolled in colleges.
      c) Line
         (1) Make graphs showing Jonesboro's population since 1860.
         (2) Make graphs showing Jonesboro's population increases during each ten-year period.
         (3) Make graph showing Jonesboro's high, normal, and low temperatures for each day.
c. Group work
   1) Continue at least once weekly with individual assignments according to needs discovered in achievement test and daily work.
K. Students share the information they have gathered by giving oral reports to the class.
L. Students make booklets, collecting information and materials which they have used in their study of the community: summaries of films, committee reports, drawings, clippings, etc.
M. Spelling bee

VI. *Evaluation*

A. Questionnaire
B. Reports, oral and written
C. Tests

Community Opportunities

NAME _____   DATE _____

Check the following community opportunities which are used by
you and/or your family:

1. Water _____
2. Electricity _____
3. Gas _____
4. Churches _____
5. Schools _____
6. Parks _____
7. Movies _____
8. Newspapers _____
9. Library _____
10. Radio _____
11. Television _____
12. City bus _____
13. Greyhound bus _____
14. Trains _____
15. Planes _____
16. Community-concert series _____
17. University programs _____
18. _____   _____
19. _____   _____
20. _____   _____

Spelling List

1	2	3	4
interview	wanted	eager	committee
rural	frightened	struggle	territory
urban	February	lawyer	village
telephone	cousin	immigration	factory
valuable	different	area	watt
magazine	sometimes	anxious	electric
bright	caught	ancient	public
industry	surprise	industrial	kilowatt
community	children	business	railroad
thousand	always	essential	utility

5	6	7	8
New York	equally	profit	regular
machinery	properly	consider	modern
Europe	process	permanent	Jonesboro
ordinary	district	enormous	caravan
commerce	doctor	meter	people
various	farmer	geography	impossible
collect	conditions	Baltimore	highway
method	ordinary	newspaper	automobile
desirable	history	articles	government
complex	attract	language	general

Bonus List

1	2	3
salutation	immigration	revolution
historical	locomotive	abandoned
recommended	dependent	solution
authority	fascinating	inventions
character	prophecy	transportation
metropolitan	census	punishment
violent	utilities	cooperate
communication	population	occasion
investigate	manufacturing	particular
individual	accustomed	superior

4	5	6
Illinois	Christmas	profitable
Jerash	necessities	acquainted
merchandise	Baptist	probably
hospitality	penetrates	subscription
religion	immigration	diagram
assembled	carpenter	experiment
resolutions	interviewee	materials
graduate	considerable	hospital
Methodist	disposal	boundary
alcohol	Asia	connection

Capital Letters

Below are some rules for capitalization which you already know.
After each statement write at least two examples of the rule.

Use a Capital Letter

1. To begin the first word of every sentence.

_____

_____

2. To begin the individual or special names of persons, places, months, and days.

_____

_____

3. To write every initial.

_____

_____

4. To begin every line of poetry.

_____

_____

5. To begin titles of dignity and position and the abbreviations of such titles.

_____

_____

6. To begin the first word of every direct quotation.

_____

_____

Circle each letter which should be capitalized in the sentences below:

my dog skippy can do several tricks. I entered him in the dog show in Chicago, illinois, last september. The judging for his class was on tuesday. on monday skippy became ill and would not pay any attention to me. Mother called dr. j. r. henderson, the veterinarian, and he gave him some medicine. the doctor said skippy was too sick to stay in the show, so we took him home. father simply said, "too bad," when he heard the news. Mother said, "don't worry about the show, jerry. there will be other times when you can enter skippy in contests. right now the important thing is for him to get well."

I still think skippy might have won the chicago show prize if he had been in the contest. He is well now, however, and we are taking him to a show in hammond, indiana, next march.

NAME _____ DATE _____

Capital Letters

Below are some rules for capitalization which you already know. After each statement write at least two examples of the rule.

Use a Capital Letter

7. To begin the word God and all names applied to God, as well as the names of all sacred books.

_____

_____

8. For I and O when these are used as words.

_____

_____

9. To begin the first word and the principal word in the greeting of a letter.

_____

_____

10. To begin the first word in the close of a letter.

_____

_____

11. To begin the first word and all other important words in the title of a story, song, poem, report, or book.

_____

_____

12. To begin every important word in the name of a newspaper or magazine, a political party, a religious group, or a department of government.

_____

_____

Circle each letter which should be capitalized in the sentences below:

my report was called "the french as aids in the american revolution." I wrote it last february. i entered it in the contest of the daughters of the american revolution, which is a national organization. Later i read an account of the contest in The new york times. a boy from arlington, vermont, won the first prize. he later went to washington, d.c.

When asked what he enjoyed most on his trip, the winner replied, "i think it was seeing the lincoln statue by daniel c. french in the lincoln memorial. i saw another of french's statues, 'the minute man,' when i was in concord, massachusetts, last july. i don't know which i really like better."

NAME _____   DATE _____

Capital Letters

Below are some rules for capitalization which you already know. After each statement write at least two examples of the rule.

Use a Capital Letter

13. When the words north, south, east, and west are used to name a particular part or section of a country.

_____

_____

14. When the words north, south, east, and west indicate direction only, they do not begin with capital letters. Give examples.

_____

_____

15. To begin the abbreviations of names of places, businesses, states, countries, months, and points of the compass.

_____

_____

Circle the letters which should be capitalized in the words below.

dr. f. n. morris	northwestern university	denver	yours truly,
lake erie	new testament	dear sir:	english
wabash river	june	algebra	island
kansas	manchester chronicle	america	continent
state	rocky mountains	hawaii	asia
u.s.a.	e.	s.w.	raleigh, n.c.
south shore drive	street	newsweek	republican party

Use the correct word in each of the following sentences. Indicate in the space to the right of each sentence how the word is used. Study the examples before you begin.

The Pacific Ocean is west (west, West) of California. <u>direction</u>
He visited Yellowstone Park while he was in the West (west, West). <u>section of country</u>

1. Our garden is _____ (east, East) of our garage. _____
2. Mexico is _____ (south, South) of California. _____
3. He visited in the _____ (south, South) last month. _____
4. He lives _____ (north, North) of the school. _____
5. The route of the Pony Express was through the _____
   (southwest, Southwest). _____

NAME _____   DATE _____

Capital Letters

Below are some rules for capitalization which you already know.
After each statement write at least two examples of the rule.

Use a Capital Letter

16. To begin the names of school subjects which are formed from
    the names of countries.

_____

_____

17. To begin words formed from the names of countries, con-
    tinents, and other proper nouns. Such words are called proper
    adjectives.

Group I	*Group II*
Europe _____	America _____
Canada _____	Mexico _____
England _____	Peru _____
Turkey _____	Boston _____
France _____	Italy _____
Spain _____	China _____
Asia _____	Africa _____

Here is a new rule to add to your list for the use of capital letters.

Use a Capital Letter

18. To begin each new topic in a topic outline or each new sentence in a sentence outline.

My Autobiography

Topic Outline	Sentence Outline
1. My ancestors	1. I can trace my ancestors through records kept by Great-Aunt Clara.
A. Relatives from Europe	
1. Grandfather Ellis from England	A. The family came from Europe in 1906.
2. Grandfather Lucain from France	1) My mother's family came from England.
	2) My father's family came from France.

Notice, that in the sentence outline, each statement is followed by a period.

NAME _____ DATE _____

English Test

Circle each letter which should be capitalized in the sentences below.

1. on our tour of jonesboro we visited the following places: keeneland, goodheart, castlewood park, and bryan station springs.
2. the total number of county schools in campbell county is 8,494.
3. there are 1,140 students enrolled at western junior high school.
4. at the university of smithville 5,636 students are enrolled.
5. dianne davidson, a student in our class, lives at 1640 lakewood drive, jonesboro, virginia.
6. the principal of western junior high school is mr. jones.

7. some of the students of our class are methodists.
8. one of the newspapers published in our community is the "jonesboro leader."
9. he lives south of jonesboro.
10. in our english class we are learning how to write good reports.
11. the "frolics," a talent show, will be held at the western senior high school auditorium on monday and tuesday, november 22 and 23.
12. the school subjects which we are studying are science, english, geography, history, mathematics, and spelling.

NAME _____   DATE _____

English Test

(Punctuation and Capitalization)

Punctuate and capitalize the following sentences correctly.

1. there are thirty-seven students in miss smith's class
2. students please listen to these announcements very carefully said mr jones
3. catherine ward a student of our class walks to school each day
4. in literature we have read the following selections: a spanking's worth trick or treat halloween eve and hans christian andersen
5. some of the things which we have studied about in english are: interviewing writing business letters telephone manners and making good written reports
6. judy barbara wayne peter catherine dianne anne and john are some of the students in our class
7. thanksgiving day is on thursday november 22
8. our class brought apples pears beans corn apple sauce and other things for thanksgiving baskets
9. oh why don't some students study their lessons
10. miss smith our teacher spoke to dr s w richards' class at goodheart college tewksbury virginia last wednesday
11. hurrah we won the game

12. the frolics a talent show given at the western senior high school auditorium on november 22 and 23 was very entertaining
13. the outstanding types of work with which special service workers are concerned are: government education health religion communication recreation and other personal and business services
14. there are ten seventh grade classes at western junior high school
15. moreover we must study if we are to make a's
16. john please close the door said the teacher
17. do not fold your english papers when you have finished with this test
18. mary said i do not know the answer to the question

Geography Test

I. Complete each of the following sentences with the correct item from the list below. The same item may be used more than once.

United States	mass production	cooperation
Industrial Revolution	rural	Brazil
commission men	urban	trade
labor	capital	2500 or more

1. It refers to the country. _____
2. It refers to the city. _____
3. More than half the people of the world live in this kind of area. _____
4. It is one of the countries in which urban people outnumber rural. _____
5. All places of this size or over are listed as cities in the United States Census reports. _____
6. It refers to the millions of dollars required to build and begin operating a factory. _____
7. It refers to the thousands of workers needed to run the plant. _____

8. They offer the animals for sale at the stockyards and are paid by the owners for doing this. _____

9. The making of thousands or millions of identical products is called _____.

10. With this change came great improvements in industry, which in turn affected the growth of cities. _____

_____

II. Write <u>L</u> in the blank before each item that names a product of light manufacturing. Write <u>H</u> before those that name products of heavy manufacturing.

_____ 11. Women's clothing
_____ 12. Tractors
_____ 13. Automobiles
_____ 14. Jewelry
_____ 15. School buses

III. Choose *five* of the following and write a complete sentence to answer each question. Write your answers on a separate sheet of paper.

16. What is household manufacturing?
17. What is the difference between New York and Greater New York?
18. Name four of the five things or essentials which every city needs in order to survive.
19. What is manufacturing?
20. How do cities differ?
21. Name the countries in which the four great clusters of urban population are located.

IV. BONUS QUESTION: Tell what the Industrial Revolution was, and describe its effect upon cities.

Geography Test

NAME _____   DATE _____

I. Complete the following sentences with the correct word or words.

    1. The exchange of goods is called _____.

    2. Every town and city has a _____ where trade is carried on.

    3. When goods are exchanged without the use of money, it is called _____.

    4. Most of the world's trade involves the use of _____ _____.

    5. Trade carried on by businesses which buy goods from the producers or manufacturers in large quantities and sell them chiefly to retail stores is called _____.

    6. Selling goods in small quantities directly to the consumer is called _____ trade.

    7. Goods which are carried abroad to other countries are known as _____.

    8. Exchange of goods between nations is known as _____ _____ trade.

    9. Trade between countries is not simple, but very _____ _____.

    10. Goods which are brought into a country from other countries are called _____.

II. Circle the T if the statement is true; circle the F if it is false.

    T. F. 11. World transportation has brought about the disappearance of all "lands of isolation."

    T. F. 12. The Industrial Revolution was the time when men invented new kinds of machines and developed new kinds of power to run them.

    T. F. 13. Transportation is the vital link between the producer and the consumer.

    T. F. 14. The three great water highways used for transportation purposes are rivers, lakes, and oceans.

T. F. 15. The United States is the only country which has good transportation.

T. F. 16. Man-made waterways, called canals, were built to connect one waterway with another.

T. F. 17. In nearly every community there are people who make a living from transportation.

T. F. 18. Some areas of the oceans are little traveled, while in others there are heavily traveled shipping routes.

T. F. 19. Because man can travel so fast, it is said that he lives in a shrinking world.

T. F. 20. Partly finished goods are products which have gone through one or more manufacturing processes but are not ready for the consumer.

Geography Test

I. In front of each of the following names of city buildings, write the name of a special-service work done there, such as health, government, education, communication, etc.

_____ 1. Public library

_____ 2. City hospital

_____ 3. Police station

_____ 4. Elementary school

_____ 5. Telephone exchange

_____ 6. Art gallery and museum

_____ 7. Church

_____ 8. Dental clinic

_____ 9. Courthouse

_____ 10. Radio station

II. Circle the T if the statement is true; circle the F if it is false.

T. F. 11. Each person in the United States is affected by the government.

T. F. 12. Government services are financed by taxes of various kinds.

T. F. 13. It is possible to measure exactly how educated a person is.

T. F. 14. In proportion to the population, the United States has one telephone for every two people.

T. F. 15. The problem of housing is found only in big cities with tenements and crowded apartments.

T. F. 16. The United States and Mexico have higher percentages of literacy than any other countries in the world.

T. F. 17. Because of the great gift of written and spoken language, we can draw upon the experience of others.

T. F. 18. More than half of the people on the earth are illiterate.

T. F. 19. Only people who are educated can understand and create the kind of government which is necessary today.

T. F. 20. In planning a city, air transportation presents one of the most difficult problems.

T. F. 21. Special-service workers include approximately three-fourths of all the workers in our country.

Electric Meters

Electric current is measured in kilowatt hours by meters that usually have four dials. A kilowatt hour is the amount of current used by ten 100-watt lamps in one hour. To read the meter begin at the left and take the number that the pointer last passed, except on the last dial at the right. For that dial, take the number nearest the pointer. The meter above shows 2383. This means that 2,383 kilowatt hours of current have been used.

Read the electric meters below.

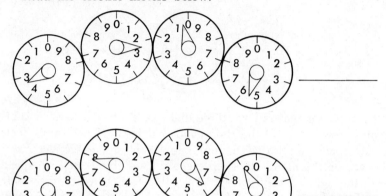

_____

_____

Draw the hands on the dials below showing the following readings:

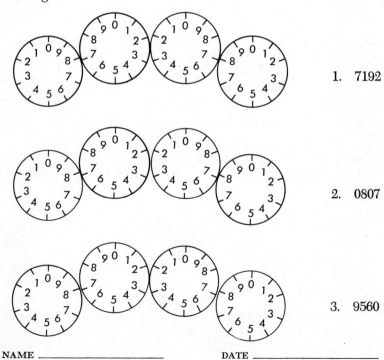

1. 7192

2. 0807

3. 9560

NAME _____   DATE _____

Gas Meters

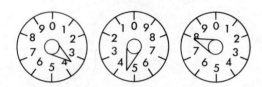

Most gas meters have three dials, as illustrated here. A complete revolution on the right-hand dial means 1,000 cubic feet; each space on this dial, therefore, represents 100 cubic feet. Each space on the middle dial represents 1,000 cubic feet; each space on the left dial represents 10,000 cubic feet. In reading the left and middle dials, use the numbers which the arrows have passed. On the right dial, use the number nearest the dial. The reading of the meter above is 34,800. On most gas bills this is written 348.

Read the gas meters below.

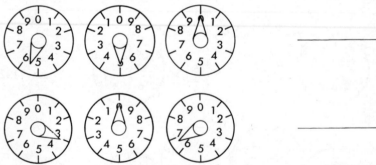

Draw the hands on the dials below showing the following readings:

1. 55,500

2. 12,300

3. 78,900

4. 30,000

NAME _____   DATE _____

Meters

NAME _____   DATE _____

Fill in the blanks.

1. The _____ _____ is the unit for measuring electricity.
2. The electric meter has _____ dials.
3. The unit for measuring the amount of gas we use is _____

   _____.
4. The gas meter has _____ dials.
5. What are two ways of telling the difference between a gas meter and an electric meter?

   a. _____
   b. _____
6. If the Gabbard family's electric meter read 3,987 KWH on September 1 and 4,321 KWH on October 1, how many kilowatt hours of electricity did they use?   Answer _____
7. If the Russel Family's gas meter read 54,600 cubic feet on October 1 and 58,400 cubic feet on November 1, how many cubic feet of gas did they use?   Answer _____

Graphs

NAME _____   DATE _____

1. Name three kinds of graphs.

        1. _____
        2. _____
        3. _____

2. Name two things which are on every graph.

        1. _____
        2. _____

3. Round off the following numbers to the nearest hundreds.

        1. 313 _____
        2. 1644 _____
        3. 777 _____
        4. 955 _____
        5. 2108 _____

4. Suzanne decided to record her weekly spelling grades on a graph. Her grades were:

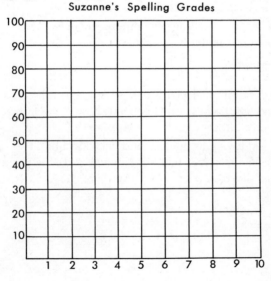

Suzanne's Spelling Grades

1st week— 60
2nd week— 70
3rd week— 50
4th week— 90
5th week— 80
6th week— 80
7th week— 90
8th week—100
9th week— 80
10th week—100

She rounded off her grades to the nearest tens, and started her graph. Finish it for her.

This graph shows automobile fatalities in this country during daylight and darkness for the period 1930–1939. Answer the following questions about it, and place the answer in the blank at the right.

a. In how many years were the number of fatalities greater during darkness than during daylight? _____

b. About how many fatalities during darkness occurred in 1932? _____ in 1935? _____

c. About how many fatalities occurred in the daytime in 1930? _____ in 1939? _____

d. In which year was the difference between the two groups the greatest? _____ the least? _____

Automobile Fatalities

During Daylight and Darkness, 1930–1939

Weather

NAME _____ DATE _____

Find definitions for the following:

1. weather	8. clouds	15. hail
2. climate	9. cirrus clouds	16. precipitation
3. wind	10. stratus clouds	17. isobars
4. saturated	11. cumulus clouds	18. isotherms
5. dew point	12. thunderheads	19. high
6. dew	13. nimbus	20. low
7. frost	14. sleet	21. evaporation

22. condensation	32. rain gauge	42. weather map
23. local storms	33. snow gauge	43. ice
24. tornadoes	34. theodolite	44. moisture
25. hurricanes	35. radiosonde	45. atmosphere
26. typhoons	36. waterspout	46. mist
27. thermographs	37. humidity	47. hygrometer
28. barometer	38. water vapor	48. water cycle
29. thermometer	39. fog	49. Weather Bureau
30. wind vane	40. lightning	50. meteorologist
31. anemometer	41. thunder	

We are studying the above words connected with a study of weather, since weather plays such a big part in the activities of the citizens of a community and we are at this time studying "our community."

Science

(Chapters 16, 17, and 18)

NAME _____   DATE _____

You may use your science book to find the answers to the following, if you so wish; however, if you do use the book, please write the number of the page on which you found the answer.

1. Meteors flash because they get [1] going through the air.   1. _____
2. Meteors have flashed as high as 150 miles above the ground; therefore there must be [2] that high.   2. _____
3. The higher you go, the [3] the air becomes.   3. _____
4. Air moves [4] where it is heated and   4. _____
5. [5] where it is cold.   5. _____
6. Cold air is [6] than hot air; therefore it can flow under and lift hot air. The flowing of   6. _____
7. the cold air is [7].   7. _____
8. Sometimes a whirling storm is set up by air becoming heated so quickly over a hot region

that cooler air blows in with violence. A
whirling storm of this nature is a [8].

8. _____

9. About four-fifths of the air is [9].

9. _____

10. About one-fifth of the air is [10].

10. _____

11. The gas that fills the red tubes in electric
signs is [11]; a small part of the air is this
gas.

11. _____

12. There is more [12] in the air near the sea-
coast than there is in the interior of a con-
tinent.

12. _____

13. When carbon unites with the oxygen of the
air, a new substance [13] is formed.

13. _____

14. [14] is the union of oxygen with another substance.

14. _____

15. Your normal body temperature is [15].

15. _____

16. We should breathe through the [16]

16. _____

17. rather than through the [17].

17. _____

18. Growths in the rear of the nasal passages are
called [18].

18. _____

19. The best temperature for our classroom is

19. _____

20. between [19] and [20] degrees.

20. _____

21. We are told that a [21] between 50 and

21. _____

22. [22] 60 per cent is best for us; however, a
range between 40 to 70 is acceptable.

22. _____

23. When the humidity is 100% the air is said
to be [23].

23. _____

24. A colorless and odorless gas, [24], even in
small quantities is dangerous to us.

24. _____

25. Supplying fresh, cleaned air, cleared of dust,
at the proper humidity and temperature is
[25].

25. _____

BONUS: If you wish to answer the bonus questions, please do so
on a separate sheet of paper and write your answers in complete
sentences.

1. Does the air weigh more or less at the bottom of a deep mine
than it does at the surface of the earth?

2. It was noticed that small articles of clothing washed in a certain home at night were dry in the morning in the wintertime but not in the summer. Explain.

3. How does nature offer you some protection from dust and cold air?

4. Why does a burning candle go out when it is lowered into a jar?

5. How does nature use oxidation in our bodies?

6. How does industry make use of oxidation?

7. Why is there less air up above us than there is around us?

8. Describe air.

9. We breathe out carbon dioxide. How is it formed?

10. Why does oil on a knife blade keep it from rusting?

Science—Air

NAME _____   DATE _____

I. If the following statements are true, write *true* in the space at the left; if they are false, write *false* in the space:

_____ 1. Air is an invisible mixture of gases that surround the earth and forms its atmosphere.

_____ 2. We can see air.

_____ 3. Air is composed of oxygen, nitrogen, carbon dioxide, neon, and traces of other gases.

_____ 4. The gases in the air are odorless.

_____ 5. Nitrogen is one of the gases in the air.

_____ 6. Oxygen has a sweet smell.

_____ 7. Air is necessary for life.

_____ 8. There is more nitrogen than oxygen in the air.

_____ 9. Air has no weight.

_____ 10. The pressure of air decreases as we go higher.

_____ 11. Mountain climbing is difficult because the air is denser at high altitudes.

_____ 12. Air is essential to fire.

_____ 13. A room is most comfortable at a temperature of 98.6 degrees.

_____ 14. Warm air is heavier than cool air.
_____ 15. Warm air moves downward.

II. Write the number of the correct answer in the space at the left.

_____ 16. Air is the (1) solid, (2) gaseous, (3) liquid part of the earth.
_____ 17. Nearly four-fifths of the air is (1) nitrogen, (2) oxygen, (3) neon.
_____ 18. (1) neon, (2) helium, (3) carbon dioxide is the part of the air that plants use.
_____ 19. Air pressure means (1) weight of air, (2) humidity of the air, (3) speed of the air.
_____ 20. (1) atmosphere, (2) wind, (3) air pressure is air in motion.
_____ 21. When air is heated, it (1) stays at the same level, (2) rises, (3) descends.

III. In the space at the left, write the word or words needed to complete the following:

_____ 22. _____ is a mixture of gases that surrounds and is a part of the earth.
_____ 23. _____ is the gas that forms about one-fifth of the air.
_____ 24. _____ is water in the air in the form of gas.
_____ 25. The higher the air rises, the less _____ there is.
_____ 26. Divers and mountain climbers carry _____ with them to supply the necessary air for breathing.

IV. From the following list of words, choose the one associated with each phrase below and write it in the space provided:

oxygen   carbon dioxide   dust and smoke   nitrogen   helium
fire   air   air pressure   ventilation   siphon

<table>
<tr><td>_____</td><td>27. A mixture of invisible gases</td></tr>
<tr><td>_____</td><td>28. Makes up about one-fifth of the air</td></tr>
<tr><td>_____</td><td>29. Makes up about four-fifths of the air</td></tr>
<tr><td>_____</td><td>30. Will not burn without oxygen</td></tr>
<tr><td>_____</td><td>31. Impurities found in the air</td></tr>
<tr><td>_____</td><td>32. Exchanging impure air for fresh air</td></tr>
<tr><td>_____</td><td>33. Gas that plant leaves take from the air</td></tr>
<tr><td>_____</td><td>34. Weight of the air</td></tr>
</table>

Science—Weather

NAME _____   DATE _____

GEOGRAPHY BOOK: Read from page 64 through page 70; refer to the pages and maps as instructed.

Read from page 372 through page 377, and study the maps on those pages.

After you have read the above material, answer the questions below; you may refer to the book if you wish; if you do so, include the page numbers where your information was located.

1. The word [1] refers to the condition of the air at a particular time.   1. _____
2. The word [2] refers to weather conditions in any one area over long periods of time.   2. _____
3. Special kinds of maps, called [3], tell about rainfall, temperature, and other weather information.   3. _____
4. There are more than [4] weather stations in the United States.   4. _____
5. Any form of falling moisture is known as [5].   5. _____
6. The average annual rainfall is the [6] rainfall.   6. _____
7. When we know the high and low temperatures for a certain day, we can figure the middle, or [7], temperature.   7. _____
8. The [8] on the weather maps answer some very important questions about the weather.   8. _____

9. In lands south of the equator, January is [9] than July.

9. _____

10. Seasons on the other side of the equator are [10] from ours.

10. _____

11. The earth turns, or revolves, on its axis [11] every 24 hours.

11. _____

12. When our side of the earth is turned away from the sun, it is [12].

12. _____

13. It takes one [13] for the earth to take a trip around the sun.

13. _____

14. In the summer the sun is [14] in the sky than in winter.

14. _____

15. On the annual rainfall maps on pages 372–373 the smallest amount of rainfall shown is [15].

15. _____

16. On the same maps the largest amount of rainfall shown is [16].

16. _____

17. Referring to the same maps, we see that most of the land of the world has less than [17] inches of rainfall.

17. _____

18. The three regions that stand out with very
19. heavy rainfall are [18], [19], and [20].
20.

18. _____
19. _____
20. _____

21. We can notice that all of the lands mentioned in 18, 19, and 20 are [21] lands.

21. _____

22. Most of the eastern half of our country has [22] rainfall.

22. _____

23. Hail and snow are measured after they are [23].

23. _____

24. When the noon sun is low in the sky, the weather is much [24] than when the sun is high in the sky.

24. _____

25. When it is summer south of the equator, it is winter [25] of it.

25. _____

26. Many lands near the [26] are hot both in summer and winter.

26. _____

27. The air tends to get [27] the higher one goes
above sea level.   27. _____

28. On the July temperature maps, hot weather
indicates temperatures of [28] degrees or
more.   28. _____

29. On the same map, cold weather is [29]
degrees or less.   29. _____

30. Winters in southern South America, southern Africa, and Australia are not as cold as
those in northern North America and Eurasia. The chief reason for this is that North
America and Eurasia extend much farther
from the [30].   30. _____

BONUS: In your geography book there is a description of a certain
kind of wind which changes with the seasons. In the
summers the winds are wet, blowing from the sea to the
land; in the winters the winds are dry, blowing from the
land to the sea. Farmers must keep these winds in mind
when planning their crops and for other work. What is
the name of these winds, in which country are they found,
and on which page did you find the answer? (Remember,
you have three things to answer).

Science—Weather

NAME _____   DATE _____

I. If the following statements are true, write True in the space
provided; if they are false, write False in the space provided.

1. Clouds are tiny drops of water which
can float in the air.   1. _____

2. Cirrus clouds are featherlike clouds very
high in the sky.   2. _____

3. Stratus clouds look like puffy cotton.   3. _____

4. Nimbus clouds are rain clouds.   4. _____

5. Thunderheads are dark cumulus clouds.   5. _____

6. Clouds that appear to be in layers are stratus clouds.

6. _____

7. A daily weather forecast is of great help to a farmer.

7. _____

8. You must be a scientist to read and understand a weather map.

8. _____

9. Climate and weather are exactly the same thing.

9. _____

10. A fog is clouds found very high in the sky.

10. _____

11. A barometer is an instrument used to measure air pressure.

11. _____

12. Water may be found as a liquid, a gas, or a solid.

12. _____

13. A meteorologist is a weather man.

13. _____

14. Saturated air contains all the moisture it can hold.

14. _____

15. A rain gauge measures the amount of snow which falls.

15. _____

II. Write the number of the correct answer in the space provided:

16. Condensation is generally caused by a change in temperature from (1) warm to cool, (2) warm to hot, (3) cold to hot.

16. _____

17. Snow, rain, hail, and sleet are forms of (1) condensation, (2) evaporation, (3) precipitation.

17. _____

18. When water vapor condenses, it (1) rises, (2) stays where it is, (3) falls.

18. _____

19. When raindrops are carried upward into cold air and freeze into ice, (1) dew, (2) hailstones, (3) frost will be formed.

19. _____

20. Clouds lose their moisture by (1) pollution, (2) condensation, (3) evaporation.

20. _____

III. Complete the following in the spaces provided:

21. The conditions of the air at any one time and place make up what we call the [21]. 21. _____

22. A [22] gives a picture of weather conditions over the entire country. 22. _____

23. An [23] tells the speed of the wind. 23. _____

24. [24] storms affect only a small area. 24. _____

25. The constant processes of evaporation and [25] are the water cycle. 25. _____

IV. From the group of words in Column A, select the one associated with each phrase in Column B and write its number in the space provided.

Column A	*Column B*	*Answer*
1. barometer	26. records temperature of	
2. rain	the air	26. _____
3. weather forecast	27. sends out storm warnings	27. _____
4. Weather Bureau	28. invisible water in the air	28. _____
5. water vapor	29. condensed water vapor	
6. thermometer	falling from clouds	29. _____
7. snow	30. a statement of future	
	weather conditions	30. _____

V. Why is the weather of great importance to any community?

LETTER TO PARENTS

Western Junior High School
Jonesboro, Virginia
November 30, 1954

Again I want to tell you some of the things our class has been doing.

You probably remember that we participated in the tour of Jonesboro and Campbell County made by the entire seventh grade. Before we made the trip, we appointed a committee to study the places we were to visit and to report to the class. They chose to use our conference room as a studio to present a TV program by using our school's PA system; the program was very interesting and informative. Later we visited Keeneland, Goodheart College, where we heard about the history of the college and saw the Patterson cabin, Gratz Park with its many famous old homes, Castlewood Park, and Bryan's Station Springs. The trip was an introduction to our unit entitled "Living in Our Community."

Following the trip we reviewed the places we visited and our reasons for visiting them and filled out a questionnaire on the opportunities offered us by our community and our responses to them. We found many things we did not know about our home town; so we listed the things in which we were interested and organized committees to locate the desired information; among these are Education and Religion, Recreation, Police and Fire Departments, Transportation and Communication, Horses and Stock Farms, and Vital Statistics. We listed the places where we could find the information and ways we could share it with the class. In English we learned how to capitalize and punctuate our written reports, how to conduct an interview, and how to outline our information. We also read several stories with rural and urban backgrounds. We kept a list of words related to our community and used those words for our spelling list. In geography we read and discussed material entitled "A Living in Town and City"; this gave us a background for our own community. In math we learned to read electric and gas meters and to figure bills; we also discussed bar and line graphs and used local school enrollments, the population of Jonesboro since 1860, the increases in the population by ten-year periods, and the city's daily high, low, and normal temperatures in constructing our graphs. In science we discussed air and weather and their influences on the activities of a community. We saw several films and one filmstrip: "Our Homes and Our Communities," "Community Governments: How they Operate," "How Weather Forecasts are Made," "The Junior Citizen," "River in the Way" (shows how natural gas is piped to us), and "Metropolitan New York." Our two student teachers have cooperated in teaching this unit. This study will be completed Friday, December 3, and at the end of the next six weeks I shall report to you our culminating activities.

During the six weeks we continued to work on our special math and spelling, according to the kind of work each of us needs. During American Education Week we wrote themes entitled "What Education Means to Me." During Book Week we had dramatizations, "Who am I?" using characters from favorite books, and reports on favorite books. Several girls made peep shows illustrating a scene from a story.

We participated in the annual hobby show sponsored by the seventh grade; our class had approximately sixteen entries. We had three representatives in the talent show sponsored by the PTA. We also filled a basket at Thanksgiving along with the other classes in our school.

The class and I appreciate the large number of parents who attended the last PTA and helped us to have the largest number in the seventh grade. We also appreciate the refreshments sent for our Halloween party.

Perhaps you will be interested in knowing that I spoke twice recently at Goodheart College: once to the Future Teachers of America and once to the class on Fundamentals in Secondary Education. I discussed the methods I use in evaluating the work of your youngsters.

Sincerely,

SPECIMEN PLAN V

History-American
Senior High School Resource Unit
Jacksonian Democracy

General Objective

To furnish experiences through which the pupils may find facts, face issues, and draw conclusions which make them worthy citizens of today, and, through opportunity for successful achievement, to create faith in themselves that will encourage them to assume civic obligations in the future.

Specific Objectives

I. Knowledges
   A. To develop knowledge of wholesome patriotism, from the study of nationalism.
   B. To develop knowledge and understanding of the Election of 1828.
   C. To develop knowledge and understanding of the forces of democracy evident during Jackson's administration.
   D. To develop knowledge and understanding of sectionalism.
   E. To develop knowledge and understanding of the influence of the frontier.
   F. To develop a sense of time relationship for this period.

II. Skills
   A. To develop ability to handle textbook material.
   B. To develop ability to read for information concerning the Jacksonian period and how it influenced the American life.
   C. To develop ability to interpret maps and pictures.

III. Attitudes
   A. To develop an appreciation of democracy, including the following related factors.
      1. Respect for the rights of others
      2. Obedience to law
      3. Willingness to abide by the decision of the majority
      4. Acceptance of the responsibilities and duties of citizenship
      5. Faith in the democratic process
      6. Love of country
   B. To develop interest in investigating, discussing, and acting upon questions of the Jacksonian era.
   C. To develop an historical attitude toward this period.
   D. To develop an appreciation of the necessity for group and individual ethics in the social studies.

Motivation—The Inaugural Scene

The scene at the inauguration of Andrew Jackson was indeed extraordinary. The day of inauguration, March 8, 1829, ten thousand visitors crowded into Washington. Droves of office seekers had come to town. Curiosity seekers were there in large numbers. There were "countrymen, farmers, gentlemen, mounted and dismounted, black and white." Some found their way into the Executive Mansion, where they "upset bowls of punch, broke the glasses, and stood with their muddy boots on the satin-covered chairs" to catch a glimpse of their hero. They saw a man sinewy and erect. He had a deep scar on his face. He bore himself with the air of a soldier. It was Jackson, "Old Hickory," exponent of frontier democracy, the hero of New Orleans, organizer of the Democratic Party and President (1829–1837).

Introduction

With the admission of new western states, a new type of politician appeared in Congress. These were men who believed not only in democracy but also in nationalism. To them it was an article of political faith that the United States was the greatest nation in the world. Their influence was seen in the War of 1812 when the Western "War Hawks," led by Henry Clay, demanded that the United States fight England. They called upon the government to spend money for internal improvements, especially for roads and canals that would make westward migration easier. The spirit of the West was well exemplified in the careers of two Westerners, Henry Clay and Andrew Jackson. Clay's career in Congress lasted from the War of 1812 until the Compromise of 1850, almost half a century.

The triumph of the Western ideas came with the election of Jackson in 1828. Jackson was a political descendant of Thomas Jefferson, a Democratic-Republican who had been succeeded in the presidency by Madison, who served two terms and who in turn was followed by Monroe, who also served two terms. All three of these presidents—Jefferson, Madison, and Monroe—belonged to the same party. Indeed, at the time of Monroe's first administration, party differences had practically disappeared so that there was really one political party. This period was called the Era of Good Feeling. But by the close of Monroe's second administration, differences of opinion among the Democrats began to appear. In 1824 there were four candidates for the presidency. The chief ones were: John Quincy Adams, member of the famous Adams family of Massachusetts; Andrew Jackson, Old Hickory, the hero of New Orleans; Henry Clay; and William Henry Crawford. The election, failing to give a majority to any one of the candidates, was settled by a vote of the House of Representatives. Clay now threw his support in the House to Adams, with the result that Adams became the sixth president of the United States.

The defeat of Jackson made the Western Democrats very bitter. Already differences of opinion had made their appearance among the Democrats; they differed on such questions as the extension of slavery, the protective tariff, the United States Bank, and internal improvements. Jackson and his supporters followed Thomas Jefferson's doctrine of strict construction of the Constitution. This group favored low tariffs and state banks rather than the United States Bank. As a political party, they became known simply as Democrats. The other division of the party adopted the party name of National Republican. John Quincy Adams and Henry Clay were the leaders of this party, which stood for high tariffs, internal improvements, and a National Bank. Both parties prepared for the campaign of 1828.

The presidential election in 1828 was in itself a democratic revolution. Andrew Jackson, the people's hero, was successful only after a spirited campaign. Jackson was the first president from the West and really the first self-made man to become president. All his predecessors in office had been men of means and members of distinguished families. But Jackson was a frontiersman and Indian fighter from the backwoods. The election of a man of the frontier type was in itself a revolutionary change. A new method of nominating candidates and campaigning for election was introduced. The old method of nominating a candidate for the presidency was by Congressional caucus. A caucus is simply a private meeting of legislators to select candidates or to discuss measures.

The Congressional caucus gave Congress control over the nomination of presidential candidates.

The Western States objected to this method of nominating candidates, believing that the nomination should be made by the state legislatures. A change also occurred in the method of winning popular support. Jackson's campaign of 1828 was the first modern campaign. His supporters ,brought him before the public whenever possible; newspapers were induced to print articles about him. So cleverly had Jackson's friends planned his campaign that he easily won. He repeated his success again in 1832, running against Henry Clay. In this election, still further and more democratic changes were made in the selection of the candidates. Instead of obtaining the nomination through a Congressional caucus or through the action of state legislatures, a nominating convention was called, made up of committees from each state. It was the duty of this convention to select candidates and to advise on issues.

During Jackson's period in office, three major issues confronted the country: (1) the tariff, (2) nullification, that is, the right of the states to declare void a law passed by Congress, and (3) the United States Bank.

Activities—Teacher

1. After the introduction, use Morrison's *Test, Teach, Test* method in addition to a short achievement quiz to determine where each student stands.

2. Read and write on blackboard: "For the first time in American history, the democratic masses had put their man in the White House" (Faulkner's American Political and Social History, p. 190). List the previous presidents.

3. Show seventeen-minute color film, "Old Hickory." (Teaching Film Custodians, Inc.)

4. Assign several reports covering Jackson's life before 1824. Confer with students who are to report, and suggest points to be included.

5. The controversy over the tariff issue of 1832–1833 is an example of the continuing dispute concerning the power of the federal government over that of the states. One way to point up this quarrel of the 1830's and, at the same time, to accustom pupils to use primary sources is to have a dialogue or informal debate between two able groups of students, who must base their arguments on copies of actual documents as recorded in Commager's *Documents of American History*. At the end of this dialogue, have members of the class summarize the main arguments on both sides.

6. To encourage research on the broad topic of Jacksonian democracy, it may be challenging to plan one or two periods for oral reports.

   Provide a series of topic sentences such as the following:

   a. Voting qualifications became more liberal.
   b. The nominating convention replaced the caucus.
   c. The "Kitchen Cabinet" was a better reflection of the people than the official cabinet.
   d. More office holders became subject to election and fewer to appointment.
   e. The spoils system became an issue.
   f. Workers of Philadelphia organized in 1828.
   g. Squatters' rights to land were recognized.
   h. Was Jackson's inauguration "the people's day" or "the reign of King Mob"?
   i. The American Peace Society was established in 1828.
   j. The American Temperance Union was organized in 1833.
   k. Dorothea Dix pioneered in prison reform and the treatment of the insane.
   l. "New Harmony" was settled in Indiana in 1825.
   m. Horace Mann promoted education in Massachusetts.
   n. Henry Barnard promoted education in New York.

   Allow several days so that pupils will have time to look up the materials for elaborating upon these topic sentences.

7. Immigration to the United States followed the ups and downs

of prosperity in America and reflected the economic and political conditions in Europe. Have the students draw a line graph or a chart showing the rise and fall of immigration to the United States during the nineteenth century, coloring in the period 1820–49. As the year's work progresses, later periods of history can be indicated with different colors. Figures for this activity may be found in the *World Almanac* or in the *Information Please* almanac.

8. Since this period of nationalism is replete with changes in American life, it may be helpful to make a summary table based on the political, economic, and social developments that are characteristic of this era. The following is the beginning of a table that will be developed much further. Start the chart on the chalk board, and fill it in from oral response.

Changes: 1816–1840

Political	*Economic*	*Social*
Reduction of property qualifications for voting	Formation of labor unions	Extension of popular education

Activities—Student

1. Discuss Jackson's Inauguration. The outcome of this discussion should be a readiness to appreciate what is meant when Jackson is referred to as the first President of the common people.

2. See film, "Old Hickory," to learn about the men with whom Jackson had dealings before and after becoming president.

3. Name special students to do assignments. The chief purpose will be to impress upon the class the fact that Jackson was really the "people's hero," not one on a pedestal, but one among them.

4. One group of students presents the arguments of the South on the subject of nullification as set forth in the "South Carolina Ordinance of Nullification." The other group of students then gives the arguments of Jackson and the advocates of national-

ism as stated in "Jackson's Proclamation to the People of South Carolina." The chairman of the first group replies by offering the ideas contained in "South Carolina's Reply to Jackson's Proclamation," following with the arguments contained in "South Carolina's Nullification of the Force Bill." Students will summarize the main arguments on both sides.

5. Write the letters A through N on small cards, and place them in a box. Students will draw out a card and speak not more than five minutes on the topic represented by the letter drawn. Class will vote to determine who made the best report.

6. Students will draw a line graph or a chart showing the rise and fall of immigration to the United States during the nineteenth century, coloring the part representing the period 1820–49. Students will make a comparison or a companion graph or chart showing the rise of population in the United States during the same period. Students will compare the proportion of the population rise due to natural increase with the rise due to immigration.

7. Students will make a chart showing the economical, political, and social developments that are characteristic of this era. Students, during review, will respond orally, completing the chart.

8. Students should understand the following terms as they are used in the text:

franchise	Jacksonian Era
nomination	shirt-sleeve diplomacy
convention	squatters
"bosses"	cheap currency
wildcat banks	removal of deposits
easy credit	"pet banks"
democracy	surplus
party machine	independent treasury

9. People and things to know about:

Workingmen's Party	William Henry Harrison
Spoils system	Martin Van Buren

"Old Hickory" .... "Tippecanoe and Tyler Too"
"Kitchen cabinet" .... John Tyler
Maysville Road .... Caroline Affairs
Specie Circular .... "King" Andrew
Anti-Masons .... Webster-Ashburton Treaty
Whigs ....

Evaluation

Examine each notebook for daily notes on outside readings, newspaper clippings, magazine articles, and other reading materials. Observe students' participation in group work to see if they were really doing something constructive and meeting their needs and goals. Give objective tests at intervals during this study to see if they were still working toward their objectives. Give essay test at the end of the unit to develop critical thinking. Observe the bulletin board to see if they were really getting good materials. Observe the action of pupils on the field trip to see if they were really meeting their needs and fulfilling their purposes. Give a few essay questions on a test, after considering all the other work that has been done, and grade the students "satisfactory" or "unsatisfactory."

On the following pages are exercises and tests that may be used in evaluating pupil progress on the learning experiences included in this unit.

Exercise I

Paragraph Meaning

Directions: Read the paragraph given below, and then fill in the outline form as follows: Make A the subject of the paragraph; make 1, 2, 3, etc., the main points; make Ex. a, b, c under the numerals the examples given.

"During the twelve years from 1763 to 1775, the colonies ceased to be contented with their relation to Great Britain and rose to the point of revolt. The main causes of this change of feeling were: the attempt to enforce the Navigation Acts, including the use of writs of assistance; taxation for revenue by Parliament, including the Stamp Act of 1765, the Townshend duties of 1767, and the tea duties in 1773; the belief that the colonists had certain rights under what they called The Constitution, noted arguments for which were framed by James Otis and Patrick Henry; the consciousness of common interest and ability to take care of themselves, shown in the Stamp Act Congress of 1765; irritation over the presence of troops in Boston, shown by the so-called Boston Massacre of 1770, and the Boston Tea Party of 1773, and by resistance in April, 1775."

A. _____

   1. _____

       Ex. a. _____

   2. _____

       Ex. a. _____

          b. _____

          c. _____

   3. _____

       Ex. a. _____

   4. _____

       Ex. a. _____

   5. _____

Exercise II

Use of Reference Materials

Below are two lists. One is a list of information you might want to find. The other is a list of general reference books. Place the letter of the reference book (A, B, C, etc.), in which you would find the information, in front of the information asked for.

_____ 1. To find the difference in meaning between two words.

_____ 2. To find the source of the Volga River.

_____ 3. To find the extent and altitude of the Rocky Mountains.

_____ 4. To locate the Aegean Sea.

_____ 5. To obtain a careful discussion of the rights and obligations of American citizenship.

_____ 6. To look up the main facts of Shakespeare's life.

_____ 7. To find out what has been written recently in magazines about evolution.

_____ 8. To obtain the address of a well-known living American author.

_____ 9. To obtain a good description of the Western Expansion Movement in the United States.

_____ 10. To find out who has won the Nobel Prizes.

_____ 11. To find out if there is a railroad connecting any two particular cities.

_____ 12. To find the total amount of wheat exported from the United States for the last ten years.

_____ 13. To find the number of students in American universities.

_____ 14. To look up information regarding Gothic Architecture.

_____ 15. To find out how many immigrants came to the United States last year.

_____ 16. To find the value of the exports and imports of the Port of New York for 1925.

_____ 17. To look up magazine articles about Mussolini.

_____ 18. To find out what other positions a certain man in public life has held.

_____ 19. To find a list of references on the Japanese Exclusion Act.

_____ 20. To find a complete technical, comparative discussion of the difference between a partnership and a corporation.

List of Reference Books

A. Atlas   F. An American History Book
B. The World Almanac   G. A Civics Book
C. Encyclopedia   H. English Language Dictionary
D. Who's Who in America   I. An Economics Book
E. Reader's Guide to Periodical Literature

Exercise III

Newspaper Reading

"A democratic government is a machine by which the people manage national and international affairs. To do this successfully, they must be well informed and intelligent. On the newspaper falls the task of keeping the public informed."

Directions: Read each statement carefully. If you consider a statement false, place a zero (0) sign in front of it. If a statement is true, place a plus (+) sign in front of it.

1. All newspapers in a city will tell the same news in the same way.
2. The newspaper is one of the most powerful means of creating public opinion.
3. Headlines are for the purpose of catching attention.
4. Facts and news are always the same thing.
5. One way to judge a newspaper's reliability is by determining the truthfulness and character of its headlines.
6. News, as published in our daily papers, always states the facts as they occur.
7. Most people read newspapers that mirror their own opinions and tastes.
8. Newspaper editorials are strictly factual articles.
9. A signed article in a newspaper is a news item expressing the writer's own opinions and conclusions.
10. All newspapers are reliable sources from which to draw facts.

_____ 11. Newspapers sometimes play upon the prejudices and fears of their readers to stir up opinion for a favored cause.

_____ 12. News reporters are highly trained, professional writers who seldom make mistakes.

_____ 13. Sometimes newspapers are used to stir up race prejudices by the use of scare headlines and partisan reports of the facts.

_____ 14. Most of a paper's news is secured indirectly through correspondents and news-collecting agencies.

_____ 15. Headlines frequently give an unfair estimate of the news contained in the article that follows.

_____ 16. A labor paper and a capitalist paper can be expected to publish identical accounts of a strike.

_____ 17. Cartoons of public events and persons in public life reflect the policies of the newspaper in which they are printed.

_____ 18. Newspapers are really run for the sole purpose of educating the public.

American History

Test—Eleventh Grade

1. What is a tariff?
2. What is a protective tariff?
3. What was President Jackson's "spoils system"?
4. For what two important things was the administration of Jackson noted?
5. What led to the panic of 1837?
6. Characterize Andrew Jackson.
7. Summarize the growth of sectionalism during this period.
8. Why was the westward movement so significant?
9. What connection can you point out between the extension of suffrage and the progress of popular education?
10. What is meant by internal improvements? Is it true that many of these were made before they were really needed? Explain.

11. Explain fully the following:

franchise	pet banks
nominating convention	Workingmen's Party
party machine	Ol' Hickory
squatters	specie circular

American History

Test—Eleventh Grade

Directions: Choose the word or phrase that will make each statement true, draw a line under it, and write the number that precedes it.

1. _____ President Jackson removed (1) many, (2) few, (3) none of the government officials.

2. _____ The spoils system referred to (1) cold-storage eggs, (2) United States Postage rates, (3) removal of officers not of the same political party as the president.

3. _____ A protective tariff protects the (1) farmer, (2) manufacturer, (3) miner.

4. _____ The (1) south, (2) north favored a high tariff to protect itself against being undersold by foreign manufacturers.

5. _____ (1) Clay, (2) Webster, (3) Hayne declared that the states had created the constitution.

6. _____ President Jackson agreed with (1) Hayne, (2) Calhoun, (3) Webster about the doctrine of nullification.

7. _____ One of the policies strongly supported by President Jackson was (1) the National Bank, (2) Civil Service, (3) the doctrine of nullification, (4) high protective tariff, (5) preservation of the Federal Union.

8. _____ The tariff of (1) 1816, (2) 1832, (3) 1828 lowered the duties on foreign goods.

9. _____ The state which threatened to withdraw from the Union in 1833 if the federal government attempted to enforce the tariff was (1) Massachusetts, (2) Georgia, (3) New York, (4) Virginia, (5) South Carolina.

10. Which of these terms is sometimes applied to the Jacksonian era?
    1. age of big business
    2. era of good feeling
    3. reconstruction period
    4. rise of the common man
11. Which of the following did President Andrew Jackson favor?
    1. abolition of the United States Bank
    2. immediate annexation of Texas
    3. doctrine of nullification
    4. civil-service reform
12. In this section, complete each statement by selecting the correct subject for it from the right-hand column. Place the letter of the subject in the space before the statement it completes.

    _____ 1. opposed Andrew Jackson   A. Robert Y. Hayne
                 in the United States Bank   B. Nicholas Biddle
                 controversy.   C. Daniel Webster
    _____ 2. argued that since the states   D. Henry Clay
                 had given the federal gov-   E. John C. Calhoun
                 ernment its powers, the
                 states could refuse to obey
                 a federal law which they
                 believed to be unconstitu-
                 tional.
    _____ 3. argued that the people had
                 created the constitution;
                 that it established a per-
                 manent union.

BIBLIOGRAPHY

Canfield, Leon H., and Howard B. Wilder, *The Making of Modern America*. Boston: Houghton, Mifflin Co., 1956 (Text).

Beard, Charles A., and Mary R. Beard, *The Making of American Civilization*. New York: Macmillan Co., 1939.

Casner, M. B., and S. P. McCutcheon, *The Story of American Democracy*. New York: Harcourt, Brace & Co., 1955.

Bragdon, H. W., and S. P. McCutcheon, *History of a Free People.* New York: Macmillan Co., 1955.

Cooperative American History Test, Cooperative Test Service, New York, N. Y.

Information Tests in American History, Education Test Bureau, Minneapolis, Minn., Grades 7–12.

Kansas American History Test, Kansas State Teachers College, Emporia, Kansas.

Test of Factual Relations in History, Educational Test Bureau, Minneapolis, Minn. Divided into six periods, Grades 10–12.

Devor, John W., *Learning Experiences for Student Teachers.*

Schorling, Raleigh, and Howard T. Batchelder, *Student Teaching in Secondary Schools.* New York: McGraw Hill, Inc., 1956.

Woodruff, Asahel D., *The Psychology of Teaching.* New York: Longmans, Green & Co., Inc., 1950.

D. Specimen Sociometric Study: Tenth Grade

AN ANALYSIS OF THE INTERPERSONAL RELATIONS IN A CLASS

The class which I have studied by means of observation and a sociometric test is a tenth-grade English class. The students average fifteen or sixteen years of age. They were classified as an honors group by tests of intelligence and reading ability administered to all students entering the high school last fall. The group did not, however, live up to the accomplishments expected of them as the only honors class in the school, and they have since been reclassified as college preparatory (the third rather than the fourth track in the curriculum). With one exception, the group is from one home room and has my supervising teacher for home room as well as English. The boy designated "1" on the diagrams is not from their home room; he was placed in this English class because of scheduling difficulties. It has been apparent to my supervising teacher and to me that this boy has neither the intelligence nor the background to compete successfully with the other members of this class. (Note on the sociometric chart that he was chosen by none of the other students, but received two definite rejections.)

When I administered the sociometric test to the class, I asked that they designate three people with whom they would like to work on a committee. This test is as likely to measure, therefore, pupil estimates of each other's ability as it is to determine close friendships. I do not think this detracts from the validity of the test; on the contrary, I believe it gives a fairly accurate picture of the pupils in their class or learning situation. Note that "21," a very smart and personable boy, was considered a good student and a hard-working committee member by most of the class. From my work with the class, I would conclude that "21" is actually the best choice the pupils could have made. He is very conscientious, industrious, and intelligent; he is earning an A in English this six weeks. I consider it significant, although not surprising, that the class as a whole made such a good judgment.

One must not discount, however, the degree to which personal friendships influence the results of such a test. On the sociogram it is easy to pick out the "best friends," indicated by mutual first choices: the girls "4" and "22," "9" and "20"; and the boys "2" and "3," "19" and "21."

I did not observe any strongly organized cliques in this class. Two factors may contribute to this situation: the racial mixture of the class (of the twenty-two students thirteen are Negro, eight are white, and one is Indian), and the great preponderance of boys (there are fifteen boys and only seven girls). As far as the racial situation goes, I feel that it has made some difference in determining the class relationships, but much less than might be expected. The most popular students included two white and two Negro boys. The officers of the class include two Negro girls and one white boy. Among the outer circle of least popular students were three white students, four Negro students, and the one Indian student. Three sets of the mutual first choices were among members of the same race, yet "9" is a Negro girl and "20" is white. The entire class includes only two white girls—"14" and "20"—yet neither chose the other at all. In this connection, it is interesting to note the rejections, which might indicate feelings of racial prejudice. This seems very unlikely, however, since the rejections of white boy "12" were both made by white boys, and the rejections of Negro boy "1" were made by a Negro girl and a white girl.

My idea that the small number of girls probably inhibits the growth of cliques is based on personal observation that girls of this age are most apt to form groups and consciously exclude others. This may or may not be true; in any case, with only seven girls in the class, it would not be logical to expect cliques. While I am discussing the girls in the class, I should like to point out another observation. Although several of the girls took boys as their first or second choices, no boys chose girls first, only one chose a girl second, and only two or three even chose girls third. Perhaps this indicates the situation peculiar to fifteen-year-olds: the girls are much more interested in the boys than the boys are in the girls.

There are several individuals in the class who require special mention. First, in all four cases the students in the inner, or most popular, circle of the sociogram do better than average work in the class. The girl who does the best work is "9"; she also was chosen several times. The students in the second and third circles all do average or better work. In every case, those students doing the poorest work in the class are in the outer circle. But the outer circle also contains "5" and "14" (shy girls who are average students) and "12" (the boy with the highest I.Q. in the class). Number "12" does not approach his capacity in English, but his work is satisfactory. His main trouble would seem to be a feeling of superiority. He manages to remain aloof from the class activities; he never volunteers any information during a class discussion.

Actually, the student in the class who constitutes the greatest discipline problem is "18," an immature, attention-seeking boy who constantly talks and argues. I was not surprised, therefore, that he was a first choice only for "17," a very shy boy who entered in the middle of the school term and has been successful neither in his schoolwork nor at making friends. The Indian boy, number "16," has had great difficulty with his schoolwork, chiefly because he has so little skill in communicating in English. In his case, I think improvement is shown even by the fact that no one rejected him as an undesirable committee member. Incidentally, he put on his preference sheet in the space where he could indicate a rejection, "Everyone is equal for me."

As I analyzed the sociogram and sociometric chart, I realized that a seating chart might be of interest and useful in substantiating several points. Note that the only students meriting rejections by other pupils—"1" and "12"—are isolated (by choice) in the seating arrangement. Note also that two sets of mutual first choices sit next to each other—"4" and "22," and "2" and "3"; the others do not. It is interesting that "15," in an isolated seat, is still one of the most popular students.

*   *   *

Making this sociometric study of my class has given me a better understanding of the class in general and several new insights of particular interest. First, I was much impressed by the sound judgment most of my class displayed in selecting coworkers. It would seem that status in this group is achieved by intelligence and hard work. Those students who were not cooperative with my supervising teacher and me were rejected by the group. But regarding these students, I can see more clearly how important it is for me to find activities in which they can experience success, so that they will not need to show off in order to gain the approval of their fellow students. I also feel a good deal more sympathetic with the shy student; in this connection, I see a similar need for providing experiences which will aid the shy pupil in building self-confidence. Most important, I have begun to see more clearly the connection between satisfaction in social relationships and success in school.

Sociometric Chart

3 pts.—first choice
2 pts.—second choice
1 pt.—third choice
R—rejection

Chosen

Chooser	1	2	3	4	5	6	7	8	9	10	11	12	13	14	15	16	17	18	19	20	21	22
1			1										2		3							
2			3				1											2				
3		3				1	2															
4			1																		2	3
5				1				2												3		
6			3												2							1
7								1	2						3							
8		2	3						1													
9				1							2									3		
10							3	1							2							
11	R			1				2														3
12								2	1											3		
13												R			1				2	3		
14	R			1																3		2
15								1	2											3		
16								1				2								3		
17								2							1			3				
18		3										1							2			
19					2							1								3		
20			1	2				3														
21												R	1		2					3		
22			1	3																	2	
No. times chosen	0	3	6	4	2	2	2	6	5	4	1	1	4	0	7	0	0	2	4	2	7	4
Total score	0	8	12	6	3	3	4	8	10	6	2	1	6	0	14	0	0	5	10	6	19	9

SOCIOGRAM

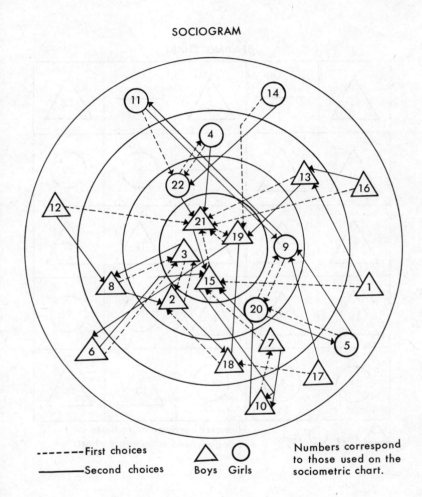

- - - - - - First choices   △ ○   Numbers correspond
————— Second choices   Boys Girls   to those used on the
                                         sociometric chart.

SEATING CHART

△ 15	——	△ 1	——	△ 12
△ 21	△ 7	——	○ 5	○ 20
△ 8	△ 2	△ 3	△ 18	△ 17
△ 10	△ 19	△ 6	○ 11	○ 9
○ 14	○ 4	○ 22	△ 13	△ 16

△ Boys ○ Girls

Numbers correspond to those on sociogram and sociometric chart.

E. Specimen Case Studies

SPECIMEN CASE STUDY I

Elementary

A. Information secured through a personal interview:

1. Name: Joe Doe
2. Age: 10
3. Residence: 804 Dolla Street, Anywhere
4. Pupil lives at home with both parents.
5. Father's name is William. He works as a traveling electrical repairman.
6. Mother's name is Geneva. She is a housewife, and she works as a saleslady for the Watkins' products.
7. There are two brothers and one sister in the family.
8. Joe's hobby is to make model planes, boats, and cars.
9. Joe has attended the Jefferson School. He transferred in 7–54 to Adams, where he is now. He left Jefferson because the family moved.
10. Pupil has never had a serious illness.

B. Data from the records or observations:

1. Previous marks in school have been satisfactory. He wants to do better in his marks because this will mean that his father will give him ten dollars in June (for the year).
2. In September he weighed 56 pounds, and now he weighs 65. Then he was 53 inches tall, and now 54 inches tall. He seems to be a little small for his age when compared with

339

other children. He has been absent only four days so far
this year.

3. Some of the results of his tests are:

    a. Metropolitan

Grade	CA	Score	Norm
3	7–2	1.7	1.9
4	10–1	5.7	4.8

    b. Age (years and months)   10.6

Word meaning	4.8
Average Reading	5.4
Spelling	4.8
Language	3.2
Average Arithmetic	5.2
Social Science	5.7
Science	4.8
Battery Median	5.0
I.Q.	105

    This test was taken 3–19–46.

4. He was born 2–19–36.

5. He attends the Christian Church. He was really display-
   ing a temper last year. A teacher suggested that his folks
   take him to church. The boy's behavior began to improve.
   Now he brags that he has not missed a Sunday for a whole
   year.

6. His attitude toward the teachers seems very good.

7. His favorite subject is mathematics.

8. School subject he most dislikes is geography.

9. While in the first or second grade he was hit by a car, and
   his mother became quite concerned, but the cause was
   said to be the boy's carelessness. He was warned and asked
   to be more careful.

10. He seems to like school fairly well and likes the teacher. It
    seems that last year he became quite a problem. He and
    another boy would climb out of the windows, run in and
    out of the room, and make themselves general pests. He
    also had quite a temper. When something would not go his

way, he would sit down on the floor and kick his heels and scream and cry. The teacher last year was put at her wit's end, because when this would happen, all the children would become upset. Then it was suggested that he go to another school and be separated from a friend of his. The family just happened to move, so that separated the two boys. Then, also, his mother started taking him to church. His teacher was wondering what he would do this year. I noticed that now he has thrown very few temper tantrums, and they have occurred mainly, I believe, when he did not understand something. At these times he went to his desk and threw everything off the top of it and then sat down. The other children seemed used to it and just ignored him. Then, later, he would go on and do his work. At home he mentioned that he "got mad, and so I went out in the kitchen and started to clean it." He finished cleaning it, and his mother was very proud of him.

11. His home life seems very involved and not too clear. It seems as though his father is gone most of the time, traveling on certain jobs. Joe is the oldest and therefore is given a great deal of responsibility when his father is gone. His father is kind to him, and he likes him very much. Sometimes his mother goes with his father and leaves the children with a cousin who comes to the house. He is never quite sure why she goes with him, but does not question it. If he is good, he will get to go to the movies twice on the next weekend after his mother and father return.

12. He seems to like his brothers and sister and is quite proud of them. He plays with them quite a bit. Every weekend the children go down to Doona and stay with their grandparents. Then on Sunday evening their folks come after them. Joe enjoys going there because he can go hunting and fishing and play with his many friends. Once he went swimming, but the next time he went, the water was down, and when he jumped in, he hit his head on the rocks. He cut it and had to have several stitches in his forehead.

He tells about hunting and killing a wild rabbit. He loves to go hiking with his grandfather.

13. Emotion, Mental Growth: Emotionally he is very hungry for honor, love, and recognition. He is a little immature for his age level. Mentally, he is up to his class level but not beyond it. He does not seem to work very hard to get his work in school; it seems to come very easily for him. He does not like to stay in his seat; as soon as he finishes his work, he is up and wandering around the room. If he is asked to give a report, he will get that and give a very pleasing report. He enjoys doing something for the teacher; but I believe this is because the teacher will thank him, giving him recognition.

C. What I believe could be done to help this boy:

1. More group work in school would help him to feel that he is wanted and give him a feeling of belonging. This might also help him to receive honor and be recognized.

2. I believe he needs more attention at home with his problems and his clothes. He is not always sent to school in clean clothes. He loves the companionship of an older person. This was partly filled by me, but mainly by his grandfather. I understand that in years past the mother has often neglected to prepare the children's meals and keep them in clean clothing.

3. Joe needs someone to talk with him and try to understand his needs.

4. He needs someone to help him analyze the reason why he gets angry and what to do when or if he does get angry. I asked him why he gets angry, and he sometimes does not know a real reason.

5. He needs to be kept from bad influences, such as his previous associate, until he learns more self-control.

D. Conclusions:

This boy has great possibilities, but needs more encouragement at home. He needs someone to keep an interest in him at school, to keep him studying. He needs to be taught more about religion so that he can understand it and live by it. The church has helped greatly in the past, and I believe that it can help him more in the future. He has greatly improved when it comes to temper, but he needs oceans of love and understanding.

SPECIMEN CASE STUDY II

Comparative Study
Two Mathematics Students
Senior High School

Personality Evaluation

1. Name____John Q. Public____   Age____15_____
   Residence_1221 Martin Road____   Telephone No. 4-7912_
2. Do you live at home with your parents?___with mother___
   If not, where do you live (with whom?) _____
3. Father's name_George A. Public_ Occupation Doctor (M.D.)
4. Mother's name__Mary K. Public_   Occupation__Housewife__
5. Number in family_5_(a) Brothers?_2_Living at home?_yes_
   (b) Sisters?_1_Living at home?_yes_
6. How far do you live from school? _____
7. How do you travel to school this summer?_Bike_
   During the regular school year?_Bike_
8. Do you work after school?_No_On weekends?_no_
   If so, what do you do?_study, develop my hobby, other activities_
9. Do you have any special interests or hobbies?_yes_
   If so, explain: Photography—school photographer_
10. Do you enjoy reading books?_yes_
    If so, what kind do you read most?_novels_. Sometimes?_mysteries_
11. Have you attended any other schools?_yes_
    If so, where and when?_Riverside, Lakeview, Central_
12. Why did you leave the previous schools?_graduation_
13. Do you belong to a church?_yes_

If so, what denomination? _Episcopal._ Do you attend:
Seldom? _____, often? ____X____, regularly? _____
(check one)

14. Have you had any serious illness? _yes_ If so, what? _pneu-
    monia_

15. Have you had any big problems during the time you have
    been in school or while you are out of school? _no_

16. What are the characteristics of your favorite teacher? _Grades
    according to what you make, with no personal favorites.
    Would explain anything._

17. Have you had any teachers that you did not like? _yes_
    If so, explain why you didn't like them. _Grades showed per-
    sonal favoritism._

18. Do you feel that your teachers have been friendly to you?
    yes

19. Do you get along with your classmates? _yes_

20. What is your favorite subject or subjects in school? _mathe-
    matics._ Why is this your favorite? _____

21. What is the school subject or subjects you most dislike?
    English. Why do you dislike it? _____

22. Do you plan to attend school after graduating from high
    school (college, university, trade school, music school, etc.)?
    yes

23. Will you please write a short autobiography of your life, giv-
    ing your interests, history, and anything interesting you have
    done, seen, or traveled to, etc.?

_Born Dec. 14, 1938, St. Louis, Mo. Shortly afterwards, moved
here. Father was in World War II._
_I have traveled to and vacationed in many parts of U.S. My inter-
ests lie chiefly in photography, electronics._
Plan to go to college after high school.

*[Following are two profile charts of John, which were plotted
while he was being observed in the classroom. It will be noticed*

that he showed a high percentage of application and was evidently interested in the work that he was doing.]

Profile Charts

Plotted by <u>John Doe</u>   School <u>Patrick Henry</u>

Date <u>   July 1, 1954   </u>   Date <u> July 1, 1954 </u>

John Q. Public (20-second intervals)

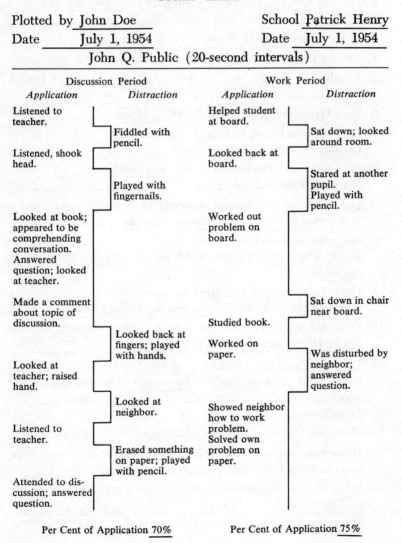

Discussion Period		Work Period	
Application	*Distraction*	*Application*	*Distraction*
Listened to teacher.		Helped student at board.	
	Fiddled with pencil.		Sat down; looked around room.
Listened, shook head.		Looked back at board.	
	Played with fingernails.		Stared at another pupil. Played with pencil.
Looked at book; appeared to be comprehending conversation. Answered question; looked at teacher.		Worked out problem on board.	
Made a comment about topic of discussion.			Sat down in chair near board.
	Looked back at fingers; played with hands.	Studied book.	
Looked at teacher; raised hand.		Worked on paper.	Was disturbed by neighbor; answered question.
	Looked at neighbor.	Showed neighbor how to work problem.	
Listened to teacher.		Solved own problem on paper.	
	Erased something on paper; played with pencil.		
Attended to discussion; answered question.			

Per Cent of Application <u>70%</u>   Per Cent of Application <u>75%</u>

Personality Evaluation

1. Name _Mary Jones_ Age __15__
   Residence _805 Oliver_ Telephone No. _9-1919_

2. Do you live at home with your parents? _yes, my mother_
   If not, where do you live (with whom?) _____

3. Father's name _J. H. Jones_ Occupation _____

4. Mother's name _Martha H. Jones_ Occupation _gift shop_

5. Number in family __4__ (a) Brothers? __1__ Living at home?
   yes (b) Sisters? __1__ Living at home? _yes_

6. How far do you live from school? __1 block__

7. How do you travel to school this summer? _walk_
   During the regular school year? _car_

8. Do you work after school? _no_ On weekends? _no_
   If so, what do you do? _____

9. Do you have any special interests or hobbies? _yes_
   If so, explain. _golf, swimming, records_

10. Do you enjoy reading books? _yes_
    If so, what kind do you read most? _novels_ Sometimes?
    classics

11. Have you attended any other schools? _yes_
    If so, where and when? _Riverside, Kellogg, E. Hi._

12. Why did you leave the previous schools? _because moved;_
    left E. Hi. because couldn't get subject I wanted.

13. Do you belong to a church? _yes_
    If so, what denomination? _Episcopal_ Do you attend sel-
    dom? _____, often? _____, regularly __X__
    (check one)

14. Have you had any serious illness? _no_ If so, what? _____

15. Have you had any big problems during the time you have
    been in school or while you are out of school? _no_

16. What are the characteristics of your favorite teacher? _friendly,_
    willing to help

17. Have you had any teachers that you did not like? _yes_

If so, explain why you didn't like them. <u>because she wasn't</u>
<u>understanding.</u>

18. Do you feel that your teachers have been friendly to you?
<u>yes</u>

19. Do you get along with your classmates? <u>yes</u>

20. What is your favorite subject or subjects in school? <u>History</u>
(<u>it's interesting</u>). Why is this your favorite? <u>English (always</u>
<u>liked teacher</u>).

21. What is the school subject or subjects you most dislike?
<u>Math, Latin</u> Why do you dislike it? <u>Because they are</u>
<u>difficult.</u>

22. Do you plan to attend school after graduating from high
school (college, university, trade school, music school, etc.)?
<u>junior college</u>

23. Will you please write a short autobiography of your life, giving your interests, history, and anything interesting you have
done, seen, or traveled to, etc.?

<u>I was born in Greenwich, Conn., on April 6, 1939. We lived there</u>
<u>for about 1 year, then my father was taken in the army, so we</u>
<u>moved around to different camps. When I was about 7, my</u>
<u>parents were divorced and we moved here to live because my</u>
<u>mother's family lives here. I have gone to 5 different schools</u>
<u>during the time I've lived here. Next year I plan to go to National</u>
<u>Cathedral School in Washington, D.C.</u>

[The profile charts for Mary, shown on the following page,
indicate a poor percentage of application during the class pe-
riods when she was being observed. This is probably due to lack
of interest in the subject matter being studied.]

Profile Charts

Plotted by John Doe   School Patrick Henry

Date   July 1, 1954   Date   July 1, 1954

Mary Jones (15-second intervals)

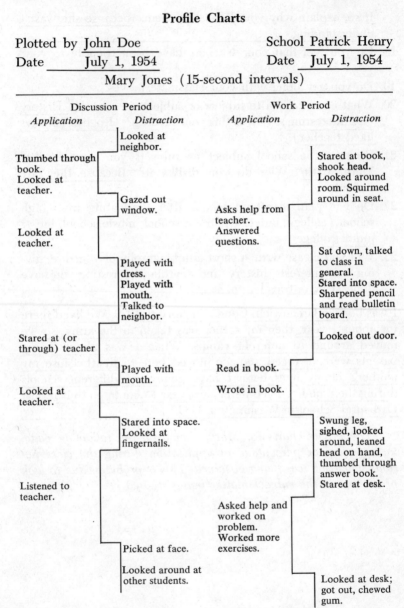

	Discussion Period		Work Period	
	Application	*Distraction*	*Application*	*Distraction*

Looked at neighbor.

Thumbed through book.
Looked at teacher.

Stared at book, shook head.
Looked around room. Squirmed around in seat.

Gazed out window.

Asks help from teacher.
Answered questions.

Looked at teacher.

Played with dress.
Played with mouth.
Talked to neighbor.

Sat down, talked to class in general.
Stared into space.
Sharpened pencil and read bulletin board.

Stared at (or through) teacher

Looked out door.

Played with mouth.

Read in book.

Wrote in book.

Looked at teacher.

Stared into space.
Looked at fingernails.

Swung leg, sighed, looked around, leaned head on hand, thumbed through answer book.
Stared at desk.

Listened to teacher.

Asked help and worked on problem.
Worked more exercises.

Picked at face.

Looked around at other students.

Looked at desk; got out, chewed gum.

Per Cent of Application 50%   Per Cent of Application 50%

Case Study

In the beginning it was my purpose to study the personality and case history of two students whose classroom conduct and activities indicated definite personality conflicts or psychological blocks. Upon investigation, I found that the past records of likely students were not available; therefore, the students presented in this study have no *definite*, easy-to-identify problems. There are, however, several weaknesses and notable personality traits that may be discussed.

Judging from my observation during the entire summer session in Algebra II, John is the better student, having greater possibilities than Mary; but upon studying records and test results, I find that this is not altogether true. From the standpoint of ninth-grade year averages (the only set of *grades* comparable, since E. Hi. lists only grade placement), Mary is a much better student than John. It may be noted, however, that in Algebra I John made an A (Grade 10) while Mary made a C+ (Grade 9).

John 9th-grade year Ave.		*Mary* 9th-grade year Ave.		*John* 10th-grade year Ave.	
English	C	English	A—	English	C
Gen. Math.	B	Algebra	C+	Algebra	A
Guidance	B	Guidance	B	Latin	A
Latin	C	Gen. Science	B	Health	B
Typing	B	Latin	B		

It must be pointed out that incentive and interest play important roles in a student's work, and I have found from talking with John and Mary that John sees a possible future use for his algebra (hobby—electronics), while Mary apparently needs only *credit* in algebra to be eligible for admission to Washington Cathedral School in September, 1954. This may be *one* factor contributing to Mary's apparent listless and inattentive attitude. As shown in the Kuder preference profile record, John proved above average in science while Mary was only average.

John	*Mary*
Above average:	Above average:
science	social service
literary	persuasive
musical	Average:
Average:	scientific
mechanical	artistic
computational	clerical
clerical	Very low:
Very low:	computational
persuasive	mechanical
artistic	

I must hasten to add that I am relatively sure that Mary's listless attitude in Algebra II is not entirely due to her lack of interest in the sciences. I shall quote from a letter to Mary's mother from her teacher in January, 1953:

"Sometimes it is very difficult to get Mary to pay attention in class. She spends most of her time looking around the room, whispering, making signs, or smiling at friends. Often, when she does pay attention, she questions the value of the teaching method."

And, from a May, 1953, letter: "Mary seems to be happy at school and is well liked by the members of her class. She is very cooperative in the class, with the exception of disturbing her neighbors at times when class attention is desired."

The profile chart included in this study will serve to show that Mary has continued to waste about half of her classroom time; in comparison, John's chart shows that he attends very well to the problem at hand, and it is my opinion that when he appears at times to be fiddling, he is actually listening and taking part mentally in the work at hand.

In the case of John, I have found, through talking with his teacher, that *one* outstanding fault is his messy handwriting and apparent hurry-up-and-get-through attitude (see analysis-quadratic functions). I found, in working with John at the board in

Algebra II, that if I could get him to slow down enough to think clearly and write legibly, he usually found the correct result. One *possible* explanation for John's "scratching" may be the fact that he is a poor speller and is trying to cover this by illegible handwriting. On the Standard Achievement Test taken in the seventh grade John scored lowest in spelling and arithmetic computation, while on the California Achievement Test taken in the eighth grade Mary scored highest in arithmetic reasoning and spelling.

John (7th grade)	*Mary (8th grade)*
Highest scores:	Arithmetic Reasoning, G.P. 11.0
Social Studies	Arithmetic Fundamentals, G.P. . . .11.5
Elementary Science	Spelling, G.P. 11.0
Word Meaning	Over-all Average, G.P. 10.7
Lowest scores:	
Arithmetic computation	
Spelling	

These results may be labeled as another signpost pointing to the fact that Mary doesn't *apply* herself as well as John, in relation to their indicated innate ability.

John

Otis Quick-Scoring Mental Ability Test, 1951: I.Q. 113

Mary

Otis Quick-Scoring Mental Ability Test, 1951: I.Q. 111
Otis Quick-Scoring Mental Ability Test, 1953: I.Q. 117
Henman-Nelson Mental Ability Test, 1953: I.Q. 129

It can be said in Mary's favor that she is well read for her age. She has read quite a number of non-fiction books, but along with these, a good group of novels. Although it didn't show very much in her algebra, she evidently comprehends what she reads, as shown by her high grade placement (12.5) in arithmetic reasoning, last taken in the eighth grade.

Mary and John have an amiable and usually pleasant attitude toward their teacher and fellow classmates, and both seem to be "a friend of all." Mary is prone to ask "Why?" at times when there seems to be no reason for the question, and I believe she is usually trying to get out of work or evade the question put to her.

Both students have evidently enjoyed good health throughout their lives and are also on a near-equal basis as far as their immediate families are concerned. The parents of both students are divorced, the mother taking the responsibility of rearing the children; and neither, I am sure, has ever been deprived of anything needed. Mrs. Public, especially, comes from a wealthy family. We all realize that children must have a sense of belonging and of being loved in order to develop a desirable personality. Both of these children seem to have had this type of home life, in spite of the absence of their fathers, and I have noted no antisocial or withdrawing tendencies. I do not attempt to put them on an equal basis just to evaluate their personal and scholastic adjustment; but considering all the presented facts and having observed them these eight weeks in class, it is my belief that both students *should* be at least B students in their school subjects.

In conclusion, I would feel more successful if I could bring out some *definite* defect or trait and give *definite* measures for its removal; since this is not so, I must offer instead a few suggestions which may be used to develop them into better students.

From a mathematical standpoint, it may be possible, through planned guidance, to channel some of the energy John uses in pursuing his hobby (photography) into a more definite interest in mathematics—for example, spatial relationships studied in geometry and angular relationships used in trigonometry. Since he is also interested in electronics, John may be more interested in the mathematics used in physics and related fields.

To me, Mary presents a more complicated problem. It would be difficult to use her hobbies (sports and popular records) to lead her away from her listless attitude toward the three R's. She has shown more improvement when attention was paid her personally to see that she did the work assigned, and perhaps this is *one* solution to her problem. In a large class, however, personal supervision is usually impossible. It might be more useful to see that she finished each assignment (not extra work) *on time,* even if this necessitated staying after class. I also think Mary would have more incentive to achieve in schoolwork if she received more encouragement in this realm from home, and less encouragement to be socially prominent.

Finally, I must add that both Mary and John have shown marked improvement during the period of my observation, and I believe that Mrs. Smith's insistence upon accuracy and precision has been extremely beneficial to both.

Index

ability to attract, interest, and get along with others, 12
achievement, measuring, 185
activities, student-teaching definitions, 10
Adams, Georgia S., 190
aims of professional laboratory experiences, 6
Alberty, Elsie J., 177
assembly programs, 69
assignment, making the, 163
Association for Student Teaching, 4, 207
Association for Supervision and Curriculum Development, 111, 157
athletic contests and pep rallies, 70
attitude of student teacher
  toward supervisors, 217
  toward the teaching profession, 219

Barron, Nora M., 176
Baruch, Dorothy, 62
Batchelder, Howard T., 35, 63
Bauer, William W., 62
Beauchamp, Mary, 177
beginning teachers, 211
  what they say, 221
Blair, Glenn M., 189
Bond, Guy L., 157
Bossing, Nelson L., 112
Bradfield, James M., 189
breadth of interests, 14
Brembeck, Cole S., 26, 34, 83, 222
bulletin boards, 45, 130
Burton, William H., 26, 62, 100, 112, 125, 157, 176, 189
Butler, Frank A., 176
Byers, Loretta, 26, 207

campus laboratory school, definition, 4
case studies, 117, 122
Chandler, J. B., 26
characteristics important to student teachers, 10
Clark, Leonard H., 100
classroom management, 54
closing the work period, 60
code of ethics, 75
community activities
  observation of, 72
  participation in, 97
cooperating school
  definition, 5
  supervising teacher, 4
Cronbach, Lee J., 189
Cunningham, Ruth, 125
curriculum materials, care of, 134

daily log of experiences, 34
Dale, Edgar, 138
decorations, room, 45, 135
difficulties, probable, 211
directed observation, definition, 5
display cases, 133
Douglass, Harl R., 26, 27, 35, 84, 112, 223
drill, review and summary, 170
Dresden, Katharine, 35, 63, 112, 138
Durrance, Charles L., 63, 100, 208

emotional balance, 11
evaluation
  by supervisors, 201
  instruments, preparation, 181
  of student progress, 179
  of student-teaching experience, 173
exhibits, 133

extra-class activities, participation in, 86

faculty meetings, 79
Faunce, Roland C., 112
Finn, James D., 138
Flanders, Ned A., 176
Forkner, Hamden L., 100
Frank, L. K., 125
Frank, M. H., 125

Gerberich, J. R., 189
Gesell, A. L., 125
getting acquainted, 46
Gowin, Lawrence E., 100
gradual induction, 30, 142
Grambs, Jean D., 26, 35, 62, 112, 126, 157, 177, 189, 222
Greene, Harry A., 189
group process techniques, 168
group work, 147
Gruhn, William J., 26, 112, 208
guiding small groups, 147

Haas, Robert B., 177
hall duty, 66
Harrison, Raymond H., 100
heating, observation of, 44
Holman, Mary V., 222
human relations with peers and adults, 12
Hymes, James L., Jr., 83

individualized instruction, 170
Ingram, Christine P., 157
insecurity, 29
instructional materials, 91
care of, 134
interest in teaching, 10
intellectual and professional energy, 13
interpersonal relations, 115
indications regarding, 120
Irish, Elizabeth, 26, 207
Iverson, William J., 26, 35, 62, 112, 126, 157, 177, 189, 222

Jenkins, Gladys Gardner, 62
Jersild, Arthur T., 126, 223

Jones, James J., 83
Jones, R. Stewart, 189
Jorgensen, Raymond J., 189

Kettlekamp, Gilbert C., 26
Klausmeier, Herbert J., 35, 63, 112, 138
Klein, Allen F., 177
Kyte, George C., 27, 35, 84, 112, 126, 209, 223

laboratory school supervising teacher, definition, 4
Lane, Howard, 177
learning by doing, 3
Leedy, Paul D., 204
Leonard, J. Paul, 112
lesson material, presenting, 144
lighting, observation, 45
Lindsey, Margaret, 208
log of experiences, 34
Logan, Lillian M., 84, 112, 126, 157, 223
Logan, Virgil G., 84, 112, 126, 157, 223
Lurry, Lucille L., 177

making the assignment, 163
management, classroom
factors affecting, 57
observing, 54
marking students, 187
McGuire, Vincent, 63, 100, 208
McKim, Margaret G., 100
measuring student achievement, 179
Mehl, Marie A., 27, 84, 223
methods, devices and procedures of instruction, 48
Miel, Alice, 177
Millard, Cecil V., 126
Mills, Hubert H., 27, 35, 84, 223
Moerdock, H. Stewart, 189
motivation, 162
Myers, Robert B., 63, 100, 208

National Education Association, Code of Ethics, 75
National Society for the Study of Education, 157